CLASSROOM INSTRUCTION
AND MANAGEMENT

CLASSROOM INSTRUCTION AND MANAGEMENT

RICHARD I. ARENDS

Central Connecticut State University

Boston, Massachusetts   Burr Ridge, Illinois   Dubuque, Iowa
Madison, Wisconsin   New York, New York   San Francisco, California   St. Louis, Missouri

This book was developed by Lane Akers, Inc.

McGraw-Hill

A Division of The McGraw-Hill Companies

Classroom Instruction and Management

This book is printed on acid-free paper.

2 3 4 5 6 7 8 9 0   DOC   DOC   9 0 9 8 7

ISBN 0-07-003082-0

This book was set in Veljovic by The Clarinda Company.
The editor was Lane Akers;
the production supervisor was Richard A. Ausburn.
The designer was Wanda Kossak.
The photo editor was Elyse Rieder.
Project supervision was done by The Total Book.
R. R. Donnelley & Sons Company was printer and binder.

Library of Congress Cataloging-in-Publication Data

Arends, Richard I.
    Classroom instruction and management / Richard I. Arends.
        p.   cm.
    Includes bibliographical references and index.
    ISBN 0-07-003082-0
    1. Teaching. 2. Classroom management   I. Title.
LB1025.3.A75 1997   96-22930
371.1'02—dc20

ABOUT THE AUTHOR

Richard I. Arends currently holds the William Allen (Boeing) Endowed Chair in the School of Education at Seattle University where he teaches and writes. He is on leave from his position as Dean in the School of Education and Professional Studies at Central Connecticut State University. Prior to his coming to Connecticut, Professor Arends was on the faculty and chair of the Department of Curriculum and Instruction at the University of Maryland, College Park. He received his Ph.D. in education from the University of Oregon where he was on the faculty from 1975 to 1983. A former elementary, junior high, and high school teacher, his special interests are the social psychology of education, teacher education, and organizational development and school improvement.

Professor Arends has authored or coauthored over a dozen books on education, including the *Second Handbook of Organization Development in Schools, Systems Change Strategies for Education,* and *Of Principals and Projects.* He is currently working on the fourth edition of *Learning to Teach* which has been used widely in teaching strategies courses throughout the world and has been translated into two foreign languages.

Arends has worked widely with schools and universities throughout North America and the Pacific Rim, including Australia, Samoa, Palau, and Saipan. The recipient of numerous awards, he was selected in 1989 as the outstanding teacher educator in the state of Maryland and in 1990 received the Judith Ruskin award for outstanding research in education given by the Association for Supervision and Curriculum Development (ASCD).

To William, who is the pride of my life and the person who inspires me to continue taking on these writing projects and seeing them through to completion.

CONTENTS IN BRIEF

CONTENTS

CHAPTER 2

DIRECT INSTRUCTION   62

CHAPTER 3
COOPERATIVE LEARNING   108

CHAPTER 4
PROBLEM-BASED INSTRUCTION   154

CHAPTER 5

CLASSROOM DISCUSSION 198

CHAPTER 6
LEARNING AND STUDY STRATEGIES 240

PREFACE

Curriculum restructuring has become an almost universal phenomenon in teacher education during the 1990s. Consequently, the number and sequence of courses found within these restructured programs and their content coverage are less predictable today than in the past. The result is a radical increase in the number of customized curricula whose courses vary in significant ways from their counterparts in other teacher education programs.

In view of this curriculum variation, it seems sensible to offer a new, more flexible teaching methods text, one that can be mixed and matched to fit a variety of curriculum arrangements. *Classroom Instruction and Management* was designed expressly for this purpose. Because of its modest length and price and its focus on core teaching functions and models, this text is ideal for any of the following situations:

- ◆ As the core text in either brief or full-length courses aimed at developing a repertoire of basic teaching models, strategies, and skills.
- ◆ As the instruction and management unit in restructured educational psychology courses.
- ◆ As the instruction and management unit in those integrated "block" courses which combine units from formerly separate courses and often last more than one term.

Classroom Instruction and Management not only helps students develop a basic repertoire of teaching models, strategies, and skills, but helps them understand their theoretical and empirical foundations and shows them how to study these behaviors in field-based settings. These goals are accomplished using the following features.

- ◆ *Content Coverage.* Chapter 1 provides an overview of classroom life and introduces students to the major functions of teaching: planning, instruction, management, and assessment. Chapters 2 through 5 present four widely used teaching models and strategies: direct instruction, cooperative learning, problem-based instruction, and discussion. Finally, Chapter 6 deals with strategy instruction, one of the most important yet neglected areas of teacher education. Altogether, these chapters present a minimum repertoire of teaching strategies that teachers at all grade levels and in all subject areas need to master.

◆ *Research Focus.* In order to develop the point of view that there is a scientific knowledge base which can and should guide teaching practice, a section entitled Theoretical and Empirical Support appears in the early part of each chapter. This section provides a broad sampling of the theory and research that supports the teaching practices recommended in the latter part of each chapter. In addition, each chapter contains a boxed summary of a classic research study pertaining to the chapter topic. Collectively, these research summaries reflect the variety and richness of methods used by educational researchers over time and around the world.

◆ *Practical Guidelines.* After examining the theoretical and empirical rationale behind a particular teaching model or strategy, each chapter provides detailed instructions on how to conduct that type of lesson. Students are shown how to carry out the planning, instruction, management, and assessment tasks associated with each model or strategy. In the process, they learn such basic teaching skills as writing objectives, establishing set, choosing content, using time and space, providing clear explanations, conducting demonstrations, forming teams, promoting collaboration, providing practice and feedback, assessing learning, and preventing or dealing with misbehavior.

◆ *End-of-Chapter Activities.* To truly understand what effective teaching is all about, students must actively observe others teach, engage in dialogues about teaching, and reflect on both their own teaching experiences and those of others. To help promote such active learning experiences, several pages of structured observation, interview, portfolio, and reflection activities are included at the end of each chapter.

◆ *Strategy Instruction.* Chapter 6 deals with one of the most important but neglected aspects of teaching—strategy instruction. This very important chapter, which is built around the cognitive learning principles that have emerged during the past three decades, adds a much needed dimension to this type of text. Its inclusion in a general methods text will reinforce the central goal of all good teachers—to produce independent, self-regulated learners.

Acknowledgments

With great appreciation, I would like to acknowledge the following reviewers whose initial support encouraged my undertaking this project: Kay Alderman, University of Akron; Hilda Borko, University of Colorado; Carol Anne Kardash, University of Missouri; Paul Pintrich, University of Michigan; and Gary Stuck, University of North Carolina. I would also like to acknowledge those reviewers of my larger text, *Learning to Teach, 3e,* whose experience with that text provided much needed guidance in designing this one. Principal among these are Mary Crisp, Western Kentucky University; Carmen Dumas, Nova University; Susan Geis and Jean Shaw, University of Mississippi; John Hoffman, Northeast Missouri State University; Harriet Johnson, Augsburg College; Larry Kortering, University of Delaware; W. C. Martin, University of West Florida; Rita Moretti, Niagara University; Karna Nelson and Sam Perez, Western Washington University; Steve Penn, Vincennes University; George Rawlins, Austin Peay State University; and Kinnard White, University of North Carolina. Finally, a very special thanks to my editor, Lane Akers, who had faith in the book from the beginning and who has provided so much valuable assistance, advice, and support over the years of our relationship.

Richard I. Arends

CLASSROOM INSTRUCTION AND MANAGEMENT

INTRODUCTION TO CLASSROOM INSTRUCTION AND MANAGEMENT

EFFECTIVE TEACHERS

TEACHING MODELS
Direct Instruction
Cooperative Learning
Problem-Based Instruction
Discussion
Learning and Study Strategies

PROVIDING LEADERSHIP

BOOKS FOR THE PROFESSIONAL

3

At one time, society was more concerned with teachers' moral character than with their ability to teach effectively.

L earning to be a good teacher in today's world is a long, complex, and exciting journey. However, this was not always the case. In earlier times, when most people farmed or worked at trades, teaching was performed mainly by young men waiting for other jobs or young women waiting for marriage. Because most occupations required only rudimentary academic skills, most communities monitored and regulated teachers' moral and social behavior far more closely than their scholarship or their teaching performance. Some communities required their teacher to go to church at least once a week; others had rules against dating or dancing. In short, society insisted that teachers be good moral examples for youth but did not hold them responsible for student learning and did not give them professional status.

This situation has changed drastically as America has moved swiftly from an agrarian to an industrialized society during the nineteenth and twentieth centuries and now moves even more swiftly into a technological and information-based society. Although still accountable for their moral behavior, teachers are now viewed as professionals who are expected to master a large **knowledge base** that covers the subject matter they teach, the methods they use to teach it, and the students to whom it is taught. It is no longer acceptable for teachers just to be "good" individuals or to use practices based on traditions, intuition, or personal preference. Today's teachers are held accountable for using teaching practices that have been shown to be effective, just as members of other professions are held accountable for **best practice** in their respective fields. It is just as unacceptable today for teachers to depend entirely on oral reading circles to teach first-graders how to read or to teach history by requiring students to answer the questions at the end of a chapter as it is for doctors to use leeches to cure infections.

Today, teachers are viewed as professionals and are held accountable for using "best practices" derived from a scientific knowledge base.

This book is about a set of best practices associated with classroom teaching and leadership. It is built on the premise that best teaching practice derives mainly from **scientific inquiry** that gradually leads to organized theories and models of instruction. This does not mean that what some refer to as the **art of teaching** should be ignored. Like most human endeavors, teaching has aspects that cannot be codified or guided by scientific knowledge alone but depend instead on complex individual judgments stemming from experience and the **wisdom of practice.** Indeed, it is the complexities of teaching and the dilemmas they produce that are most difficult for beginners. Experience and reflection, however, help bring some of these complexities into focus as teachers integrate the science and the art of teaching and learn to make both scientific and artistic choices on a day-to-day basis.

Experience and reflection help teachers become artistic practitioners of the science of teaching.

EFFECTIVE TEACHERS

Efforts to define the effective teacher have a long history. Instead of producing a single consensus view, however, research and experience have produced a variety of views on this topic. Some have argued that effective teachers are people who can establish rapport with students and create nurturing, caring classroom environments. Others have defined an effective teacher as a person who has a love for learning and a superior command of their subject matter. Still others view an effective teacher as an individual who can motivate students to work toward a more just and humane society.

The view of effective teaching used in this book embraces all these views but also extends beyond them. Effective teaching requires as its baseline individuals who care for young people, who are academically able, and who have a strong command of the subjects they teach. It also requires individuals who can foster their students' academic achievement and guide them toward important social, moral, and ethical goals. Teaching is complex work and, to be an effective teacher necessitates the **attributes** listed below.

Effective teachers seek authentic relationships with their students, have positive dispositions toward knowledge, command a repertoire of teaching practices, and are reflective problem solvers.

1. Effective teachers have personal qualities that allow them to develop **authentic human relationships** with their students, as well as with parents and colleagues.

2. Effective teachers have *positive dispositions toward knowledge.* They have command of the knowledge bases on teaching and learning: about the subject matter they teach, about human development and learning, and about classroom instruction and management.

3. Effective teachers command a **repertoire of teaching practices** known to stimulate student engagement and to enhance student learning. For example, they are adept at such things as planning and sequencing lessons, asking questions, evaluating student learning, and executing a variety of teaching models.

4. Effective teachers have attitudes and skills that facilitate **reflection** and **problem solving.** They understand that learning to teach is a lifelong process that, like other professions, requires ongoing study and interaction with professional colleagues.

Figure I.1 illustrates the point of view taken here about effective teaching and the four attributes deemed essential for an effective teacher.

The focus of this text is on attribute 3, acquiring a repertoire of teaching practices that can be adapted to a variety of teaching and learning situations for the purpose of motivating and enhancing student learning. In the process, however, we inevitably touch on the other attributes as well. Now let's turn to the two major jobs of teaching—providing instruction to students and exerting leadership to classroom groups.

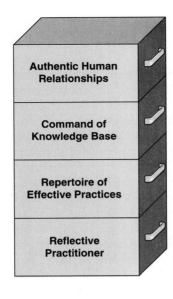

FIGURE 1.1

*Attributions of
Effective Teachers*

TEACHING MODELS

Over the years, many different approaches to teaching have been created and studied. Some have been developed by educational researchers investigating the learning process and how particular teaching behaviors affect student performance. Other approaches have been developed by classroom teachers experimenting with their own teaching to solve specific classroom problems. Still others have been invented by psychologists, industrial trainers, and philosophers such as Socrates, Rousseau, and John Dewey. Some of these approaches, the use of scientific method in instruction or large-scale group investigations, for instance, are large and complex and can be fully implemented only over a period of several days or even weeks. Other approaches, such as specific questioning techniques, are rather simple and straightforward. To help cut through the complexity of classroom instruction, the instructional approaches described in this book will be based on the concept of the teaching model and a taxonomy developed initially by Bruce Joyce and his colleagues (Joyce & Weil, 1972; Joyce, Weil, & Showers, 1992).

In the late 1960s, Bruce Joyce and Marsha Weil began tracking down and describing the various teaching approaches then in use. In the process of recording and describing each approach, they developed a system for analyzing a particular approach in terms of its theoretical base, its educational purposes, and the teacher and student behaviors required to successfully execute it. Joyce and Weil (1972) and Joyce, Weil, and Showers (1992) labeled each of these approaches a *teaching model,* although one of several other terms, such as *teaching strategy, teaching method,* or *teaching principle,* could have been used. The term *model* was chosen by Joyce, Weil, and Showers and will be used in this book for two important reasons.

First, the term *model* implies something larger than a particular strategy, method, or procedure. As used here, the term **teaching model** encompasses a broad, overall approach to instruction. For example, the problem-based model of instruction involves small groups of students working together to solve a problem of mutual interest to the group. Within this general model, students often employ a variety of problem-solving and critical thinking skills and procedures. Thus, a single instructional model can employ a number of methodological or procedural skills such as defining a problem, asking questions, doing research, holding discussions and debating findings, working collaboratively, creating artifacts, and making presentations.

As used in this book, the term *teaching model* has four attributes that specific strategies or procedures do not have. These are (1) a coherent theoretical rationale made explicit by its creators or developers; (2) a point of view about what and how students learn (intended learning outcome); (3) required teaching behaviors that make the model work, and (4) required classroom structures for bringing about intended outcomes. As an example, you will see in Chapter 4 that the problem-based model of instruction derives from a constructivist theory of learning; holds that instruction should be driven by real problems whose solution requires collaboration among students; sees the teacher's role as helping students break the project down into manageable tasks and then modeling the skills and strategies needed in order to complete these tasks; and depends on maintaining a flexible, inquiry-oriented classroom environment. Figure I.2 illustrates the four features of a teaching model.

The term teaching model *refers to a particular approach to instruction that includes its goals, syntax, environment, and management system.*

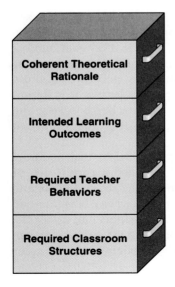

FIGURE I.2

Features of a Teaching Model

Second, models can serve as important communication devices, whether talking about classroom teaching, automobiles, or child-rearing practices. As is described in subsequent chapters, teaching models are classified according to their instructional goals, their syntaxes (sequential patterns), and the nature of their learning environments. The use of a particular model allows teachers to achieve some instructional goals, but not others. Direct instruction, for instance, is a good method for helping students learn basic skills such as the multiplication tables or place geography. However, it is not suitable for teaching higher-level mathematical concepts or helping students understand the influence of the earth's topography on agricultural production.

A model's syntax *is the sequence of steps that a lesson usually follows.*

A model's **syntax** refers to the overall flow or sequence of steps that a lesson usually follows. A lesson's syntax specifies what kinds of teacher and student actions are required, the order in which these actions normally occur, and the particular task demands placed on students. The syntaxes of most models have certain things in common. For instance, almost all instruction begins by gaining students' attention and getting them motivated to engage in learning activities. Likewise, most models employ some form of closing procedure in which the teacher and students summarize or review what has been learned. Syntaxes also differ. The sequencing of activities in a direct instruction lesson is much different, for instance, from that in a group discussion lesson. It is these differences, particularly between the opening and closing of lessons, that must be understood if the various models are to be used effectively by teachers.

Each teaching model requires slightly different physical arrangements and classroom management systems.

Finally, each model employs a slightly different **learning environment** and **management system.** Each approach places different demands on the learner, on the physical space, and on the classroom social system. Cooperative learning, for example, requires a flexible physical environment that includes such features as moveable desks. Discussions are usually conducted when students are seated in a circle or horseshoe arrangement. Conversely, most direct instruction lessons work best if students are seated so that they face their teacher, who is often stationed at the chalkboard in the front of the room. Similarly, different teaching approaches make different task demands on students, and these require particular managerial strategies. In a direct instruction lesson, it is important for students to be quiet and attend to what the teacher is saying and doing. However, during cooperative learning lessons, it is important that students talk with one another.

In order to meet the diverse goals and teaching situations of today's schools, teachers need a repertoire of teaching practices.

The point of view taken in this text is that no model of instruction is innately better than any other. Classroom teachers need a **repertoire of teaching practices** for instruction in order to meet the diverse goals and situations that characterize today's schools. A single approach or method is no longer sufficient. With a sufficient repertoire, teachers can select the model that best achieves particular objectives or that best suits a particular situation or group of students. Also, alternative models can sometimes be used in tandem. For example, a teacher may use direct instruction to teach new subject matter or skills, followed by a classroom discussion to extend student thinking about the topic, and then divide students into cooperative learning groups to practice their newly acquired skills and to construct their own meaning about the subject.

Mastering the most widely used teaching models is a lifelong learning process. This book focuses on four of these models (Chapters 2 through 5) as well as a set of learning strategies (Chapter 6) that can help direct students toward being independent, self-regulated learners. If learned well, these teaching models and learning strategies will meet the needs of most teachers in their initial years of teaching. To extend the notion of instructional flexibility, we also take the position that there is no single correct way of enacting a particular model. Rather, artful teachers adapt these models to fit specific situations. Bear in mind, however, that if teachers deviate too far from a model's syntax or environmental demands, they are no longer using a variation of the model, and the learning goals intended for the lesson will likely not be accomplished. Teachers should try to master a limited number of well-established instructional models that will cover most teaching situations. Then, after repeated use of the models, they should begin to adapt them to fit their own situation and teaching style. A brief preview of each model follows.

Direct Instruction

Much of a teacher's work is aimed at helping students acquire **procedural knowledge**—how to do something. Procedural knowledge includes such things as how to write a sentence, perform a mathematical operation, climb a rope, or read a map. Teachers also want their students to acquire straightforward **declarative knowledge**—basic knowledge about the world such as the names of the state capitals or spelling rules. Finally, teachers want their students to develop **study skills** such as underlining, taking notes, and outlining. Acquiring basic procedural and declarative knowledge consists in most instances of mastering specific and, often, sequential tasks. For example, learning how to drive a car requires declarative knowledge about the rules of the road as well as procedural knowledge about how to steer, how to shift gears, and how to accelerate and brake appropriately. **Direct instruction,** which rests on ideas from behavioral psychology and social learning theory, has been specifically designed to promote student learning of well-structured procedural and declarative knowledge that can be taught in a step-by-step fashion. The model has an extensive research base, it requires a tightly structured learning environment, and its direct and straightforward explication makes it a learnable model for beginning teachers.

Direct instruction enables teachers to promote student learning of procedural knowledge, straightforward declarative knowledge, and study skills.

Cooperative Learning

The cooperative learning model provides a framework within which teachers can foster important social learning and human relations goals.

This model presents the sharpest contrast to direct instruction. It can be used to teach rather complex academic materials and, more important, can help teachers accomplish important social learning and human relations goals. For instance, it has been shown to be extremely effective in improving race and ethnic relationships within multicultural classrooms as well as relationships among regular and handicapped students. **Cooperative learning** stems from both social learning theory and cognitive-constructivist perspectives of learning. The classroom environment is characterized by cooperative task and incentive structures and by small-group activity. As you will learn, there are several variations of cooperative learning, some of which are rather simple and can be readily learned. Other variations are more complex and may take longer to master.

Problem-Based Instruction

Higher-level thinking, knowledge processing, and knowledge constructing are furthered by problem-based instruction.

The teaching model, which dates back to as early as John Dewey, has had a very strong revival during the past decade. This model is a most effective approach for teaching higher-level thinking processes, helping students process information already in their possession, and assisting students to construct their own knowledge about the social and physical world around them. Contemporary approaches to **problem-based instruction** rest on cognitive psychology and constructivist perspectives about learning. This model has a reasonably well-developed knowledge base and, although complex, can be learned and executed by classroom teachers with sufficient instruction and practice.

Discussion

No matter what approach to instruction is used, at some point student-teacher or student-student dialogue is desired. **Discussion** is an approach to teaching that affords this dialogue. It differs in its syntax from the other teaching models and is used most often in conjunction with another teaching model. For instance, discussion can occur in small groups during cooperative learning, between a teacher and particular students during a problem-based lesson, and with the class as a whole during a direct instruction recitation. There is a moderate research base that supports the use of discussion and extensive practice-based guidelines for holding discussions. Becoming a proficient manager of classroom discussions is difficult for inexperienced teachers and often takes more persistence and practice than other teaching models.

Learning and Study Strategies

Finally, it is important for teachers to help students master learning and study strategies. Sometimes called **cognitive strategies,** these processes are aimed at helping students learn how to learn; that is, how to comprehend, store, and recall information and skills. Learning and study strategies rest firmly on cognitive and information processing theories of learning. Some strategies date back to ancient times, but most have been developed during the past 2 decades. There is a strong knowledge base showing the positive effects of learning strategies on students' academic performance. Learning strategies can be mastered by teachers rather quickly and can then be taught to students. This, however, requires a shift in teacher thinking, because traditionally teachers have spent very little time on this aspect of teaching.

Table I.1 provides a summary of the teaching models that will be covered in this text and describes the key features of each: its theoretical underpinnings, major theorists, instructional goals, instructional characteristics, and environmental characteristics. Although used here as an advance organizer, the reader is encouraged to refer back to this table from time to time in order to maintain a comparative perspective on the various models.

PROVIDING LEADERSHIP

Providing students with face-to-face instruction is the most visible and perhaps the most glamorous aspect of teaching. Equally important, however, is the job of providing leadership and motivation to groups of students so they will engage and accomplish the academic and social goals of schooling. This text examines three of the most important leadership functions of teaching: planning, managing classroom life, and assessing and evaluating student progress.

A teacher's ability to provide leadership and motivation is as important as his or her ability to provide instruction.

An overview of each of these **leadership functions** is provided in Chapter 1, followed by detailed accounts of how each function is carried out within the confines of particular teaching models. Although treated independently in this and other texts, in real day-to-day teaching, the various leadership functions overlap and interact with one another and are interrelated with particular teaching models being employed. As teachers carry out face-to-face instruction, they check comprehension by asking questions and reading the expressions of their students (assessment). If they decide a lesson is not going well, they revise their plans and, possibly, their instructional approach (planning).

Moreover, each of the teaching models requires slightly different planning, management, and assessment activities. For instance, planning a

TABLE 1.1   SUMMARY AND COMPARISON OF TEACHING MODELS AND LEARNING STRATEGIES

Key Features	Direct Instruction	Cooperative Learning	Problem-Based Instruction	Discussion	Learning Strategies
Theoretical underpinnings	Behavioral psychology; social learning theory	Social learning theory; constructivist theory	Cognitive theory; constructivist theory	Cognitive theory; social interactionist theory	Information processing theory
Major theorist(s)/ developers	Bandura; Hunter	Dewey; Vygotsky; Slavin	Dewey; Vygotsky	Bruner; Cazden; Vygotsky	Bruner; Ausubel; Vygotsky
Instructional outcomes	Basic declarative knowledge; academic skills	Academic and social skills	Academic and inquiry skills	Discourse and thinking skills	Cognitive and metacognitive skills
Instructional features	Clear presentation and demonstration of learning materials; task analysis and behavioral objectives	Group work with cooperative reward and task structures	Inquiry-based projects conducted in groups	Group discourse	Explicit teaching; reciprocal teaching
Environmental characteristics	Tightly structured, teacher-centered environment	Flexible, democratic, student-centered environment	Flexible, inquiry-focused environment	Reflective, emphasis on open dialogue	Reflective, emphasis on learning how to learn

direct instruction lesson on how to set up and use a microscope necessitates carefully analyzing the specific tasks to be learned (learning the parts, assembling, focusing) and the logical ordering of these tasks. Planning for a cooperative learning lesson, on the other hand, will likely not require this type of detailed task analysis but, instead, demand that the teacher think through the numerous logistical issues (movement, talk, access to materials) associated with small-group work.

Similarly, assessment and evaluation of student learning must be tailored to the instructional goals of particular teaching models. Constructing a performance test to measure how well students have learned to multiply whole numbers following a direct instruction lesson is different from assessing their ability to define a problem and to conduct a scientific experiment in a problem-based lesson. Moreover, both these types of tests differ from procedures that might be devised to assess students' social skills.

Finally, and perhaps most important, each of the teaching models differ in terms of their classroom leadership and management demands. For each model, we examine ways of designing the physical environment to fit the type of lesson being taught. We also examine how particular tasks and activities associated with the various instructional models require different time frames, different expectations for students, and different management behaviors for teachers.

It is difficult to overemphasize the leadership tasks of teaching. If students are not motivated to persist in academic tasks, or if they are not managed effectively, all the rest of teaching and learning is lost. Yet, performing these leadership tasks is no easy matter. Leadership behaviors must be performed in classrooms characterized by fast-moving events and a large degree of unpredictability. Learning to plan, to assess, and to read specific classroom situations and then provide effective leadership and management are some of the most difficult yet most rewarding challenges of teaching.

As you use this book, we hope that you will aspire to be the type of teacher described, to learn the existing knowledge base on teaching and learning, and to master a repertoire of best teaching practices. Linking what is known about teaching and learning to your own experiences will help bring the complexities of teaching into focus and equip you with the confidence and skill to be an effective teacher.

BOOKS FOR THE PROFESSIONAL

Barzun, J. (1991). *Begin here: The forgotten conditions of teaching and learning.* Chicago: University of Chicago Press. This little book features various essays and articles written by Jacques Barzun during his long career which describe his vision about what it means to teach and to learn and what is required of teachers and schools if they are to be effective.

Joyce, B., Weil, M., & Showers, B. (1992). *Models of teaching* (4th ed.). Englewood Cliffs, N.J.: Prentice-Hall. This book is a must. It provides more information on the models of teaching described here, plus many others.

CHAPTER 1

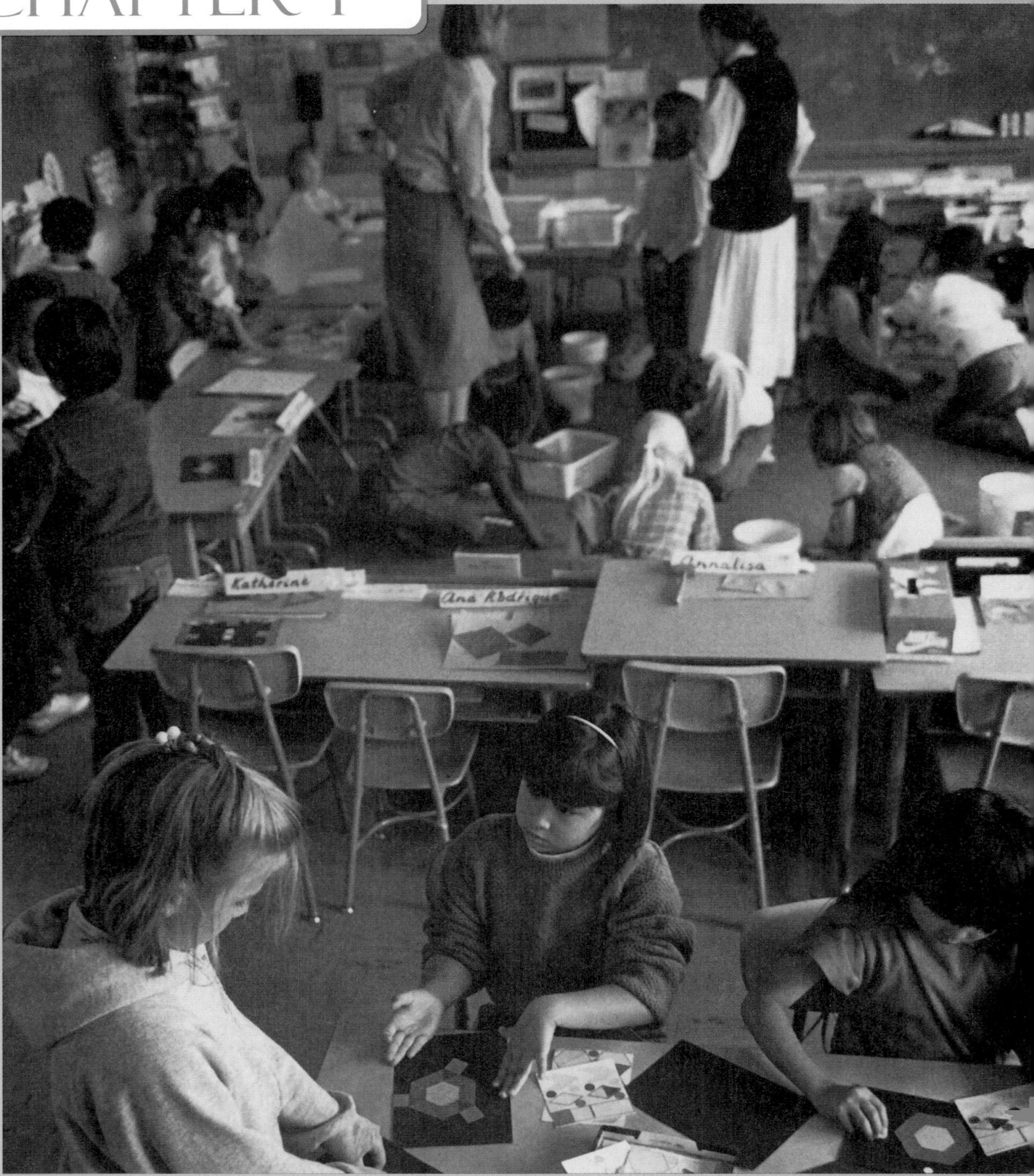

CLASSROOM TEACHING: A DEMANDING JOB IN A COMPLEX SETTING

M arie Cuevas is a sixth-grade teacher at Martin Luther King Middle School. She meets daily with her students in an integrated science and language arts class. The students in her class have been hetrogeneously grouped, meaning that all ability levels are represented. If we were to visit Ms. Cuevas's classroom on a typical day, we would likely see the following things going on.

> Ms. Cuevas sits with a cluster of students in one corner of the room discussing a story they have just read on the life cycle of the Pacific Coast salmon, while several other students are working alone at their desks. They are writing their own stories about how salmon are threatened with extinction because hydro-electric activities have disturbed their breeding grounds. In another corner, a special education teacher is working with Brenda, a young girl who still reads at a second-grade level. Elsewhere, Ms. Cuevas's aide is administering a test to three children who were absent last Friday. At a far science table, a pair of students who are supposed to be practicing with a microscope are really discussing yesterday's football game. Overhearing their discussion, Ms. Cuevas stops to get them back on task. At the same moment, a squabble erupts between two students who are returning from the library. Ms. Cuevas asks the teacher's aide to resolve the conflict, then returns to the life-cycle discussion, where irrelevant comments from Joey about last week's fishing trip with his father has caused it to drift.

> As the class period draws to a close, the principal slips in to remind Ms. Cuevas that they have a short meeting scheduled during the lunch break and also to ask if she objects to having a small group of parents visit her next period. All this occurs as learning materials are being returned and readied for the next class, today's homework assignments are collected, and the squabble between the two students continues.

Becoming a teacher involves learning to confront a complex work environment in which many activities are going on simultaneously.

This scenario is not an atypical one. Classrooms everywhere are extremely busy places, characterized by a variety of simultaneous activities: individual and group instruction, socializing, conflict management, evaluation activities, and in-flight adjustments for unanticipated events. In addition to being a specially designed learning environment, classrooms are social settings where friendships form and conflicts occur. The classroom is a setting for parties, visits, and a myriad of other activities. This book is about teaching in schools and these complex places called classrooms.

The aim of this chapter is to provide a set of conceptual lenses for viewing and thinking about classroom teaching. The first section looks at the classroom itself, because this is the setting where most teaching and learning occurs. Section two focuses briefly on the two major jobs of teaching: providing instruction and exerting leadership. **Instruction** is concerned mainly with what teachers do as they interact face-to-face with their students, whereas **leadership** is a more general term and covers such diverse activities as planning, managing, and evaluating students. An introduction to teacher planning, classroom management, and classroom evaluation and assessment compose the final three sections of the chapter.

CLASSROOM LIFE

Although teaching and learning happen in many settings (work, family, peer group), school teaching in our society occurs mainly in a setting we call a *classroom*. Classrooms are very familiar places; the average college senior has spent 16 years there interacting with fellow students, lining up for gym or recess, listening to lectures, doing seatwork, taking tests, and cringing at the smells in the lunchroom and biology labs. They have watched teachers "read, talk, and scold" over and over again.

Most students preparing to be teachers, however, have known classrooms only from in front of the teacher's desk. Viewed from behind that desk, classroom events take on a very different perspective. What from in front was a covert whisper to the little girl at the next desk, from behind, is now a potential disruption. A fourth-grader's attempt to make a new friend is now viewed in terms of its effects on the learning group. In short, the way one experiences classroom life is very much influenced by whether one's classroom role is played out from in front of or from behind the teacher's desk. Our familiarity with classrooms sometimes gets in the way of appreciating and understanding the complexity of classroom life and the job of teaching.

Features of Classrooms

There are numerous ways to think about classrooms. One way is to think about them as **ecological systems** in which a set of inhabitants (teachers and students) interact within a specific environment (the classroom) for the purpose of completing valued activities and tasks. Using this perspective to study classrooms, Walter Doyle (1979, 1986) pointed out that classrooms have six intrinsic features that make them complex and demanding places. Becoming familiar with these features of classroom life is a good place to begin one's change in perspective from that of a student to that of a teacher.

Classrooms can be viewed as ecological systems in which inhabitants interact within a specific environment to complete valued tasks.

Multidimensionality

This refers to the fact that classrooms are crowded places where many people with different backgrounds, interests, and abilities compete for scarce resources. Unlike a dentist's or an optician's office where a narrow range of predictable events occur, a multitude of diverse events are planned and orchestrated in classrooms. Teachers explain things, give directions, manage conflict, collect milk money, make assignments, and keep records. Students listen, read, write, engage each other in discussion and conversation, form friendships, and experience conflict. Teachers must learn to take these multidimensional activities into account and accommodate them in some manner.

Simultaneity

While helping an individual student during seatwork, a teacher must monitor the rest of the class, handle interruptions, and keep track of time. During a presentation, a teacher must explain ideas clearly while watching for signs of inattention, noncomprehension, and misbehavior. During a discussion, a teacher must listen to a student's answer, watch other students for signs of comprehension, and think about the next question to ask. Each of these situations illustrates a basic feature of classroom life, the simultaneous occurrence of different events that effective teachers must be able to recognize and manage.

Immediacy

Because of the rapid pace of classroom events, teachers need to react immediately, often with little time to reflect.

A third important feature of classroom life is the rapid pace of classroom events and the immediate impact they have on the lives of teachers and students. Teachers have hundreds of daily exchanges with their students. They are continuously praising, reprimanding, explaining, scolding, and challenging. Students also have hundreds of interactions with their teachers and with each other. Pencils are dropped, irrelevant comments occur, squabbles surface, and conflicts are resolved. Many of these events are unplanned, and their immediacy gives teachers little time to reflect before acting.

Unpredictability

Classroom events not only demand immediate attention, many take unexpected turns and confront teachers in unpredictable ways. Distractions and interruptions are frequent. Sudden illnesses, announcements over the intercom, and unscheduled visitors are common. Consequently, it is difficult to anticipate how a particular lesson or activity will proceed on a particular day with a particular group of students. What worked so well last year may be a complete flop this year. Even a lesson that produced enthusiasm and full participation first period may be greeted with stony silence during sixth period.

Publicness

In many settings, people perform their work mostly in private or in view of only a few others. Doctors diagnose patients' illnesses in the privacy of their offices; clerks and waitresses attend to their customers without much attention from others; technicians and accountants do their work unobstructed by an observing public. Classrooms, however, are very public places, and almost all events are witnessed by others. Teachers describe their existence as "living in a fishbowl." This feature of publicness or lack of privacy is just as acute for students. Students' behavior is constantly being scrutinized by their teachers, many of whom seem (from the students' perspective) to have "eyes in the back of their heads." Students also watch each other with considerable interest. It is very difficult, therefore, for any aspect of one's classroom life, whether it is a score on the latest test or a whisper to a neighbor, to go unnoticed.

History

Finally, classrooms and their participants gradually become a community that shares a common history. Classes meet five days a week for several months and thereby accumulate a common set of experiences, norms, and routines. Early meetings shape events for the remainder of the year. Each classroom develops its own social system with particular structures, organization, and norms. Though classrooms may look alike from a distance or on paper, each class is actually as unique as a fingerprint. Each develops its own internal procedures, patterns of interaction, and limits. It is as if imaginary lines were guiding and controlling behavior within the group. In spite of day-to-day variation, there is a certain constancy in each class which emerges from its individual history.

Classrooms gradually form into unique learning communities, each with its own norms, structure, and organization.

These properties directly affect the overall classroom environment and shape the behavior of participants. They have profound effects on teaching. As you will learn, some of these features can be altered by teachers, others cannot—at least not very significantly. This aspect of teaching will be revisited later in this chapter under the discussion of how teachers can provide leadership to students and help them manage group life.

The Two Big Jobs of Teaching

The intrinsic features of classrooms just discussed are not the only forces shaping classroom life. Equally important are the expectations of the public and the profession regarding the personal characteristics of teachers and their professional knowledge and skills. In the introductory section, you read how the public's and the profession's expectations for teachers have changed over time. Today, the emphasis is no longer on the teacher's moral and social behavior (although those are still important) but instead on the teacher as a professional, who can be held accountable for using best teacher practices in two important aspects of his or her work, providing instruction and exerting leadership.

Providing instruction and exerting leadership are the two big jobs of teaching. Providing instruction includes what most people think about when they think of teaching, that is, face-to-face interaction with students. Exerting leadership and motivating students to accomplish the academic and social

Providing instruction and exerting leadership are a teacher's two major jobs.

RESEARCH BOX CONSIDERING THE ROLE OF RESEARCH

Knowledge Base

Scientific knowledge in education, as in other fields, is essentially knowledge about relationships between variables. In education, this means basically that knowledge exists about how one set of variables (teacher behaviors) is related to another set of variables (student learning) and how these interact under varying conditions. Educational researchers strive to discover true relationships in regard to teaching and learning, and they seek answers to questions and problems facing teachers. All kinds of questions, however, cannot be answered through research. The type of problems that can be studied scientifically are those that focus on relationships and can be tested from a scientific perspective. Questions that cannot be studied this way are those that pose questions of value or opinion. Many important questions fall into this latter category.

Use of Research

Educational philosopher Gary Fenstermacher (1986) has taken the position that the major value of educational research for teachers is that it can lead to the improvement of their *practical arguments*. His own argument for this position goes something like the following.

For teachers, as well as for other professional practitioners, the knowledge and beliefs held are not only important for their own sake but also because they prompt and guide action. Actions taken by teachers are guided by a number of premises—beliefs held to be just and true and linked together in some logical format. Sometimes these premises and the underlying logic have been made explicit by the teacher; many times, however, they are not consciously aware of their practical arguments. Fenstermacher provides the following example of a teacher's practical argument used to support the methods she used to teach reading.

1. It is extremely important for children to know how to read.
2. Children who do not know how to read are best begun with primers.
3. All nonreaders will proceed through the primers at the same rate (the importance of learning to read justifies this standardization).
4. The skills of reading are most likely to be mastered by choral reading of the primers, combined with random calling of individual students.
5. This is a group of nonreaders for whom I am the designated teacher.

Action: (I am distributing primers and preparing the class to respond in unison to me.) (p. 46)

In this example, premise 1 is a statement of value, on which most people would concur. Premise 5 is a statement of fact, presumed to be accurate. Premises 2, 3, and 4, however, are beliefs held by the teacher about how children learn and about pedagogy. These beliefs influence the actions of using primers and choral reading. In this particular instance, these beliefs are simply not supported by the research on reading instruction.

Fenstermacher points out that if the results of research were known in this instance, they could lead this teacher to doubt her beliefs and subsequently rethink the premises undergirding her pedagogical behavior and instructional practices. Knowing about and using research becomes a process of understanding, doubting, and challenging the beliefs we hold about how children learn and about the best practices to employ to enhance this learning. This approach is in contrast to taking actions based on tradition, conventional wisdom, or folklore. In fact, it can be said that educational research produces information that helps describe relationships and phenomena more accurately than folklore and popular impressions do.

Research on teaching can dispel old wives' tales about teaching, just as other research can dispel myths about the physical and social world outside of education. For this reason, it is important that teachers have a firm grasp of the knowledge base on teaching, including its application in various settings. Everyone, however, should be cautious and remember that teaching is a tremendously complex process that continually departs from fixed recipes and formulas.

Limits of Educational Research

We should also remember the limits of educational research and current knowledge about teaching, particularly because it tends to focus on practices currently employed by teachers, not those yet to come. The valuable descriptions and explanations about what teachers currently do should not forestall discovery of new practices. Further explanation of this idea may help highlight its importance.

Many of the research-based practices for classroom management described in this text stem from studies in which researchers compared the classroom management procedures used by researcher-defined effective teachers with those used by less effective teachers. From this research, patterns of effective classroom management practices have emerged. However, these results do not preclude the development of better practices in the future. They mean simply that in regard to the range of current practices, some classroom management procedures can be said to be better than others under certain conditions.

Along the same line, much of the research on effective teaching has been done in classrooms that represent the more traditional patterns of teaching—a single teacher working with whole groups of students for the purpose of achieving traditional learning objectives, student acquisition of basic information and skills. Although this research, like the classroom management research, can inform us about best practices within the confines of the traditional paradigm, it does not tell us very much about worthwhile innovations that may occur in the future.

goals of schooling include what teachers do when they plan for instruction, manage classroom life, and assess and evaluate student progress.

Interactive Aspects of Teaching

When most people think about teaching, they think of face-to-face classroom instruction. This aspect of teachers' work has been labeled the **interactive function of teaching** (Arends, 1994). It includes the direct application of various teaching models described in this book as well as the use of a variety of teaching strategies and techniques aimed at helping students learn. It includes explaining and demonstrating ideas to students, helping them with seatwork assignments, showing a film to introduce a unit of work, and conducting a review prior to a test. It could also include organizing students in study groups, taking them on a field trip, or sitting around and reading a story. An interesting study on the nature of teacher's work found that instruction-centered activities accounted for about 30 percent of a teacher's total work week (Cypher & Willower, 1984).

Leadership Aspects of Teaching

Three important leadership functions of teaching are planning, managing classroom life, and assessing student progress.

Providing students with face-to-face instruction is the most visible and perhaps the most glamorous aspect of teaching. Equally important, however, is the job of providing leadership to motivate students to accomplish the academic and social goals of schooling. This text will examine three of the most important leadership functions of teaching: planning, managing classroom life, and assessing and evaluating student progress. An overview of each of these leadership functions is provided in this chapter and is then followed by detailed accounts of how each function is carried out within the confines of the particular teaching models presented. Although treated independently in this and other texts, in real day-to-day teaching, the various leadership functions overlap and interact with one another. Performing leadership tasks is no easy matter. Leadership behaviors are essential in classrooms like Ms. Cuevas's, characterized by fast-moving events and a large degree of unpredictability. Learning to read specific classroom situations in order to provide effective leadership is one of the most difficult, yet most rewarding, challenges of teaching.

Both jobs of teaching, face-to-face instruction and leadership, can best be carried out by teachers with the use of best practice supported by the professional knowledge that has been acquired through research. This text will continually refer to "best practice" stemming from research and to the **knowledge bases** on teaching and learning. The research box in this chapter considers what is meant by a knowledge base, how research is created and used in education and its strengths and weaknesses. Research boxes in subsequent chapters will expand on ideas introduced here and will illustrate research studies and methods specific to the particular teaching model being considered.

TEACHER PLANNING

Particular lessons taught by teachers do not just happen. Successful classroom learning nearly always is the result of considerable planning prior to actual instruction. Teacher planning sets the conditions for allocating the use of time, choosing an appropriate method of instruction, creating student interest in the lesson, and building a productive learning environment. Planning also helps control the unpredictability and the fast-moving pace of classroom life. Similarly, once a lesson has been taught, a teacher must evaluate how much was learned and then use that information to plan subsequent lessons. In short, planning is a crucial and ongoing part of effective teaching.

Good planning involves allocating the use of time, choosing an appropriate method of instruction, creating student interest, and building a productive learning environment.

The Three Phases of Teacher Planning

Teacher planning and decision making normally have three phases: before instruction, during instruction, and after instruction. These three phases of teacher planning and the types of decisions associated with each are summarized in Table 1.1.

The important point to understand here is that teacher planning is an ongoing process that covers almost everything teachers do in their instructional and leadership functions. It is also important to note that the mental processes involved in planning vary from one phase of teaching to the next. For example, choosing lesson content can be done after careful analysis and inquiry about students' prior knowledge, the teacher's understanding of the subject, and the nature of the subject matter itself. Similarly, many postinstructional decisions, such as the type of test to give or how to assign grades, can be made after careful reflection. On the other

TABLE 1.1 THREE PHASES OF TEACHER PLANNING

Preinstructional Phase	Interactive Phase	Postinstructional Phase
Choosing content	Presenting	Checking for understanding
Choosing approach	Questioning	Providing feedback
Allocating time and space	Assisting	Praising and criticizing
Determining structures	Providing for practice	Testing
Determining motivation	Using wait-time	Grading
	Making transitions	Reporting
	Assisting	
	Managing	

hand, planning and decision making during instruction must often be done spontaneously, based on little more than intuition about student interest and comprehension.

The remainder of this chapter focuses mainly on the planning tasks and decisions associated with the **preinstructional** phase of **planning. Interactive** and **postinstructional planning** and decision making will be examined later as part of the particular teaching models described in Chapters 2 through 6.

Planning Cycles

A planning cycle is the time span for preparing instruction: daily, weekly, unit, term, or yearly.

Teachers must prepare for different **planning cycles** or time spans, ranging from the next minute or hour to the next week, month, or year. If schoolwide planning or one's own career planning is involved, time spans may even cover several years. Obviously, planning what to accomplish tomorrow is much different from planning for a whole year. However, both are important. Also, plans carried out on a particular day are influenced by preceding events and will in turn influence plans for the days and weeks ahead.

Robert Yinger (1980) conducted an interesting and important study a few years ago that provides teachers with a way of thinking about the time dimensions of teacher planning. Using participant-observation methods, Yinger spent 40 full days over a 5-month period observing and recording activities of one primary grade teacher. From this work, Yinger was able to identify the five time spans that characterized this teacher's planning: daily planning, weekly planning, unit planning, term planning, and yearly planning. Figure 1.1 illustrates these five basic levels of planning and plots their occurrence across the school year.

Yinger also found that for each level of planning, the teacher attended to the following four items: goals of planning, sources of information, form of the plan, and criteria for judging the effectiveness of planning. Table 1.2 summarizes these four aspects of planning for each of the five levels. Later, specific information about the tasks and purposes associated with the various time dimensions of planning will be provided in some detail in both this and subsequent chapters.

The Specifics of Planning

It must be obvious by now that planning is important and that it has many dimensions. This section describes the primary tasks associated with teacher planning, starting with the use of instructional objectives and followed by the use of lesson plans and other planning tools.

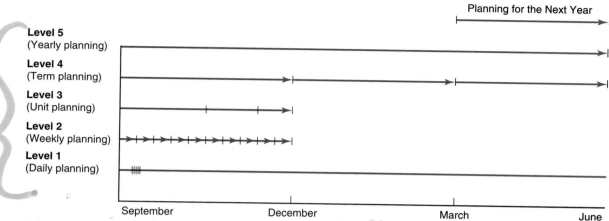

FIGURE 1.1

Five Levels of Teacher Planning

SOURCE: From R. J. Yinger (1980), A study of teacher planning. *The Elementary School Journal, 80,* 113. Copyright © 1980 The University of Chicago Press. Reprinted with permission.

Instructional Objectives

By definition, teaching is a process of attempting to promote change in students. The intended change may be far-reaching, such as developing a whole new conceptual framework for thinking about science or acquiring a new appreciation for literature. It may be as precise and simple as learning how to tie a shoestring. **Instructional objectives** are statements that describe a teacher's intent about how students should change. Instructional objectives are like road maps: They help teachers and their students know where they are going and when they have arrived at their location. Like different kinds of road maps, some instructional objectives are simple. They are easy to make and read. Others are more complex. For this reason, there are several different approaches to guide the writing of instructional objectives and a variety of formulas to use. Differing opinions among theorists and teachers about how specific or general instructional objectives should be written have at times become controversial issues.

Instructional objectives describe a teacher's intent about what students should learn.

Behavioral Objectives.   In 1962, Robert Mager wrote a book entitled *Preparing Instructional Objectives,* which set off a debate over the most desirable form in which to write an objective. Mager and his disciples argued that for instructional objectives to be meaningful, they must clearly communicate a teacher's instructional intent and should be very specific. Objectives written in the Mager format became known as **behavioral objectives** and required three parts:

Well-written behavioral objectives give students a clear statement of what is expected of them.

TABLE 1.2 PLANNING AT EACH LEVEL OF THE MODEL

	Goals of Planning	Sources of Information	Form of the Plan	Effectiveness of Planning
Yearly Planning	1. Establishing general content (fairly general and framed by district curriculum objectives) 2. Establishing basic curriculum sequence 3. Ordering and reserving materials	1. Students (general information about numbers and returning students) 2. Resources available 3. Curriculum guidelines (district objectives) 4. Experience with specific curricula and materials	1. General outlines listing basic content and possible ideas in each subject matter area (spiral notebook used for each subject)	1. Comprehensiveness of plans 2. Fit with own goals and district objectives
Term Planning	1. Detailing the content to be covered in next 3 months 2. Establishing a weekly schedule for term that conforms to teacher's goals and emphases for the term	1. Direct contact with students 2. Time constraints set by school schedule 3. Resources available	1. Elaboration of outlines constructed for yearly planning 2. A weekly schedule outline specifying activities and times	1. Outlines—comprehensiveness, completeness, and specificity of elaborations 2. Schedule—comprehensiveness and fit with goals for term, balance 3. Fit with goals for term
Unit Planning	1. Developing a sequence of well-organized learning experiences 2. Presenting comprehensive, integrated, and meaningful content at an appropriate level	1. Students' abilities, interests, etc. 2. Materials, length of lessons, setup time, demand, format 3. District objectives 4. Facilities available for activities	1. Lists of outlines of activities and content 2. Lists of sequenced activities 3. Notes in plan book	1. Organization, sequence, balance, and flow of outlines 2. Fit with yearly and term goals 3. Fit with anticipated student interest and involvement
Weekly Planning	1. Laying out the week's activities within the framework of the weekly schedule 2. Adjusting schedule for interruptions and special needs 3. Maintaining continuity and regularity of activities	1. Students' performance in preceding days and weeks 2. Scheduled school interruptions (for example, assemblies, holidays) 3. Materials, aides, and other resources	1. Names and times of activities in plan book 2. Day divided into four instructional blocks punctuated by A.M. recess, lunch, and P.M. recess	1. Completeness of plans 2. Degree to which weekly schedule has been followed 3. Flexibility of plans to allow for special time constraints or interruptions 4. Fit with goals
Daily Planning	1. Setting up and arranging classroom for next day 2. Specifying activity components not yet decided on 3. Fitting daily schedule to last-minute intrusions 4. Preparing students for day's activities	1. Instructions in materials to be used 2. Setup time required for activities 3. Assessment of class "disposition" at start of day 4. Continued interest, involvement, and enthusiasm	1. Schedule for day written on the chalkboard and discussed with students 2. Preparation and arrangement of materials and facilities in the room	1. Completion of last-minute preparations and decisions about content, materials, etc. 2. Involvement, enthusiasm, and interest communicated by students

SOURCE: R. J. Yinger (1980), A study of teacher planning, *The Elementary School Journal, 80*, 114–115. Copyright © 1980 by The University of Chicago Press. Reprinted with permission.

1. *Student behavior.* What the student will be doing or the kinds of behavior the teacher will accept as evidence that the objective has been achieved
2. *Testing situation.* The condition under which the behavior will be observed or expected to occur
3. *Performance criteria.* The standard or performance level defined as acceptable

A simple mnemonic for remembering the three parts of a behavioral objective is to think of it as the STP approach: student behavior (S), testing situation (T), and performance criteria (P). Table 1.3 illustrates how Mager's three-part approach works and provides examples of each.

When teachers write behavioral objectives using the Mager format, the recommendation is to use precise words that are not open to many interpretations. Examples of precise words include *write, list, identify, compare.* Examples of less precise words are *know, understand, appreciate.* There are also recommendations about how to link the three parts of the instructional objective together using the following steps: Begin by noting the testing situation, follow this by stating the student behavior, and then write the performance criteria. Table 1.4 illustrates how behavioral objectives written in this format might look.

Mager's behavioral approach has been widely accepted among teachers and others in the educational community during the past 3 decades. Well-written behavioral objectives give students a clear statement about what is expected of them and help teachers when it is time to measure student progress. The behavioral approach, however, has not been free of criticism.

Critics have argued that Mager's format leads to *reductionism,* that is, to reducing complex learning goals into small, overly simplified responses which may or may not provide evidence of the larger, wholistic learning goal. When used exclusively, those critics argue, behavioral objectives lead to

Some critics believe that reliance on specific student behaviors as the sole measure of learning does not provide evidence of larger learning goals that may not be observable.

TABLE 1.3 SAMPLE BEHAVIORAL OBJECTIVES USING MAGER'S FORMAT

Parts of the Objective	Examples
Student behavior	Identify nouns
Testing situation	Given a list of nouns and verbs
Performance criteria	Mark at least 85 percent right
Student behavior	List five causes of the Civil War
Testing situation	Essay test without use of notes
Performance criteria	Four of five reasons

TABLE 1.4   THREE PARTS OF BEHAVIORAL OBJECTIVES APPLIED

Testing Situation	Student Behavior	Performance Criteria
Given a map . . .	The student will be able to:	At least 85 percent
Without notes . . .	Identify	Four of five reasons
With the text . . .	Solve	Correct to nearest
	Compare	percentages
	Contrast	
	Recite	

neglect of many of the unmeasurable but most important goals of education. Always emphasizing precision and observable student behaviors forces teachers to be too specific in their objectives. To accomplish this specificity, they must break (reduce) larger, more global educational goals into overly small pieces. The number of objectives for almost any subject or topic could run well into the thousands, an unmanageable list for most teachers and their students. The teacher also runs the risk of paying attention only to specific objectives, which are of minor importance in themselves, while neglecting the sum total, which is more important than all the parts.

Critics have also pointed out, and rightfully so, that behavioral objectives are not compatible with contemporary constructivist perspectives on learning and that many of the more complex cognitive processes are not readily observable. It is easy, for instance, to observe a student adding two columns of numbers and to determine if the answer is correct. It is not easy to observe the thought processes or the mathematical problem solving that goes into this act. Along the same line, it is rather easy to observe students recall the major characters in a Tolstoy novel. It is not so easy to observe and measure their appreciation of Russian literature or the novel as a form of creative expression. Critics worry that the emphasis on behavioral objectives may cause teachers to neglect the more important aspects of education merely because the latter are not readily observed and measured.

Gronlund advocates first writing global objectives and then writing specific objectives that are consistent with the larger (usually unobservable) ones.

An Alternative Format.   Several curriculum theorists, as well as measurement specialists, have developed alternative approaches to handling behavioral objectives. Norman Gronlund (1978, 1982), for example, illustrated how objectives can be written first in more general terms, with appropriate specifics added later for clarification. Unlike the strict behaviorists, Gronlund is willing to use words such as *appreciate, understand, value,* or *enjoy* with his approach. He believes that although these words are open to a wide range of interpretations, they more clearly communicate the educational intents of many teachers. Table 1.5 illustrates how an objective might look using this more general format.

Notice that the initial objective is not very specific and perhaps not very meaningful or helpful in guiding lesson preparation or measuring student

TABLE 1.5 MORE GENERAL APPROACH TO WRITING OBJECTIVES	
Format	**Example**
Overall objective	Understands and appreciates the diversity of the people who make up American society
Subobjective 1	Can define diversity in the words of others and in his or her own words
Subobjective 2	Can give instances of how diverse persons or groups have enriched the cultural life of Americans
Subobjective 3	Can explore in writing how maintaining appreciation for diversity is a fragile and difficult goal to achieve

change. It does, however, communicate the overall intent the teacher desires. The subobjectives help clarify what should be taught and what students are expected to learn. While they provide more precision, they are still not as precise as Mager's three-part behavioral objective.

As in many other aspects of teaching, which type of objectives to use is likely to remain a controversial subject for years to come. The approach used by teachers will be influenced somewhat by schoolwide policies, but in most instances considerable latitude will exist for individual preferences and decisions. It is important to remember that the purposes behind instructional objectives are to communicate clearly to students the teacher's intents and to aid the teacher in evaluating student growth. Common sense as well as accumulated research suggest adopting a middle ground between overly abstract objectives and a strict adherence to the behavioral approach. Gronlund's approach of writing a more global objective first and then clarifying it and getting as specific as the subject matter allows is probably the best advice at this time.

Lesson Plans

Instructional objectives are used in conjunction with *lesson plans* and, as you saw from Yinger's research, teachers construct both short-term and long-term plans.

Daily Lesson Plans.   Teacher's daily plans are the ones that receive the most attention from practitioners. Many schools require teachers to write daily lesson plans in a prescribed format. Normally, daily plans outline content to be taught, motivational techniques to be used, specific steps and activities for students, needed materials, and evaluation processes. The amount of detail can vary. During student teaching, cooperating teachers may require a beginning teacher to write very detailed daily plans, even though their own plans may be briefer.

Daily lesson plans normally outline the content to be taught, motivational techniques to be used, materials needed, specific steps and activities, and evaluation procedures.

Most teachers can understand the logic behind requiring rather detailed daily plans. Think of the daily lesson plan as similar to the text of a speech to be delivered to a large audience. Speakers giving a speech for the first time need to follow a set of detailed notes or perhaps even a word-for-word text. As they gain experience, or as their speeches are gradually committed to memory through repeated presentations, speakers find less and less need for notes and can proceed more extemporaneously.

Lesson plans tend to vary according to the type of teaching model used.

Daily plans can take many forms. The features of a particular lesson often determine the lesson plan format. For example, each of the teaching models described in Chapters 2 through 6 requires a somewhat different format, as you will see. A teacher will find, however, that some schools have a preferred format. Normally that format contains most, if not all, the features included in the sample lesson plan developed by faculty at Augsburg College and illustrated in Figure 1.2. Notice that this lesson format includes a clear statement of objectives and a sequence of learning activities for the lesson, beginning with a way to get students started and ending with some type of closure and assignment. It also provides a means to

Lesson Topic/Subject _____ Grade Level _____

Preinstructional Planning

Objectives

_____

_____

_____

Domains
Cognitive
Affective
Motor/Skill

Materials/special arrangements/individual modifications

During Instruction

Introduction/establishing set

Sequence (syntax) of learning activities

Closure

Assignment

Postinstructional

Evaluation of student learning

   Formal

   Informal

Evaluation of the lesson (How did the lesson go? Revisions needed.)

FIGURE 1.2
Sample Lesson Plan
SOURCE: Dr. Ann Fleener, Augsburg College, Minneapolis, Minn., 1990. Reprinted with permission.

evaluate student learning as well as the lesson itself. More sample lesson plans will be provided in subsequent chapters.

Weekly and Unit Plans.   Most schools and teachers organize instruction around weeks and units. A *unit* is essentially a chunk of content and associated skills that fit together in a logical way. Normally more than one lesson is required to accomplish a unit of instruction. The content for instructional units might come from chapters in books or from major sections of curriculum guides. Examples of units could include such topics as sentences, the Civil War, fractions, thermodynamics, the heart, Japan, or Hemingway's short stories.

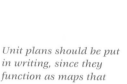

Most teachers organize instruction around units that require multiple lessons spread over several days.

Unit planning is, in many ways, more critical than daily planning. A unit plan links together a variety of goals, content, and activities a teacher has in mind. It determines the overall flow of a series of lessons for a period of several days, weeks, or perhaps even months and often reflects the teacher's understanding of both the content and processes of instruction.

Most people can memorize plans for an hour or a day, but they cannot remember the logistics and sequencing of activities over several days or weeks. For this reason, teachers' unit plans are generally written with a fair amount of detail. When unit plans are put into writing, they also serve as a reminder that some lessons require supporting materials, equipment, motivational devices, or evaluation tools that cannot always be obtained on a moment's notice. If teachers are working together in teams, unit planning and assignment of responsibilities for various unit activities are important factors to include.

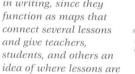

Unit plans should be put in writing, since they function as maps that connect several lessons and give teachers, students, and others an idea of where lessons are going.

Unit plans can also be shared with students, because they provide the overall scheme that explains where the teacher or a particular lesson is going. Communicating unit goals and activities to students helps them recognize what they are expected to learn. Knowledge of unit plans can help older students allocate their study time and monitor their own progress as well.

Over a period of time, experienced teachers develop unit plans and supporting materials that can be reused. Most beginning teachers, however, will have to rely on textbooks and curriculum guides. There is nothing wrong with doing this, and a beginning teacher should not feel guilty about it. Most curriculum guides have been developed by experienced teachers, and although their approach to subjects cannot be expected to fit the preferences of an individual teacher, they do provide a helpful overall design to follow.

Two notes of caution are worth mentioning, however. First, some teachers, particularly in middle schools and high schools, rely heavily on their college textbooks or on the course and unit plans of their college instructors. These plans and materials are always inappropriate for younger learners who are not ready for the advanced content found in college courses. Second, there are teachers who, after several years of experience, still rely on textbooks for planning and sequencing their instruction. Teaching and learning are creative evolutionary processes that should be keyed to a particular group of students at a particular point in time. Only when this is done can lessons rise above the humdrum and offer intellectual excitement to students.

Yearly Plans.   Yearly plans are also critical but, because of the long time frames, cannot be done with as much precision as daily or unit plans. The effectiveness of yearly plans generally revolves around how well they handle the following three features.

Most teachers have a few long-term global goals that can be achieved only by infusing them into many lessons and units during the year.

Overall themes.   Most teachers have some global attitudes, goals, and themes they would like to leave with their students. Perhaps a teacher in a mixed-race elementary classroom would like students to end the term with less bias or misunderstanding and more tolerance for people who are racially different. No specific lesson or unit can teach this attitude, but many carefully planned and coordinated experiences throughout the year can. Perhaps a high school biology teacher would like students to understand and embrace a set of attitudes associated with scientific methods. A single lesson on the scientific method will not accomplish this goal. However, personal modeling and formal demonstrations showing respect for data, the relationships between theory and reality, and the process of making inferences from information can eventually influence students to think more scientifically. A history teacher may want students to leave class with an appreciation of the lengthy time frame associated with the development of democratic traditions. Again, a single lesson on the Magna Carta, the Constitution, or the Fourteenth Amendment will not develop this appreciation. Building a succession of lessons that come back to a common theme on the "cornerstones of democracy" may.

Careful planning for the year helps teachers avoid the trap of covering too much content too superficially.

Coverage.   There are few teachers who run out of things to do during the course of a school year. Instead, the common lament is that time runs out with many important lessons still to be taught. Experienced teachers carry many of their year-long plans in their heads. Beginning teachers, however, take care to develop year-long plans if they want to get past the Civil War by March. Planning to cover desired topics requires asking what is really important to teach, deciding on priorities, and attending carefully to the instructional hours actually available during a year's time. In most instances, teachers strive to teach too much too lightly. Students may be better served if a reduced menu is planned. In short, most inexperienced teachers overestimate the amount of time actually available for instruction and underestimate the amount of time it takes to teach something well. Careful planning can help minimize this error in judgment.

School year. Experienced teachers know that the school year is cyclical and that some topics are better taught at one time than another. School cycles and corresponding emotional or psychological states revolve around the opening and closing of school, the days of the week, vacation periods, the changes of season, holidays, and important school events. Some of these can be anticipated; some cannot. Nonetheless, it is important to plan for school cycles as much as possible. Experienced teachers know that new units or important topics are not introduced on Friday or on the day before a holiday break. They know that the opening of school should emphasize processes and structures to facilitate student learning later in the year. They know that the end of the school year will be filled with interruptions and decreasing motivation as students anticipate summer vacation. They also know that it is unwise to plan for a unit examination the night after a big game or the hour following a Halloween party.

Planning for Time and Space

A final overall aspect of teacher planning has to do with the use of time and space, resources over which teachers have considerable control. This includes how much time to spend on academic tasks in general, how much time to allocate to particular subjects, and where to place students, materials, and desks. Because there has been much useful research on the relationship between teachers' use of classroom time and student achievement, we will now look more carefully at this topic. Following that, we will briefly consider the topic of classroom space. A more thorough discussion about the use of space can be found in Chapters 2 through 6, where particular teaching models are examined.

Time

The management of classroom time is a complex and difficult task for teachers, although on the surface it appears to be a rather simple and straightforward matter. Fortunately, there is a well-developed knowledge base on the use of classroom time that can guide teacher planning in this area. Essentially, the research has validated what experienced teachers have always known: The time available for instruction that appears to be so plentiful when the year begins, soon becomes a very scarce resource. Too often inexperienced teachers find themselves racing through topics in as little time as possible in order to cover targeted content. Unfortunately, what appears to them an efficient use of time often produces little, if any, student learning. This suggests that the effective use of time is just as important as the amount of time spent on a topic. Current interest in the use of classroom time stems mainly from thought and research done in the 1960s and 1970s. A number of studies during that era produced three

Research has validated that time available for instruction is far less than one would believe even though it seems plentiful at the beginning of the year.

important findings (Stallings & Kaskowitz, 1974; Fisher, Filby, Marliave, Cahen, Dishaw, Moore, & Berliner, 1978; Rosenshine, 1980):

1. Time allocated and used for specific tasks is strongly related to academic achievement. What the researchers found was that regardless of the specific methods used by teachers in particular programs, classrooms where students spent the most time *engaged in academic work* were those in which students were making the highest achievement gains in reading and mathematics.

2. Teachers vary considerably in the amount of time they allocated to to particular studies. For instance, in one study researchers found some fifth-grade classrooms allocated 60 minutes each day to reading and language arts whereas others spent almost $2\frac{1}{2}$ hours on these subjects.

3. Regardless of the amount of time a teacher might allocate to a particular topic, there was considerable variation in the amount of time students were actually engaged in learning activities. A large proportion of time was found to be devoted to nonacademic, noninstructional, and various housekeeping activities.

A direct relationship exists between time engaged in academic tasks and high achievement gains.

These time studies of the 1970s led Carol Weinstein and Andrew Mignano (1993) to differentiate instructional time into seven categories:

1. *Total time.* This is the total amount of time students spend in school. In most states the mandated time consists of 180 days of school per year and from 6 to 7 hours of school each day.

2. *Attended time.* This is the amount of time that students actually attend school. Sickness, broken heating systems, and snow days reduce the amount of attendance time from the total time required by law.

3. *Available time.* Some of the school day is spent on lunch, recess, pep rallies, and other extracurricular activities and, consequently, is not available for academic purposes.

4. *Planned academic time.* When teachers fill in plan books, they set aside a certain amount of time for different subjects and activities, called planned academic time.

5. *Actual academic time.* The amount of time the teacher actually spends on academic tasks or activities is called allocated time. This is also called **opportunity to learn** and is measured in terms of the amount of time teachers have their students spend on a given academic task.

6. *Engaged time.* The amount of time students actually spend on learning activity or task is called engaged time (also called **time on task**). This type of time is measured in terms of on-task and off-

task behavior. If a teacher has allocated time to seatwork on math problems, and the student is working on these problems, the student's behavior is on task. Conversely, if the student is doodling, or talking about football with another student, the behavior is counted as off task.

7. *Academic learning time (ALT)*. This is the amount of time a student spends engaged in an academic task at which he or she is successful. It is the aspect of time most closely related to student learning.

The graph shown in Figure 1.3, developed by Carol Weinstein and Andrew Mignano (1993), shows how much time is available in each of the seven categories. Figure 1.3, based on the time studies described previously, shows how the almost 1,100 hours of mandated time for schooling is reduced to slightly over 300 hours when it comes to actual academic learning time, because there is slippage each step of the way. Thus, although there is great variation in the way school and classroom time is managed, the lesson from the research on how time is used clearly shows that far less academic learning time is available to teachers and students than initially meets the eye.

Time studies done by prominent educational researchers gained worldwide attention from both practitioners and researchers alike. If strong relationships existed between time-on-task and academic achievement, the obvious follow-up research would be to discover what some teachers do to produce classrooms with high on-task ratios and what can be done to help other teachers improve in this direction. Two domains of immediate concern were the ways teachers organized and managed their classrooms and

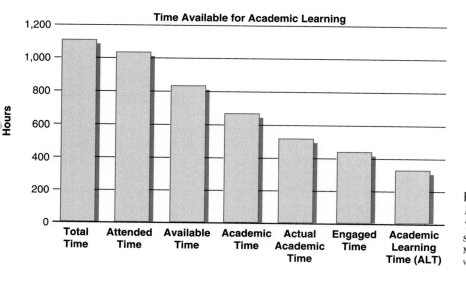

FIGURE 1.3
How Much Time is There, Anyway?
SOURCE: Weinstein & Mignano (1993). Reprinted with permission.

the particular teaching methods they employed. More is said about these two topics in subsequent sections and chapters.

Space

The use of classroom space is a major influence on communication patterns and power relationships among teachers and students.

The arrangement of classroom space is critical and does not have simple solutions. Most important is the fact that the way space is used influences the way classroom participants relate to one another and what students learn. Consider, for example, how a teacher might conduct a discussion with students. The teacher and students could be arranged in a circle that permits equal communication among all parties or, as is more usual, the students could be arranged in straight rows with all information directed to and from a central figure (the teacher). In the latter arrangement, the discussion does not occur among students but between the students and the teacher. As this example shows, the way space is designed influences both communication patterns and power relationships among teachers and students. These relationships are important, because they may affect the degree to which students take ownership of the lesson and become independent learners.

Arrangements of students, desks, and chairs not only help determine classroom communication patterns and interpersonal relationships but also influence a variety of daily decisions teachers must make concerning the management and use of scarce resources. The choices involved are not clear-cut. Fortunately, a substantial body of research provides guidelines for teachers as they think about these decisions. Space arrangements to facilitate particular teaching models will be described in some detail in subsequent chapters.

CLASSROOM MANAGEMENT

Teachers consistently rank classroom management and discipline among their most difficult tasks.

When teachers talk about the most difficult problems they experienced in their first years of teaching, classroom management and discipline consistently rank among the most difficult. Although a rich knowledge base and many guidelines on classroom management have been developed over the past two decades, beginning teachers continue to feel insecure about managing their first classrooms. This remains one of the most critical leadership aspects of teaching.

Many of the anxieties inexperienced teachers have in regard to classroom management are, in fact, the natural reaction of people in any field when they are asked to assume positions of leadership and to exert influence and authority for the first time. Gaining basic management understanding and skills will do much to reduce the natural anxiety that accompanies one's first classroom assignment. This section introduces several important concepts and skills associated with classroom management in any setting. These concepts will be revisited in subsequent chapters along with other aspects of classroom management that are closely associated with specific models of instruction. The discussion here begins with three big ideas that form this book's overall perspective on classroom management.

First, classroom management is not an end itself; it is merely one part of a teacher's overall instructional and leadership role. It cannot be separated from the other functions of teaching. For example, teachers who plan their lessons carefully and thereby ensure a well-paced and engaging lesson are doing much to assure good classroom management. When teachers plan ways to allocate time to various learning activities or consider how classroom space should be used, they are making important decisions that will affect classroom management. Similarly, all the strategies for building positive learning environments described in subsequent chapters, such as helping a class develop into a learning community and attending to student motivation, are also important components of classroom management. In short, since the use of effective teaching practices helps prevent classroom management problems from arising, it is helpful to think of classroom management and instruction as two sides of the same coin. An important theme stressed throughout this text is what has been labeled **preventive management.** Teachers who plan appropriate classroom activities and tasks, who make wise decisions about time and space allocation, and who have a sufficient repertoire of instructional strategies will be building learning environments that gain **student cooperation** and minimize management and discipline problems.

The term preventive management *refers to planning and teaching strategies that minimize management and discipline problems.*

Second, each teaching model described in subsequent chapters has its own unique classroom **management demands** that influence the behaviors of both teachers and learners. The instructional tasks and classroom arrangement associated with giving a lecture, for example, call for different student behaviors than would be appropriate if students were trying to master a new skill. Similarly, behavioral demands are different for students working together in groups as compared to working alone on a seatwork assignment. In short, the appropriateness of particular classroom management actions is determined by circumstances surrounding particular lessons and particular students.

Each teaching model has its own unique classroom management demands.

Finally, classroom management is possibly the most important challenge facing teachers, since their reputation among colleagues, school authorities, and even students will be largely influenced by their ability to create and to maintain an orderly and effective learning environment. Sometimes inexperienced teachers think this judgment is unfair and argue that schools and principals put too much emphasis on order as contrasted to learning. Perhaps it is unfair. Nonetheless, teachers are quickly tested in the management and discipline arenas, and when something goes wrong, their reputations as effective classroom leaders are questioned. More important, without adequate management, effective classroom instruction can-

Since good classroom management is a prerequisite to effective classroom instruction, teachers are often judged on their ability to create an orderly learning environment.

not occur. Dunkin and Biddle (1974) pointed out this important fact many years ago, when they wrote that "management of the classroom . . . forms a necessary condition for cognitive learning; and if the teacher cannot solve problems in this sphere, we can give the rest of teaching away" (p. 135).

In the following sections, the findings from research will be described followed by recommendations for teachers that stem from several important classroom management studies.

Help from Research

The research base on classroom management is quite well developed. Rather extensive studies have been conducted on the way teachers manage their classrooms. Particular attention has been paid to what effective teachers do to gain and sustain student engagement with academic tasks.

The Kounin Studies

One approach to studying classroom management has stemmed from the ecological view of classroom life described earlier. A teacher's major function from this point of view is to plan and orchestrate well-conceived activities that flow smoothly. Student misbehavior is conceived as actions that disrupt this activity flow. Examples of disruptions might include students talking when quiet is desired, students not working on a seatwork assignment, or students getting out of their seats at inappropriate times.

The classic research in this tradition was done by Jacob Kounin and his colleagues. After spending several years trying to understand how order and discipline are maintained in classrooms, Jacob Kounin (1970) hypothesized that the key was not so much the way teachers controlled and disciplined individual students but the ways they managed groups and developed smooth instructional procedures. In the late 1960s, Kounin decided to study these phenomena directly by videotaping 49 teachers and their students in upper-elementary classrooms. Many variables were measured in this complex study, but essentially Kounin sought to find relationships between student **work involvement** on the one hand and the means teachers used to keep lessons *flowing smoothly* on the other.

Teachers who are aware of classroom events and maintain good momentum and activity flow have fewer classroom disruptions.

Of particular importance for our discussion here are Kounin's findings regarding how some teachers were able to keep students engaged and on task. Kounin found that teachers who could maintain good activity flow, who were "with it," and who used concepts he labeled **overlappingness, smoothness,** and **momentum** all appeared to increase student work involvement. Similarly teachers who exhibited **with-it-ness** and who had smooth-flowing lessons decreased student deviancy and had fewer disruptions.

Kounin's research has provided a rich source of ideas for how teachers can approach the problem of classroom management, and guidelines emanating from his work will be incorporated into several subsequent discussions of classroom management.

The Texas Studies

Another set of classroom organization and management studies was done by researchers Edmund Emmer, Carolyn Evertson, Julie Sanford, and a number of their colleagues at the University of Texas in the late 1970s and early 1980s. The methods used by these researchers across a number of studies consisted mainly of visiting teachers in a number of schools throughout a school year and intensively observing their management behaviors using a number of observational tools (Emmer, Evertson, & Anderson, 1980; Sanford, 1981; Evertson, Emmer, Clements, & Worsham, 1989). By observing teachers closely, the researchers were able to identify teachers who after several months had few management problems and teachers who had serious problems. They then compared the behaviors of the effective and ineffective classroom managers to find what seemed to contribute to the effective teacher's successes. A study done by Sanford (1981) while she was with the Texas group is illustrative of the work of this group of researchers.

Sanford was interested in two important questions: (1) Which classroom management practices are most related to student on-task behavior and disruptive behavior? and (2) What similarities and differences exist between the practices of more and less effective classroom managers. To answer these questions, she studied 13 middle school science teachers and their students. She observed each teacher 16 to 18 times in two different classes during September and October and 8 times during January and February of the same school year. Detailed narratives of teacher and student behaviors were kept, with particular attention paid to keeping records of student on-task behavior. A second step in Sanford's study was to rank the management practices of the 13 teachers and sort them into three groups: three teachers called best managers, seven teachers called average managers, and three teachers called poor managers.

Sanford found strong relationships between student on-task behavior and a number of teacher behaviors. Specifically, when she compared the best and poorest classroom managers, she found the following. Note the similarity with Kounin's findings.

◆ The more effective classroom managers had *procedures* that governed student talk, participation, movement, turning in work, and what to do during instructional downtimes.
◆ Classroom activities in the effective managers' classrooms ran smoothly and efficiently. *Instructions were clear* and student *misbehavior was handled quickly.*
◆ Effective managers had very *clear work requirements* for students and monitored student progress carefully.

◆ Effective managers gave *clear presentations and explanations* and their directions about note taking were explicit.

Effective classroom managers provide clear instructions regarding student assignments, handle misbehavior quickly, and give clear presentations and explanations.

While Sanford was identifying effective classroom management behaviors, researchers Emmer, Evertson, and Anderson (1980) were discovering that effective classroom managers start their school years differently than less effective classroom managers do. These researchers studied 27 third-grade teachers and their students in eight elementary schools. As in the Sanford study, teachers were intensively observed. Twelve teachers in this study were observed during the first day of school and the remainder during day 2. Teachers were then observed at least eight times during the first 3 weeks and then again later in the year. The researchers in this study were able to identify seven teachers who were very effective classroom managers and seven who were clearly less effective in producing student engagement compared to off-task behavior.

◆ More effective managers had more contact with students during the first few days and spent considerable time explaining rules and procedures.

◆ More effective managers had better instructional procedures and made the first academic activity enjoyable.

◆ More effective managers were sensitive to student needs and concerns during the first few days of school, specifically in gauging attention span, levels of lesson difficulty, and overall judgment about what to do.

◆ More effective managers exhibited better listening and affective skills.

Establishing a smooth-running classroom at the beginning of the year helps maintain a good learning environment later in the year.

The most important finding of this study, however, was the stability between beginning-of-the-year management effectiveness and what happens later on. In other words, teachers who establish smooth-running classrooms in the beginning of the year maintain them throughout the school year. Those who get off to a bad start face troubles later on.

The Kounin and Texas classroom management studies significantly influenced the way educators approach classroom management and produced the recommendation and guidelines for creating and maintaining well-managed classrooms that follow.

Conditions and Procedures for Good Management

Practicing Prevention

The old adage "an ounce of prevention is worth a pound of cure" accurately reflects what Kounin, the Texas group, and almost all other classroom management research have shown over the years. The problems associated with student misbehavior are best dealt with through preventive management which focuses on how teachers gain student cooperation and how they establish and teach clear rules and procedures. The following recommendations stem mainly from the University of Texas researchers. (Evertson, Emmer, Sanford, & Clements, 1983, 1993).

Gain Student Cooperation through Well-Planned Activities. Earlier in this chapter the intrinsic features of classrooms such as multidimensionality, simultaneity, unpredictability, and history were defined, and it was shown how these features of classroom life create pressures that affect teachers and students alike. Within such a complex setting, a big part of a teacher's job is to secure student cooperation for engaging in specified activities and tasks. If you reread the opening vignette about Ms. Cuevas's classroom, you will see that students were simultaneously engaged in various activities such as carrying on a discussion, working in small groups, and taking a test. Such activities form the basic units of classroom organization and can be described in a number of ways including the following.

- ◆ *Student groupings.* In addition to the sheer number of students present, classroom organization and management is affected by how the students are arranged in their seats, in small groups, or in large groups. As will be described in more detail in subsequent chapters, the challenge of gaining student cooperation during a large-group lecture is quite different from the challenge of getting students to work together in small groups.

- ◆ *Physical space.* The physical space in which activity occurs—the classroom, the gym, the playground, or the assembly—also affects teachers' management behavior. For example, teachers generally don't care how loudly students yell on the playground, but they are very concerned about behaviors that may cause injury. In an assembly, however, talking and movement are normally discouraged.

- ◆ *Content focus.* The activity's focal content, such as art, social studies, the Pledge of Allegiance, requires different behaviors from students and has an impact on teachers' managerial behavior. For instance, a social studies lecture requires listening and taking notes; a discussion of literature requires both listening and focused dialogue; an art lesson may require drawing.

Classroom management demands vary according to the type of student activity being used: whole-group, small-group, or seatwork.

The key to successful classroom teaching and management is gaining **student cooperation** in classroom activities and their **engagement** in the appropriate learning tasks. From this point of view, a teacher's main function is to plan and orchestrate well-conceived activities that flow smoothly. Actions by students that disrupt this activity flow constitute misbehavior. Appropriate teacher interventions to disruptions, as will be described later, should be quick and as nonintrusive as possible in order to keep learning activities flowing smoothly.

Establish Clear Rules and Procedures.   In classrooms, as in most other interactive settings, a great percentage of potential problems and disruptions can be prevented by planning rules and procedures beforehand. To understand the truth of this statement, think for a moment about the varied experiences you have had in nonschool settings where fairly large numbers of people come together. Examples most people think about include driving a car during rush hour in a large city, attending a football game, going to Disneyland, or buying tickets for a movie or play. In all these instances, established rules and procedures indicated by traffic lights and waiting lines help people who do not even know each other to interact in regular, predictable ways. Rules, such as "the right of way" and "no cutting in line," help people negotiate rather complex processes safely and efficiently.

Consider what happens when procedures or rules suddenly break down or disappear. You can probably recall an instance when a power outage caused traffic lights to stop working, or when a large crowd arrived to buy tickets for an important game before the ticket sellers set up the queuing stalls. Recently, a teacher was in Detroit for a conference, and her return flight was booked on an airline that had merged with another airline on that particular day. When the two airlines combined information systems, something went wrong with the computers, making it impossible for the ticket agents to know who was on a particular flight and preventing them from issuing seat assignments. Disruptive behavior and bedlam resulted. People shoved each other as they tried to ensure a seat for themselves; they yelled at each other and at the cabin crew. Members of a normally well-disciplined crew spoke sharply to each other and to the passengers. Eventually a seat was found for everyone. The boarding process, however, had not proceeded in the usual orderly, calm manner, because some well-known procedures were suddenly unavailable.

Rules are statements specifying what students can and cannot do, while procedures are routines used to get work and activities accomplished.

Classrooms are not too different from busy airports or busy intersections. They, too, require rules and procedures to govern important activities. As used here, **rules for behavior** are statements that specify the things students are expected to do and not do. Normally, rules are written down, are made clear to students, and are kept to a minimum.

Whereas rules specify the "dos and don'ts" of classroom life, **procedures** are the routines used to accomplish work and other activity. They are seldom written down, but effective classroom managers spend considerable time teaching routine procedures to students in the same way that they teach academic content. Student movement, student talk, and what to do with instructional downtime are among the most important factors that require rules and procedures to govern behavior and make work and lessons flow efficiently.

◆ *Student movement.* In many secondary classrooms, such as a science laboratory, an art room, or a physical education facility, and in all elementary classrooms, students must move around to accomplish important learning activities. Materials have to be obtained or put back, pencils need sharpening, small groups are formed, and so on. Effective classroom managers devise ways to make such necessary movement flow smoothly. They devise waiting and distribution procedures that are efficient; they establish rules that minimize disruptions and ensure safety. Examples of rules might include those that limit the number of students moving at any one time or those that specify when to be seated. How to line up, move in the halls, and go unattended to the library are procedures that assist with student movement.

◆ *Student talk.* Effective classroom managers have a clear set of rules governing student talking. Most teachers prescribe when no talking is allowed (when the teacher is lecturing or explaining), when low talk is allowed and encouraged (during small-group work or seatwork), and when anything goes (during recess and parties). Effective classroom managers also have procedures that make classroom discourse more satisfying and productive, such as talking one at a time during a discussion, listening to other people's ideas, raising hands, and taking turns.

◆ *Downtime.* Sometimes lessons are completed before a period is over, and it is inappropriate to start something new. Similarly, when students are doing seatwork, some finish before others. Waiting for a film projector to arrive for a scheduled film is another example of instructional **downtime.** Effective classroom managers devise rules and procedures to govern student talk and movement during these times. Examples include: "If you finish your work, you can get a book and read silently until everyone is finished." "While we wait for the film to start, you may talk quietly to your neighbors, but you may not move around the room."

Table 1.6 shows the type of rules recommended by Evertson, Emmer, and their colleagues (1989) for elementary and secondary classrooms. Although these rules are just examples, they conform to general recommendations for classroom rules, namely that they are designed to encourage positive student behavior and consist of a few general rules rather than a long list of specific ones.

Teach Rules and Procedures

Rules and procedures are of little value unless participants learn and accept them. This requires active teaching to make them routine through their consistent use. In most classrooms only a few rules are needed, but it is important for the teacher to make sure students understand the purpose for a rule and its moral or practical underpinnings. Concepts and ideas associated with rules have to be taught just as any other set of con-

It is important that students understand the purpose behind rules and routines and that teachers use them consistently.

TABLE 1.6 SAMPLE RULES FOR ELEMENTARY AND SECONDARY CLASSROOMS	
Sample Rules for Elementary Classrooms	**Sample Rules for Secondary Classrooms**
1. Be polite and helpful 2. Respect other people's property 3. Listen quietly while others are talking 4. Do not hit, shove, or hurt others 5. Obey all school rules	1. Bring all needed materials to class 2. Be in your seat and ready to work when the bell rings 3. Respect and be polite to everyone 4. Respect other people's property 5. Listen and stay seated while someone else is speaking 6. Obey all school rules

cepts and ideas is. For instance, very young children can see the necessity of keeping talk low during downtime when it is explained that loud talk disturbs students in neighboring classrooms who are still working. Taking turns strikes a chord with older students who have heightened concerns with issues of fairness and justice. Students understand that potential injury to self and others governs movement in a science laboratory. One point of caution about teaching rules should be noted, however. When teachers are explaining rules, they must walk a rather thin line between providing reasonable explanations and sounding patronizing or overly moralistic.

Most movement and discourse procedures have not only a practical dimension but also a skill dimension, which, like academic skills, must be taught. In subsequent chapters, several strategies are described for teaching students how to listen to other people's ideas. Student movement skills also need to be taught. Even college-age students need instruction and two or three practices to make forming into a circle, a fishbowl arrangement, or small groups move smoothly. Effective classroom managers devote time in the first week or so of the school year to teaching rules and procedures and then provide periodic review as needed.

Maintain Consistency

Finally, effective classroom managers are consistent in their enforcement of rules and their application of procedures. If they are not, any set of rules and procedures soon dissolves. For example, a teacher may have a rule for student movement that says, when you are doing seatwork and I'm at my desk, only one student at a time can come for help. If, at any time, a second student is allowed to wait at the desk while one student is being helped, soon several others will be there too. If the rule is important to the teacher, then whenever more than one student appears, the teacher must firmly remind the waiting student of the rule and ask him or her to sit down. Similarly, a teacher has a rule that no talking is allowed when he or she is giving a presentation or explaining important ideas or procedures. If two students are then allowed to whisper in the back of the room, even if they are not disturbing others, soon many students will follow suit. Or, if the teacher wants students to raise their hands before talking during a discussion and then allows a few students to blurt out whenever they please, the hand-raising rule is soon rendered ineffective.

It is often difficult for inexperienced teachers to establish consistency for at least two reasons. One, rule breaking normally occurs when more than one event is going on simultaneously. Maintaining total awareness of the complex classroom environment requires experience, and a novice teacher may not always see everything that occurs. Two, it takes considerable energy and even personal courage to enforce rules consistently. Many inexperienced teachers find it easier and less threatening to ignore certain student behavior rather than to confront and deal with it. Experienced teachers know that avoiding a difficult situation only leads to more problems later.

CLASSROOM ASSESSMENT AND EVALUATION

Like leaders in all situations, teachers are responsible for the assessment and evaluation of students in their classrooms, an aspect of their work that some find unpleasant. Nonetheless, assessment, evaluation, and grading are of utmost importance to students and parents, and the way these processes are performed have long-term consequences. Assessment and evaluation processes also consume a fairly large portion of teachers' time. For instance, a review by Shaefer and Lissitz (1987) reported that teachers spend as much as 10 percent of their time on matters related to assessment and evaluation. Stiggins (1987) found that teachers can spend as much as one-third their time on assessment-related activities. For these reasons, it is critical that teachers build a repertoire of effective strategies for performing this leadership role.

Some studies have found that teachers spend as much as one-third their time in assessment-related activities.

Although certain measurement techniques associated with assessment and evaluation are beyond the scope of this book, many basic concepts and procedures are well within the grasp of all teachers. This section explains why assessment and evaluation are important and introduces key concepts. Subsequent chapters explore specific assessment and evaluation procedures and concerns as they relate to each specific approach to teaching.

Purposes of Assessment and Evaluation

If you will think back to your own school days, you will recall the excitement (and the anxiety) of getting back the results of a test or of receiving your report card. When these events occurred, they were almost always accompanied by the student question, "Wad-ja get?" You also will remember (in fact, you still hear) another favorite student question, "Is it going to be on the test?" These questions and the emotion behind them highlight the importance assessment and evaluation play in students' lives.

Assessment and evaluation are not only fundamental functions of teaching, they are also controversial. Some people argue that grades dehumanize education and establish distrust between teachers and students. Others say that grading and comparing students lead to harmful anxiety and to low self-esteem for those who receive poor grades. Even those who acknowledge the importance of assessment and evaluation have often condemned current practices for the emphasis on testing basic skills out of context and the excessive competition that results. Still others believe grades are really a "rubber yardstick," measuring the whims of particular teachers rather than mastery of important educational goals. Regardless of the criticism and controversy surrounding this topic, the process of assessing and evaluating students has persisted, and basic practices have remained essentially constant for most of the twentieth century. Two important conditions of schools and teaching help explain this fact.

Sorting Functions of Schools

The job of assessing and evaluating student growth and potential is assigned to teachers, whose decisions affect students' life chances.

Sociologists have observed on numerous occasions that schools in large, complex societies are expected to help sort people for societal roles and occupations. Although some may wish for the day when better and fairer means are found for making these judgments, at present, the larger society assigns the job of assessing and evaluating student growth and potential, in large part, to teachers. How well students perform on tests, the grades they receive, and the judgments their teachers make about their ability have important, long-run consequences for both students and society. These judgments can determine who goes to college, the college they attend, the type of career open to them and their first jobs, and the lifestyles they maintain. Enduring perceptions about self-esteem can also result from the way students are evaluated in school.

This aspect of a teacher's work is one that parents are also very concerned about. They are fully aware of the important sorting going on in schools. Most parents can recall critical judgments made about their own work and the consequences these had for them. Similarly, they are keenly aware of the judgments being made when their children are placed into a higher- or lower-level reading group or into general math instead of algebra.

Teachers have been known to complain about this type of parental concern, and sometimes these complaints are justified. For instance, some parents let unrealistic expectations for their children interfere with teachers' professional judgment about the most appropriate level of work for their child. Conversely, other parents seem indifferent to their children's academic evaluation and offer little encouragement at home for doing good work or getting good grades.

Most parental concern is natural, however, and potentially can be beneficial. There is a growing research literature showing that parental concern can be tapped and used by effective teachers for the purpose of enhancing student learning. For instance, actions by teachers that show regard for parental concerns by using more frequent reporting procedures and by getting parents to support the school's reward systems at home can result in more homework completed, better attendance, more academic engagement, and generally increased student output.

Grade-for-Work Exchange

Much of what students choose to do, or not do, is determined by what Walter Doyle labeled the *grade-for-work exchange*. This idea describes how students, like the rest of us, can be motivated to do certain things for extrinsic rewards. We may work hard and do what employers want in order to receive a merit raise; we may volunteer for community service hoping to receive public recognition for our work. This does not mean that our work has no intrinsic value or that altruistic reasons do not prompt us to help others. It simply means that for many human beings extrinsic rewards are valued and provide a strong incentive to act in particular ways. Academic tasks such as completing assignments, studying for tests, writing papers, and carrying on classroom discourse are the work of students. It is important to remember that just as adults work for a salary, students work for grades. These exchanges are critically important and help explain much of classroom life.

Just as adult behavior is influenced by extrinsic rewards, such as money, student behavior is influenced by the extrinsic rewards of the grading system.

Key Assessment and Evaluation Concepts

Assessment and evaluation are related functions carried out by teachers in order to make wise decisions about their students and about their instruction. Since we know the important long-term consequence that these decisions have for students, it follows that such teacher decision making should be based on information that is as relevant and as accurate as possible. Several key concepts can help you understand how to gather reliable data.

Assessment

The term **assessment** usually refers to the full range of information gathered and synthesized by teachers for the purpose of making decisions

Assessment refers to the process of gathering and synthesizing information to make decisions about something, while evaluation is the process of judging the worth or value of something.

about their students and their classrooms. Information about students can be gathered in informal ways, such as through observation and verbal exchange. It can also be gathered through formal means, such as homework, tests, and written reports. Information about classrooms and a teacher's instruction can also be part of assessment. The range of information can also vary from informal feedback provided by students about a particular lesson to more formal reports resulting from course evaluations and standardized tests.

Evaluation

Whereas assessment focuses on gathering and synthesizing information, the term **evaluation** usually refers to the process of making judgments, assigning value, or deciding worth. A test, for example, is an assessment technique used to collect information about how much students know about a particular topic. Assigning a grade, however, is an evaluative act, because the teacher is placing a value on the information gathered on the test.

Formative evaluations are made prior to or during instruction so that teachers can match instruction to students' knowledge; summative evaluations are made after instruction to determine how much students have learned from instruction.

Most evaluation specialists talk in terms of either formative or summative evaluations, depending on how the evaluation is to be used. **Formative evaluations** are made *prior to or during* instruction and are intended to inform teachers about their students' prior knowledge and skills in order to assist with planning. Information from formative evaluations is used to make judgments about such matters as student grouping, unit and lesson plans, and instructional strategies. **Summative evaluations,** on the other hand, are made *after* a set of instructional activities has occurred. Their purpose is to summarize how well a particular student, group of students, or a teacher has performed on a set of learning goals or objectives. Summative evaluations are designed so that judgments can be made about accomplishments. Information obtained from summative evaluations is used by teachers to determine grades and to inform the reports sent to students and their parents.

A Teacher's Assessment Program

Classroom teachers are responsible for the assessment, testing, and grading related to their own specific classrooms and courses. In general, a teacher's assessment activities are aimed at one of the following three important goals: diagnosing prior knowledge and skills, providing corrective feedback, and making judgments and grading student achievement. These three purposes have some similarities and also have some important differences.

Diagnosing Prior Knowledge

To individualize instruction for specific students or to tailor instruction for a particular classroom group requires reliable information about students' capabilities and their prior knowledge. Standardized tests attempt to measure many areas of student achievement. These tests are most highly developed and most readily available in reading, language development, and mathematics. Unfortunately, they are less available in other subject areas.

In many school systems, teachers will be assisted by test and measurement personnel or by counseling and special education staff who have been specifically trained to help diagnose student capabilities and achievement. In other school systems, this type of assistance may not be available. If formal diagnostic information is not available, teachers will have to rely on more informal techniques for assessing prior knowledge. For example, teachers can observe students closely as they approach a particular task and get some sense about how difficult or easy it is for them. Similarly, by listening carefully to students and by asking probing questions, a teacher can ascertain additional cues about students' prior knowledge about almost any topic. In fact, teacher and student questions are a major means of ascertaining student understanding. Verbal responses help teachers decide whether to move forward with a lesson or to back up and review. Nonverbal responses such as frowns, head nodding, and puzzled looks also provide hints about how well students understand a topic. However, teachers should be aware that sometimes these nonverbal behaviors can be misinterpreted.

Because many students will not admit their lack of knowledge or understanding in large groups, some teachers have found that interviewing students in small groups can be a good way to get the diagnostic information they need. This technique is particularly useful for getting information from students who do not participate regularly in classroom discussions or those who offer few nonverbal signals.

Providing Corrective Feedback

A second important purpose of assessment and evaluation is to provide students with feedback on how they are doing. As with diagnosing students' prior knowledge, this is easier to do for some topics and skills than others. Test makers have developed rather sophisticated and reliable procedures for measuring discrete skills such as word recognition or simple mathematical operations. It is also quite easy to collect information on how fast a student can run the 100-yard dash or how long it takes to climb a 30-foot rope. Biofeedback techniques are also available to help students monitor their own physical reactions to stress and certain types of exertion. However, as instruction moves from a focus on basic skills and abilities to a focus on more complex thinking and problem-solving skills, the problem of providing corrective feedback becomes more difficult, because there are few, if any, reliable tests for these more complex processes. Later chapters provide some principles for giving feedback to students and will explain the importance of feedback for student improvement.

REFLECTION BOX   BECOMING A REFLECTIVE TEACHER

Becoming truly accomplished in almost any human endeavor takes a long time. Many professional athletes, for example, display raw talent at a very early age, but they do not reach their athletic prime until their late twenties and early thirties. Many great novelists have written their best pieces in their later years, only after producing several inferior works earlier on. Becoming a truly accomplished teacher is no different. It takes time to gain command of the knowledge base that guides effective teaching. But as important, it takes purposeful actions in which one gradually discovers one's best style through experience and **reflection** on that experience.

But what is reflection and how does one learn from experience?

Many of the problems and dilemmas faced by teachers in real classrooms are characterized by their uniqueness, meaning that the more generalized knowledge from research is often of little help. This same problem is faced by other professionals, such as doctors, lawyers, and architects, as the following observations by Donald Schon (1983) illustrate:

> The situation of practice is characterized by unique events. Erik Erikson, the psychiatrist, has described each patient as a "universe of one," and an eminent physician has claimed that "85 percent of the problems a doctor sees in his office are not in the book." The unique case calls for "an art of practice which might be taught," if it were constant and known, but it is not constant.

> Practitioners are frequently embroiled in the conflicts of values, goals, purposes and interests. Teachers are faced with pressures for increased efficiency in the context of contracting budgets, demands that they rigorously "teach the basics,": exhortations to encourage creativity, build citizenship, and help students to examine their values.

> If it true that there is an irreducible element of art in professional practice, it is also true that gifted engineers, teachers, scientists, architects, and managers sometimes display artistry in their day-to-day practice. If the art is not invariant, known and teachable, it appears nonetheless, at least in some individuals, to be learnable. (pp 16–18)

Learning from experience and through reflection differs from more formal learning. Instead of starting with a set of academic principles or rules, experience-based learning starts with concerted experiences, followed by observation and reflection and culminating in personal conception of knowledge that can be applied to new situations. John Dewey (1938) suggested

Testing for Summative Evaluation and Reporting

For most teachers, the bulk of their assessment time and energy is spent on assessing student progress, determining grades, and reporting progress. Although some teachers do not like this aspect of their work, that to learn from experience and reflection is to make a backward-forward connection between what we do to things and what we learn from those things and experiences. This perspective is illustrated in Figure 1.4

Experience is especially useful in complex learning situations and for learning those aspects of teaching for which pat answers do not exist. Experience alone, however, is not sufficient. For best results, learners must be able to step back and observe their own behavior and their personal reactions to it so they can reflect on the experience. Indeed, some observers have argued that the key to becoming an autonomous professional rests partly on a teacher's disposition and ability to engage in self-study. It also rests on their ability to reflect on and critically judge their teaching and formal and informal testing.

The reflection boxes found in each chapter, as well as several of the learning aides found at the end of each chapter, have been designed to alert readers to areas of teaching where knowledge is incomplete and where teaching situations require individual problem solving and reflection.

Think for a moment about what you have learned from experience and from reflection. How does this type of learning differ for you from more formal types of learning? Do you reflect on your experiences regularly by keeping a journal? What steps do you need to take to become a reflective practitioner?

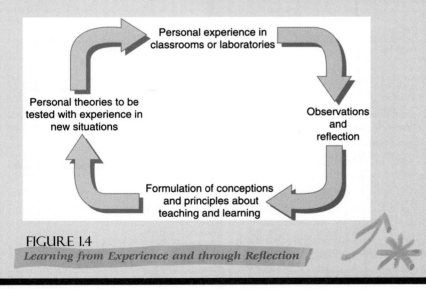

FIGURE 1.4
Learning from Experience and through Reflection

it must be done and, for reasons enumerated earlier, done well. Students perform academic work for grades and they expect their work to be evaluated. Teachers who take this work-for-grade exchange lightly, or who do their part poorly, usually are faced with serious classroom problems.

TABLE 1.7   THREE MAJOR PURPOSES OF CLASSROOM ASSESSMENT

	Diagnostic	Feedback	Reporting
Function	Placement, planning, and determining the presence or absence of skills and prior knowledge	Feedback to student and teachers on progress	Grading of students at the end of a unit or semester
When used	At the outset of a unit, semester, or year, or during instruction when student is having problems	During instruction	At the end of quarter, semester, or year's work
Type of test	Standardized diagnostic tests; observations and checklists	Quizzes and special tests or homework	Final exams
Scoring	Norm- and criterion-referenced	Criterion-referenced	Norm- or criterion-referenced

The key concepts and procedures associated with the three major purposes of classroom assessment are summarized in Table 1.7. Later chapters will provide more specific information about a teacher's assessment program.

SUMMARY

◆ Teaching is a demanding job that takes place in a complex and dynamic setting, the classroom.

◆ Although classrooms are familiar places for beginning teachers, most have known the classroom from in front of rather than behind the teacher's desk. A new set of lenses is required to understand classroom life as the teacher experiences it.

◆ One way to view classrooms is to think about them as "ecological systems" where the inhabitants (teachers and students) interact within a specific environment for the purpose of accomplishing valued learning goals and activities.

◆ Classrooms have six intrinsic features that make them complex to understand and demanding to teach in: multidimensionality, simultaneity, immediacy, unpredictability, publicness, history.

◆ Over time the public's and the profession's expectations for teachers have changed. In earlier times teachers were expected to be moral examples for their students and to conform to the social norms of the community. Today, teachers are increasingly being held accountable for using "best practice" in order to maximize their students' achievement.

◆ The two big jobs of teaching are providing instruction and exerting leadership. Providing instruction refers to what most people think about when they think of teaching, that is, face-to-face interaction with students. Exerting leadership and motivating students to accomplish the academic and social goals of schooling include what teachers do when they plan for instruction, manage classroom life, and assess and evaluate student progress.

◆ Planning and making decisions about instruction are among the most important aspects of teaching, because they are major determinants of what is taught in schools and how it is taught.

◆ Teacher planning is multifaceted but relates to three phases of teaching: the pre-instructional phase, in which decisions are made about what will be taught and for how long; the interactive phase, in which decisions are made minute to minute; and the postinstructional phase, in which decisions are made about how to evaluate student progress and what type of feedback to provide.

◆ Planning cycles include not only daily plans but also weekly, monthly, and yearly plans. The details of these various plans differ. Plans carried out on a par-ticular day are influenced by preceding events and will in turn influence future plans.

◆ Instructional objectives and lesson plans are the specific tools that assist with teacher planning.

◆ Instructional objectives are statements that describe what students should learn as a result of instruction. They can be written in behavioral or more general forms. A good behavioral objective includes statements about expected student behavior, the testing situation in which the behavior will be observed, and per-formance criteria. An objective written in the more general form communicates a teacher's overall intent but lacks the precision of a behavioral objective.

◆ Formats for lesson plans can vary, but most good plans include a clear statement of objectives, a sequence of learning activities, and a means of evaluating stu-dent learning.

◆ Effective teachers know how to make good formal plans. They also know how to make adjustments when plans prove to be inappropriate or ineffective.

◆ Time and space are scarce commodities in teaching, and their use should be planned with care and foresight.

◆ Research on time shows that there is considerable variation from teacher to teacher on the amount of allocated time devoted to different subject areas. The amount of time students spend on a task is related to how much they learn. Stu-dents in classrooms in which allocated time is high and a large proportion of stu-dents are engaged learn more than in other classrooms.

◆ Space—the arrangement of materials, desks, and students—is another important resource planned and managed by teachers. The way space is used affects the learning atmosphere of classrooms, influences classroom dialogue and commu-nication, and has important cognitive and emotional effects on students.

◆ The uses of time and space are related to each other around learning tasks. Effective teachers develop an attitude of flexibility and experimentation about these features of classroom life.

◆ Classroom management is not an end in itself but one part of a teacher's over-all leadership role. Managerial and instructional aspects of teaching are highly interrelated and, in actual teaching, cannot be clearly separated.

◆ Unless classroom management issues are solved, the rest of teaching is wasted.

◆ A large portion of disruptive student behavior can be eliminated by using pre-

ventive classroom management measures such as having clear rules and procedures and carefully orchestrated learning activities.

◆ Effective managers have well-defined procedures that govern student talk and movement, make work requirements clear to students, and emphasize clear explanations.

◆ Effective managers establish clear rules and procedures, teach these rules and procedures to students, and carefully orchestrate classroom activities during such unstable periods as the beginning and end of class and transitions.

◆ Regardless of their planning and orchestration skills, teachers are still often faced with difficult or unmotivated students who will choose to be disruptive forces rather than involve themselves in academic activity. Effective managers have intervention skills for dealing quickly with disruptive students in direct but fair ways.

◆ As with other teaching functions, effective teachers develop an attitude of flexibility about classroom management, because they know that every class is different and plans, rules, and procedures must often be adjusted to particular circumstances.

◆ Assessment and evaluation are functions performed by teachers to make wise decisions about their instruction and about their students. A fairly large portion of a teacher's time is consumed with assessment and evaluation, and the consequences of this work are immense.

◆ Distinctions can be made between assessment and evaluation. Assessment refers to the full range of information gathered by teachers about their classrooms and their students. Evaluation refers to the process of making judgments and assigning value and worth.

◆ Evaluation specialists make key distinctions between formative and summative evaluation. Formative evaluations are made prior to or during instruction and are intended to inform teachers of their students' prior knowledge and skills in order to assist with planning. Summative evaluations come at the end of a term and summarize how well students have done.

◆ A teacher's assessment program is aimed at accomplishing three goals: diagnosing students' prior knowledge, providing students with corrective feedback, and making judgments for grading and reporting. Because the evaluation decisions teachers make are so important, it is essential that their assessment and evaluation information be of high quality.

L   E   A   R   N   I   N   G   A   I   D   1 . 1

INTERVIEWING TEACHERS ABOUT
THE SCIENTIFIC BASIS OF THE ART OF TEACHING

PURPOSE: Teaching is both science and art. This aid will help you to uncover an experienced teacher's perceptions about the scientific basis of the art of teaching and to develop your own appreciation of teaching as art and science.

DIRECTIONS: Use the following questions to guide you as you interview a teacher about his or her understanding and application of the scientific basis of the art of teaching. (Note: Many experienced teachers may not be aware of the research base and yet may be using best practice. Some effective teaching research is based on what excellent experienced teachers do.)

1. To what extent has the way you plan your teaching been influenced by: *(Estimate the percentage contribution of each.)*

   _____ research on planning

   _____ your own experience and intuition

   _____ other (*please specify*) _____

2. Can you give an example of a planning principle you have learned from each source?

   Research: _____

   Experience: _____

   Other: _____

3. Do you find you sometimes need to modify these principles in practice? If so, in what way(s)?

   _____

   _____

   _____

4. To what extent has the way you allocate resources like time and space in your classroom been influenced by: *(Estimate the percentage contribution of each.)*

   _____ research on allocating time and space

   _____ your own experience and intuition

   _____ other (*please specify*) _____

5. Can you give an example of a principle of allocating resources that you have learned from each source?

Research: _____

Experience: _____

Other: _____

6. Do you find you sometimes need to modify these principles in practice? If so, in what way(s)?

_____

_____

_____

7. To what extent has the way you organize your classroom to create a productive learning environment been influenced by: *(Estimate the percentage contribution of each.)*

_____ research

_____ your own experience and intuition

_____ other *(please specify)* _____

8. Can you give an example of a principle underlying the creation of productive learning environments you have learned from each source?

Research: _____

Experience: _____

Other: _____

9. Do you find you sometimes need to modify these principles in practice? If so, in what way(s)?

_____

_____

_____

10. To what extent has the way you manage your classroom been influenced by: *(Estimate the percentage contribution of each.)*

_____ research

_____ your own experience and intuition

_____ other *(please specify)* _____

11. Can you give an example of a classroom management principle that you have learned from each source?

Research: _____

Experience: _____

Other: _____

12. Do you find you sometimes need to modify these principles in practice? If so, in what way(s)?

_____

_____

_____

13. To what extent are the teaching strategies you use influenced by: *(Estimate the percentage contribution of each.)*

_____ research

_____ your own experience and intuition

_____ other *(please specify)* _____

14. Can you give an example of a teaching strategy that you have learned from each source?

Research: _____

Experience: _____

Other: _____

15. Do you find you sometimes need to modify these strategies in practice? If so, in what way(s)?

_____

_____

_____

L   E   A   R   N   I   N   G   A   I   D   1 . 2

OBSERVING LEADERSHIP AND INSTRUCTIONAL FUNCTIONS OF TEACHING

PURPOSE: Teaching is a complex, multifaceted activity. This aid will help sensitize you to the multiple functions of teaching.

DIRECTIONS: Shadow a teacher for at least half a day. Make sure you have a chance to observe him or her either before school starts or after class is let out. Make a "tick" whenever you see the teacher perform one of the listed activities. At the same time, estimate the amount of time the teacher spends on that activity, and jot down any other observations you make. Perhaps certain activities tend to occur at certain times, or a particular emotional tone is evident, or several activities occur simultaneously. Note anything you think will help you refine your understanding of the two teaching functions.

Function	Observed	Time	Comments
Leadership			
Planning	_____	_____	_____
Allocating time and space	_____	_____	_____
Organizing for a productive learning environment	_____	_____	_____
Managing the classroom	_____	_____	_____
Assessing or evaluating	_____	_____	_____
Instruction			
Using the direct instruction model	_____	_____	_____
Using the cooperative learning model	_____	_____	_____
Using discussion models	_____	_____	_____
Using the problem-based instruction model	_____	_____	_____
Using other strategies (specify)	_____	_____	_____

Analysis and Reflection: Tally the number of ticks for each category, and add the amount of time spent on each category. What did this teacher spend the most time doing? What did he or she do most often? How much time is spent on average on any one episode within a category? (Divide time spent by number of ticks.) Does this seem to be the most productive allocation of the teacher's time? Why or why not?

P   O   R   T   F   O   L   I   O

MY TEACHING PLATFORM

DEFINITION: A portfolio is a collection of ideas, artifacts, and products. It provides an authentic means for teachers to represent and assess their views and practices in regard to teaching and the results of their work.

Portfolios are useful for keeping a record of professional growth during a lifelong process of learning to teach. They are also useful for displaying a candidate's strengths when interviewing for a teaching position.

Today most teacher education programs recommend that teacher candidates begin the process of building a portfolio early in their program so the portfolio can evolve and mature as the candidate grows and changes.

At the end of each chapter in this text, portfolio activities are included and recommendations will be provided for creating or collecting particular artifacts and products. There is not a particular format to follow. However, the portfolio should be neat, organized, and creative. But most important, when completed, it should be a clear representation of you.

PURPOSE: This first portfolio activity has been designed to help you describe your current thinking about teaching and learning by creating a *teaching platform.*

DIRECTIONS: Create a teaching platform by doing the following:

Step 1: Write a two- or three-page paper that describes your platform for teaching and learning. This platform should represent your thinking at this point in time about how learning occurs and the implications this has for teaching practices. Your platform should be supported by clear and specific "planks" that would include the beliefs and values you hold and guide the way you would construct your classroom and perform your teaching.

Think of the platform as the overall concept you hold about teaching and learning and the planks as your more specific beliefs and values. An example of a plank might be that "learning is an active process where knowledge is socially constructed."

Step 2: Your platform should be started now, preferably early in the semester. It should be revised weekly as you study and learn more about all aspects of teaching and learning.

Step 3: You may also wish to use your platform as a device to organize other aspects of your portfolio. For instance, you may wish to illustrate your attitudes with photographs, videos, papers, lesson plans, and examples of student work.

*The ideas in this activity have been adapted from work done by Dr. Paulette Lemma and her colleagues in the Elementary Education Program at Connecticut State University.

BOOKS FOR THE PROFESSIONAL

Classroom Teaching

Fenstermacher, G. D., & Soltis, J. F. (1986). *Approaches to teaching.* New York: Teachers College Press. Drawn from classical conceptions of teaching, this book can help beginning teachers analyze alternative approaches to teaching.

Fosnot, C. T. (1989). *Inquiring teachers, inquiring learners.* New York: Teachers College Press. This book does a wonderful job of taking concepts such as constructivist perspectives, teacher empowerment, and reflection and showing how they relate to classroom learning and how they can be put into practice for helping beginners learn to teach.

Joyce, B., Weil, M., & Showers, B. (1992). *Models of teaching* (4th ed.). Englewood Cliffs, N.J.: Prentice-Hall. This book is a must. It provides more information on the models of teaching described here, plus many others.

Schön, D. A. (1983). *The reflective practitioner.* San Francisco: Jossey-Bass. This book explores the complexity of learning to become a professional and emphasizes the importance of developing skills for "reflection in action."

Wittrock, M. C. (ed.). (1986). *Handbook of research on teaching* (3d ed.). New York: Macmillan. This is the most authoritative review of the mountain of research on teaching. Beginning teachers will find many of the chapters tough going; however, it is an invaluable reference work. A new edition will be coming soon, perhaps by 1998.

Teacher Planning and Classroom Management

Emmer, E., Evertson, C., Clements, B., & Worsham, W. E. (1994). *Classroom management for secondary teachers* (3d ed.). Boston: Allyn & Bacon.

Evertson, C., Emmer, E., Clements, B., & Worsham, M. (1994). *Classroom management for elementary teachers* (3d ed.). Englewood Cliffs, N.J.: Prentice-Hall.

These two volumes, one aimed at secondary teachers, the other for elementary teachers, describe in more detail many of the procedures and techniques mentioned in this chapter. Together these books offer a comprehensive approach to classroom management from the perspective of the teacher effectiveness research.

Weinstein, C. S., & Mignano, A. J., Jr. (1993). *Elementary classroom management: Lessons from research and practice.* New York: McGraw-Hill. This highly readable book on classroom management combines both the research and the wisdom of practice on this topic. It shows how various learning tasks make different demands on the management structure and how different management approaches are required.

Assessment and Evaluation

Airasian, Peter W. (1996). *Assessment in the classroom.* New York: McGraw-Hill. An excellent text written specifically for teachers. This book includes both informal as well as formal assessment procedures.

Gronlund, N. E., & Linn, R. L. (1990). *Measurement and evaluation in teaching* (6th ed.). New York: Macmillan. This book offers the most thorough treatment available on issues related to classroom measurement and evaluation. It is filled with practical advice and tools for teachers to assist with both planning and evaluation tasks.

DIRECT INSTRUCTION

S kills, cognitive and physical, as well as certain kinds of information, are the foundations on which more advanced learning is built. Before students can discover powerful concepts, think critically, solve problems, or write creatively, they must first acquire basic skills and information. Before students can acquire and process large amounts of information, they need command of such learning strategies as note taking and summarization and the skills involved in encoding and decoding printed words. Before students can think critically, they must have basic skills associated with logic, drawing inferences from data, and recognizing bias in presentation. Before students can write an eloquent paragraph, they must master basic sentence construction, rules about correct word usage, and the self-discipline to keep with a writing task.

A major difference between novices and experts in any field is the degree to which they have mastered the basic skills of their trade.

In fact, the difference between novices and experts in almost any field is that experts have so mastered certain basic skills that they can perform them unconsciously and with precision under new or stressful situations. For example, expert teachers worry little about classroom management, because years of experience have engendered an unconscious mastery of human interaction and group dynamics skills. Similarly, top NFL quarterbacks read every move of a defense without conscious thought and automatically respond with skillful actions to a safety blitz or double coverage of prize receivers, something novice quarterbacks cannot do.

This chapter focuses on an approach to teaching that helps students learn basic skills and acquire information that can be taught in a step-by-step fashion. We refer to this approach as the **direct instruction** model, although it is often referred to by other names, such as **active teaching** (Good & Grouws, 1983), **mastery teaching** (Hunter, 1982), and **explicit instruction** (Rosenshine & Stevens, 1986). Although not synonymous, lecture, presentation, and classroom recitation are also closely related to the direct instruction model.

Even though you may never have thought about this model in any systematic way, you will undoubtedly be familiar with certain aspects of it. The rationale and procedures underlying it were probably used by adults to teach you to drive your first car, to brush your teeth, to hit a solid backhand, to write a research paper, or to solve algebraic equations. For some, this model may have been used to correct a phobia about flying or to wean them from cigarettes. Direct instruction is rather straightforward and can be mastered in a relatively short period of time. It is a "must" in the repertoire of all teachers.

[handwritten marginal note: Other names: active teaching, mastery " ", explicit instruction]

OVERVIEW OF DIRECT INSTRUCTION

This section provides a general overview of the direct instruction model using the analytical scheme introduced in the Introduction, which provides the following features:

◆ The model's **instructional goals** and the effects the model has on learners including required assessment procedures

◆ The model's **syntax** or overall pattern and flow of instructional activity

◆ The model's **learning environment** and **management system** required to make particular lessons employing it effective

Following this overview, we will take a brief look at the theoretical and empirical support for this model, after which we will provide a detailed discussion of how to conduct a direct instruction lesson. This same chapter structure will be followed in subsequent chapters with additional models.

Instructional Goals and Learner Outcomes

Learning theorists normally distinguish between two types of knowledge: **declarative knowledge** and **procedural knowledge** (Marx & Winne, 1994; Ryle, 1949; Gagné, 1977; Gagne, 1985). Declarative (verbalizable) knowledge is knowledge *about* something or that something is the case. Procedural knowledge, on the other hand, is knowledge about *how to do something*. An example of declarative knowledge is knowledge about the three branches of government: that the legislative branch has two chambers (the house and the senate) and that representatives to the house are elected to 2-year terms while senators are elected to 6-year terms. Procedural knowledge about this same topic is knowledge about, if one is a citizen, how to go to the polling place and vote on election day and how to write a letter to a senator, or if one is a senator, how to guide a bill through the Senate until it becomes a law.

> Declarative knowledge *is knowing about something, whereas* procedural knowledge *is knowing how to do something.*

Many **taxonomies,** or classification systems, exist for categorizing knowledge according to levels of thought. At the lowest level is straightforward factual information, simple declarative knowledge that one acquires but may or may not use. Memorizing the rules of poetry written in iambic pentameter is an example of factual knowledge. In contrast, the higher levels of knowledge generally involve using knowledge in some way, such as critiquing one of Robert Browning's poems or comparing and contrasting it with work by Keats. Often, procedural knowledge requires the previous acquisition of declarative knowledge, in this case, basic concepts of poetry. Teachers want their students to have both kinds of knowledge. They want them to acquire large bodies of basic declarative knowledge; they also want them to acquire important procedural knowledge, so they can take action and do things effectively.

The nature of knowledge and how it is acquired is explored in more detail in Chapter 6. The distinctions between types of knowledge and the various levels of knowledge are introduced here because they are acquired

Direct instruction was specifically designed to promote student learning of procedural knowledge and declarative knowledge that can be taught in a step-by-step fashion.

differently. The direct instruction model was specifically designed to promote student learning of procedural knowledge and declarative knowledge that is well structured and can be taught in a step-by-step fashion. Table 2.1 illustrates instructional objectives aimed at promoting the acquisition of basic declarative knowledge and straightforward procedural knowledge and compares this type of objective with those that promote social learning and higher-level thinking.

Differences can be observed in the various types of objectives listed in Table 2.1. For instance, the first objective expects the student to be able to identify the rules of ice hockey. This is important declarative knowledge for students who wish to be involved in the game. However, being able to identify the rules does not mean that the student can perform any skills associated with hockey (like passing on the move), the content of the procedural knowledge objective found in column 2. Further, neither knowing the rules nor having specific hockey skills will necessarily lead to being a good teammate or to bringing critical judgment to the way the sport is conducted, the aim of the objectives found in columns 3 and 4. Direct instruction is a suitable approach to instruction when the teacher wants students to learn particular skills or straightforward declarative knowledge such as those found in columns 1 and 2. Other models are required to promote social learning and higher-level thinking.

Syntax

Direct instruction is a teacher-centered model that has five steps: set induction, demonstration, guided practice, feedback, and extended practice.

Although experienced teachers learn to adjust their use of direct instruction to fit various situations, there are five essential phases or steps in most direct instruction lessons. The teacher begins the lesson by providing a rationale for the lesson, establishing set, and getting students ready to learn. This preparational and motivational phase is then followed by presentation of the subject matter being taught or demonstration of a particular skill. The lesson concludes with opportunities for student practice

TABLE 2.1 SAMPLE DIRECT INSTRUCTION OBJECTIVES COMPARED TO SOCIAL LEARNING OR HIGHER-LEVEL THINKING OBJECTIVES

Acquisition of Basic Knowledge	Skill Acquisition	Social Understanding	Higher Level
Student will be able to list the basic rules of ice hockey	Student will be able to pass while moving	Student will display cooperation while playing a hockey game	Student will express an opinion in regard to the presence of violence in hockey

TABLE 2.2 SYNTAX OF THE DIRECT INSTRUCTION MODEL

Phases	Teacher Behavior
Phase 1 Provide objectives and establish set	Teacher goes over objectives for the lesson, gives background information, and explains why the lesson is important. Gets students ready to learn.
Phase 2 Demonstrate knowledge or skill	Teacher demonstrates the skill correctly or presents step-by-step information.
Phase 3 Provide guided practice	Teacher structures initial practice.
Phase 4 Check understanding and provide feedback	Teacher checks to see if students are performing correctly and provides feedback.
Phase 5 Provide extended practice and transfer	Teacher sets conditions for extended practice with attention to transfer to more complex and real life situations.

and teacher feedback on their progress. During the practice-feedback phase of this model, teachers should always try to provide opportunities for students to transfer the knowledge or skill being taught to real life situations. The five phases of the direct instruction model are summarized in Table 2.2. A more detailed discussion of each phase is presented later in this chapter.

Learning Environment and Management System

A direct instruction lesson requires a most careful structuring and orchestration by the teacher. To be effective, the model necessitates that every detail of the skill or content be carefully defined and that the demonstration and practice session be carefully planned and executed. Even though there are opportunities for teachers and students to jointly identify goals, the model is primarily teacher directed. The teacher's management system must ensure student engagement, mainly through watching, listening, and structured recitations. Lessons must proceed at a brisk pace and not get sluggish. This does not mean that the learning environment and the management system have to be authoritarian, cold, or free of humor. It means that the environment is task oriented and provides high expectations for student accomplishment.

THEORETICAL AND EMPIRICAL SUPPORT

A number of historical and theoretical roots come together and provide the rationale for the direct instruction model. These include ideas from systems analysis, social or behavioral modeling theory, and teacher effectiveness research. Historically, some aspects of the model derive from training procedures developed in industrial and military settings. Barak Rosenshine and Robert Stevens (1986), for example, reported that they found a book published by the War Manpower Commission in 1945 entitled *How to Instruct* that includes many of the ideas and steps associated with the contemporary definition of direct instruction.

Systems Analysis

Systems analysis, which studies how to break down the parts of a whole so that they can be taught in small steps, provides one theoretical support for direct instruction.

Systems analysis has its roots in many fields, and it has influenced thinking in many areas of human research and development including biology, organizational theory, social theory, and learning. Basically, it is the study of the various relationships that exist between the interdependent parts of some whole. Examples of two well-known systems are the intricate relationships among the various living organisms that make up an ecosystem and those among the production, distribution, and communication parts of the incredibly complex system of international trade. Most often, people become aware of the part-whole relationships of systems when they break down. An example of such a breakdown is the overpopulation of rabbits that developed in Wyoming after the coyote population was systematically eliminated in that area. In a similar instance, purchasers are unable to buy a Japanese car in Chicago because East Coast dock workers are on strike.

In the area of instruction and learning, systems analysis emphasizes how knowledge and skills are organized and how to systematically break down complex skills and ideas into component parts so that they can be sequentially taught. Theorists Robert Gagné and Leslie Briggs (1987) represent the systems point of view in education:

> Systematically designed instruction can greatly affect individual human development. Some educational writings . . . indicate that education would perhaps be best if it were designed simply to provide a nurturing environment in which young people were allowed to grow up in their own ways, without the imposition of any plan to direct learning. We consider this an incorrect line of thinking. Undirected learning, we believe, is very likely to lead to the development of many individuals who are in one way or another incompetent to derive personal satisfaction from living in our society of today or tomorrow. (p. 5)

Later you will see how the ideas of systematically designed instruction and task analysis (a tool used by systems analysts) have contributed to the direct instruction model.

Behavioral Modeling Theory

The learning theory that seems to have contributed most to the direct instruction model is one that is variously known as *social learning theory, observational learning,* or as it is called in this book, **behavioral modeling** theory.

Behavioral modeling theory, which studies how people learn from watching others, provides another theoretical support for direct instruction.

Originated by John Dollard and Neal Miller in the 1930s and 1940s, behavioral modeling theory attempted to use the mechanisms of observation and vicarious reinforcement to explain the acquisition of various social behaviors such as aggression and cooperation. Later, Albert Bandura and his colleagues, the most famous proponents of this theory, began broadening it to include the learning of academic skills and concepts such as those taught through direct instruction.

According to Bandura, most human learning is done by selectively observing and memorizing the behavior of others. Bandura (1977) wrote:

> Learning would be exceedingly laborious, not to mention hazardous, if people had to rely solely on the effects of their own actions to inform them of what to do. Fortunately, most human behavior is learned observationally through modeling: from observing others one forms an idea of how new behaviors are performed, and on later occasions this coded information serves as a guide for action. Because people can learn from example what to do, at least in approximate form, before performing any behavior, they are spared needless errors. (p. 22)

Unlike pure behaviorists, behavioral modeling theorists believe that something is learned when the observer consciously attends to some behavior (e.g., striking a match) and then commits that observation to long-term memory. The observer hasn't yet *performed* the observed behavior, so there have been no behavioral consequences (reinforcements), which behaviorists maintain are necessary for learning to occur. Nevertheless, as long as the memory is retained, the observer knows how to strike a match, whether or not he ever chooses to do so. The same claim can be said for thousands of simple behaviors, such as braking a car, eating with a spoon, and opening a bottle.

According to Bandura, behavioral modeling theory is a three-step process involving attention, retention, and production. That is, it depends on the observer's attending to some behavior, then placing his or her perception of the behavior in long-term memory, and finally, retrieving the memory in order to produce the behavior when motivated to do so. For someone using the direct instruction model of teaching, these research findings might translate into the following teaching behaviors.

Attention

According to Bandura's research, observers attend best to behaviors that are distinctive and not too complex. This knowledge might elicit the following behaviors from a direct instruction teacher at the outset of a lesson and also at critical points during a lesson.

1. *To initially gain students' attention,* the teacher might use an expressive gesture like clapping her hands or introduce an unusual, attention-getting object such as a large pumpkin or a mysterious box with holes in it. To direct attention to some important part of the lesson a firmly delivered verbal remark, such as "gather round now and pay close attention," can be effective.

2. *To ensure that the observation is not too complex* to be accurately observed, the teacher might subdivide some complex skill, such as a tennis serve, into its component parts and then teach each part (e.g., the grip, toss, and swing) separately. Exposure to the total performance might overwhelm students' attention capacity and result in errors.

Retention

Behavioral learning involves three steps: attention, retention, and production.

Bandura also found that retention of an observed behavior was strengthened if the observer could link the observation with previous experiences that were personally meaningful and engage in cognitive rehearsal of the activity. Knowing this, a direct instruction teacher might do the following.

1. *To link the new skill to the students' prior knowledge,* the teacher might ask students to compare the newly demonstrated skill with something they already know and can do. For instance, the teacher might say that setting up a microscope in the laboratory reminds her of reassembling her kitchen mixer after cleaning it piece by piece.

2. *To ensure long-term retention,* the teacher might set aside a practice period in which students alternately rehearse the new skill mentally and physically. They could, for example, visualize themselves going through the demonstrated steps in setting up a microscope before actually doing it.

Production

Providing students with opportunities to practice new skills is important. However, Bandura found that the timing and type of feedback provided by the teacher is crucial if practice is to be beneficial. Especially during initial learning, feedback should be immediate, positive, and corrective. One way that a direct instruction teacher can use this knowledge is through *corrective modeling,* which involves the following.

1. *To ensure a positive attitude toward the new skill,* the teacher should immediately praise those aspects of the skill that the student performs correctly, then identify any problematic subskill. For example, if a student holds and swings the tennis racket correctly when learning to serve but tosses the ball off-line, the teacher should immediately point out the student's correct behaviors and then identify the problem area.

2. *To correct the troublesome subskill,* the teacher should first model the correct performance, then let the student rehearse it until mastered.

Teacher Effectiveness Research

The research base for the direct instruction model and its various components comes from many fields. However, the clearest empirical support for the model's effectiveness comes from the teacher effectiveness research conducted in the 1970s and 1980s.

The study by Jane Stallings and her associates (Stallings & Kaskowitz, 1974) was described in Chapter 1 to illustrate the importance of time on task. This study also contributed empirical support for the use of direct instruction. Remember this was an investigation conducted in first- and third-grade Project Follow Through classrooms. The Follow Through classrooms the researchers observed were characterized by several programmatic approaches. Some teachers used highly structured and formal methods, while others used more informal methods associated with the open-classroom movement of the time. Stallings and her colleagues wanted to find out which of the various programs were working best in raising student achievement. The behaviors of teachers in 166 classrooms were observed and their students were tested for achievement gains in mathematics and reading. Although many findings emerged from this large and complex study, two of the most pronounced were that time allocated and used for specific tasks was strongly related to academic achievement and that teachers who were businesslike and used teacher-directed or direct instruction strategies were more successful in obtaining high engagement rates than those who used more informal and student-centered teaching methods.

Several studies in the 1970s, such as the work by Stallings and her colleagues, found that teachers who had well-organized classrooms where structured learning experiences prevailed produced higher student *time-on-task* ratios and higher student achievement than teachers who used more informal and less teacher-directed approaches. Most of these studies observed teachers in natural classroom settings, and they usually identi-

RESEARCH BOX   PROCESS-PRODUCT RESEARCH:
DISCOVERING RELATIONSHIPS BETWEEN TEACHER
BEHAVIOR AND STUDENT ACHIEVEMENT

Prior to the 1970s, many educational researchers focused mainly on teachers' personal characteristics and how they related to student learning, or they examined the correlation between a principal's judgment of a teacher's effectiveness and student achievement scores. Researchers eventually became disillusioned with this line of inquiry, and in the early 1970s, a new paradigm for research on teaching and learning emerged. Called **process-product research,** this approach to research had profound effects on our views of effective teaching. For example, many of the tests used today to certify teachers have test items based on this research, and most state departments of education have developed evaluation systems for beginning teachers that require observers to validate the correct application of certain teaching behaviors deemed effective from the process-product research.

Process-Product Research

Process-product research was characterized both by the type of questions asked and by the methods of inquiry used by the researcher. The overriding question guiding process-product research was, What do individual teachers do that makes a difference in their students' academic achievement?

There are two key words in this question. One, the word *do*, suggests the importance of teachers' actions or behaviors, in contrast to earlier concerns about their personal attributes or characteristics. These teacher behaviors were labeled *process* by the researchers. The second key word is *achievement.* For the process-product researchers, achievement was the *product* of instruction. In most instances, achievement was defined as the acquisition of those skills and that knowledge which could be measured on standardized tests. Teachers were judged effective if they acted in ways that produced average to above-average achievement for students in their class. Process-product research, thus, can be summarized as the search for those teacher behaviors (process) that led to above-average student achievement scores (product).

Process-product research was also characterized by particular methods of inquiry. Typically, process-product researchers went directly into classrooms and observed teachers in natural (regular) classroom settings. Teacher behaviors were recorded using a variety of low-inference observation devices, and student achievement was measured over several time periods, often at the beginning and at the end of a school year. Particular teacher behaviors were then correlated with student achievement scores, and successful and unsuccessful teacher behaviors were identified. Anderson, Evertson, and Brophy (1979) described the key features of process-product research as follows:

> to define relationships between what teachers do in the classroom (the processes of teaching) and what happens to their students (the products of learning). One product that has received much attention is achieve-

ment in the basic skills. . . . Research in this tradition assumes that greater knowledge of such relationships will lead to improved instruction: once effective instruction is described, then supposedly programs can be designed to promote those effective practices. (p. 193)

The Good and Grouws Studies

Let's now look at what process-product research has contributed to our understanding of teacher effectiveness in general and to direct instruction specifically. Although hundreds of such studies were completed in the 1970s and 1980s, the work of Good and Grouws between 1972 and 1976 is illustrative of process-product research at its best, and it is illustrative of the type of evidence that supports the effectiveness of the direct instruction model.

THE INITIAL STUDY: Between 1972 and 1973, Good, Grouws, and their colleagues studied over 100 third- and fourth-grade mathematics teachers in a school district that skirted the core of a large urban school district in the midwest. The Iowa Test of Basic Skills was administered to students in their classrooms in the fall and spring for two consecutive years. From analyses of achievement gains made by students, the researchers were able to identify nine teachers who were relatively effective in obtaining student achievement in mathematics and nine teachers who had relatively low effectiveness. This led the researchers to plan and carry out an **observational study** to find out how the effective and ineffective teachers differed.

THE OBSERVATIONAL STUDY: To protect the identity of the "effective" and "ineffective" teachers, the researchers collected observational data from 41 classrooms, including those in which the nine effective and nine ineffective teachers taught. Trained observers visited each classroom six or seven times during October, November, and December of 1974. *Process* data were collected on many variables including: how instructional time was used, teacher-student interaction patterns, classroom management, types of materials used, and frequency of homework assignments. Student achievement was measured with the Iowa Test of Basic Skills in October 1974 and in April 1975. The classroom process data were analyzed to see if there were variables on which the nine high-effective and nine low-effective teachers differed. Teacher effectiveness was defined as obtaining high mathematics achievement on a standardized test. From the comparisons, Good and Grouws concluded that teacher effectiveness was strongly associated with the following clusters of behaviors. Notice how closely these behaviors correspond to the required teacher behaviors for direct instruction.

◆ *Whole-class instruction.* In general, whole-class (as contrasted to small-group) instruction was supported by this study, particularly if the teacher possessed certain capabilities such as an ability to keep things moving along.

(cont.)

RESEARCH BOX CONTINUED   PROCESS-PRODUCT RESEARCH: DISCOVERING RELATIONSHIPS BETWEEN TEACHER BEHAVIOR AND STUDENT ACHIEVEMENT

◆ *Clarity of instructions and presentations.* Effective teachers introduced lessons more purposively and explained materials more clearly then ineffective teachers did.

◆ *High performance expectations.* Effective teachers communicated higher performance expectations to students, assigned more work, and moved through the curriculum at a brisker pace than ineffective teachers did.

◆ *Task-focused but productive learning environment.* Effective teachers had fewer managerial problems than ineffective teachers. Their classrooms were task focused and characterized by smoothly paced instruction that was relatively free of disruptions.

◆ *Student-initiated behavior.* Students in effective teachers' classrooms initiated more interactions with teachers than students in the classrooms of ineffective teachers did. The researchers interpreted this as students' perceiving the effective teachers as being more approachable than the ineffective teachers.

◆ *Process feedback (knowledge of results).* Effective teachers let their students know how they were doing. They provided students with process or developmental feedback, especially during seatwork, and this feedback was immediate and nonevaluative.

◆ *Praise.* Effective teachers consistently provided less praise than ineffective teachers. This reflected the nonevaluative stance of the effective teachers. This finding (consistent with the results of other studies done in the early 1970s, e.g., Brophy & Evertson, 1974; Stallings, 1976), flew in the face of the common wisdom at that time that praise was to be used by teachers very liberally. The result of process-product research showed that praise was effective only when used under certain conditions and in particular ways and that too much praise, or praise used inappropriately, did not promote student learning.

In sum, process-product researchers found that teachers who had well-organized classrooms where structured learning experiences prevailed produced certain kinds of student achievement better than teachers who did not use these practices. It is important to note that process-product researchers did not try to invent and test new ways of teaching. Mainly, they were content to study teaching as it occurred in regular classroom settings. This point will be discussed in more detail in subsequent chapters.

fied two groups of teachers: those who were effective in producing student achievement and those who were not. Observation of the effective teachers showed that, in most instances, they were applying direct instruction procedures. The research box for this chapter describes briefly the nature of process-product research and a set of studies that directly influence our view of the direct instruction model.

CONDUCTING DIRECT INSTRUCTION LESSONS

Like any approach to teaching, expert execution of a direct instruction lesson requires specific behaviors and decisions by teachers during planning, while conducting the lesson, and while evaluating its effects. Some of these teacher actions can be found in other instructional models, and other behaviors are unique to direct instruction. The unique features involved in conducting a direct instruction lesson are emphasized here.

Planning Tasks

As already stated, the direct instruction model is applicable to any subject, but it is most appropriate for performance-oriented subjects such as reading, writing, mathematics, music, and physical education. It is also appropriate for teaching the skill components of more information-oriented subjects such as history or science. Wherever the information or skill to be taught is well structured and can be taught in a step-by-step fashion, the direct instruction model is usually suitable. It is less appropriate when the teacher is trying to promote social skills or to teach creativity, higher-level thinking, or abstract concepts and ideas. Neither is it appropriate for teaching attitudes or understandings of important public issues. Table 2.1 (p. 66) illustrated the kinds of objectives for which the direct instruction model is most appropriate. The following section provides more detail on how to prepare objectives for this model.

Direct instruction is most applicable for skill-oriented subjects such as math and reading where the subject matter can be taught in a step-by-step manner.

Prepare Objectives

When preparing objectives for a direct instruction lesson, the Mager format described in Chapter 1 is usually the preferred approach. Remember the STP guidelines specifying that a good objective should be *student-based* and specific, specify the *testing* situation, and identify the level of expected *performance.* The major difference between writing objectives for a skill-oriented lesson and for lessons with more complex content is that skill-oriented objectives usually represent easily observed behaviors that can be stated precisely and measured accurately. For example, if the objective is to have students climb a 15-foot rope in 7 seconds, that behavior can be observed and timed. If the objective is to have students go to the world globe and point out Kuwait, that behavior can also be observed. On the other hand, performance tests to measure the use of more complex skills, such as the use of the various teaching models described in this book, would be much more difficult to construct.

Choose Content

Most beginning teachers cannot expect to acquire a high level of mastery of the subjects they teach for many years. For those who are still in the process of mastering their subject matter, the recommendation for choosing content is to rely on the framework and ideas provided in curriculum guides and some textbooks. Most curriculum guides and textbooks have been written by subject matter specialists and reflect the latest thinking about how a particular subject should be structured and what should be taught at particular grade levels. They also reflect experienced teachers' estimates of students' prior knowledge. If good curriculum guides or texts do not exist in a particular school system, they can be found in the libraries of most major universities or resource centers within any state department of education. Whether beginning teachers use their own knowledge of the subject or knowledge that has been organized by others, several principles can assist in choosing content for particular lessons.

The economy principle in teaching means that teachers should limit their objectives and strive for economy in their explanations and demonstrations.

Economy. It has been observed that most presentations and demonstrations by teachers contain too much information, much of which is irrelevant. Students are hampered from learning key ideas or skills because of verbal clutter. Jerome Bruner (1962) said teachers should strive for economy in their explanations and demonstrations. What he meant is that teachers should be very careful regarding the amount of information presented at any one time. Economy encourages providing concise summaries of key ideas several times during the lesson. The economy principle argues for taking a difficult concept and making it clear and simple for students rather than taking an easy concept and making it vague and difficult because of verbal overkill.

Power. Bruner also described how the principle of power should be applied when selecting content for instruction. Power exists when basic information from a subject area is chosen and presented in straightforward and logical ways. It is through logical organization that students learn relationships between the key facts and concepts that make up any topic. To achieve economy and power depends not so much on a teacher's delivery style as it does on planning. In fact, a carefully organized demonstration or presentation done in monotone might well produce more student learning than a dynamic, highly enjoyable presentation void of powerful ideas and logical organization.

Perform Task Analysis

Task analysis is a tool used by teachers to define with some precision the exact nature of a particular skill or piece of well-structured knowledge they want to teach. Some people believe that task analysis is something that is unreasonably difficult and complex, when in fact, it is a rather straightforward and simple process, particularly for teachers who know their subjects well. The central idea behind task analysis is that complex understandings and skills cannot be entirely learned at any one time. To promote ease of understanding and eventual mastery, complex skills and understandings should first be divided into their component parts so that they can be sequentially taught in a logical, step-by-step fashion. Task analysis helps the teacher define precisely what it is the learner needs to do to perform a desired skill. It can be accomplished through the following steps:

Task analysis involves dividing a complex skill into its component parts so it can be taught in a sequential, step-by-step fashion.

Step 1   Find out what a knowledgeable person knows or does when the skill is performed
Step 2   Divide the overall skill into subskills
Step 3   Order subskills logically so that some are prerequisite to others
Step 4   Design strategies to teach each of the subskills and then to combine them

Figure 2.1 (p. 78) shows a task analysis done for a skill objective in mathematics, how to subtract whole numbers.

It would be a mistake to believe that teachers do a task analysis for every skill they teach. Even though the process is not difficult, it is time consuming. Effective teachers, however, do rely on the main concept associated with task analysis, that is, that most skills have several subskills and that learners cannot learn to perform the whole skill until they have mastered the parts.

Plan for Time and Space

Planning and managing time is very important for a direct instruction lesson. Two concerns should be foremost in teachers' minds: (1) ensuring that allocated time matches the aptitudes and abilities of the students in the class, and (2) motivating students so that they remain attentive and on task throughout the lesson. Knowing one's students is enormously helpful in allocating time for particular lessons. Many teachers, particularly inexperienced teachers, underestimate the amount of time it takes to teach something well. Later in this chapter, assessment strategies that help teachers check for understanding are presented. Such assessment information is used by teachers to determine whether or not they have allocated sufficient time to a particular topic. Making sure that students understand the purposes of direct instruction lessons and tying lessons into students' prior knowledge and interests are ways of increasing student attention and engagement. Guidelines for doing this are provided in the next section.

Many inexperienced teachers underestimate the amount of time it takes to teach something well and, consequently, don't allocate enough instructional time.

Planning and managing space for a direct instruction lesson is equally important. In most situations, teachers prefer the more traditional **row-**

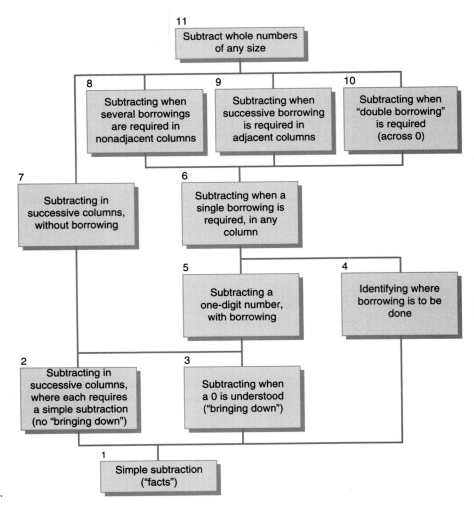

FIGURE 2.1

Task Analysis for Subtracting Whole Numbers

SOURCE: From R. M. Gagné and L. J. Briggs (1979), *Principles of instructional design.* © Holt, Rinehart and Winston. Reprinted with permission of Holt, Rinehart and Winston Inc.

and-column formation as illustrated in Figure 2.2. This is the most-used space arrangement and was so prevalent during earlier times that desks in rows were attached to the floor so they could not be moved. This formation is best suited to situations in which students need to focus attention on the teacher or on information being displayed on the chalkboard or overhead projector. A variant on the traditional row-and-column arrangement is the horizontal row arrangement illustrated in Figure 2.3.

In this arrangement, students sit quite close to each other in a fewer number of rows. The horizontal arrangement is often useful for direct instruction demonstrations in which it is important for students to see what is going on or to be quite close to the teacher. Neither of these spatial arrangements is conducive to student-centered teaching approaches

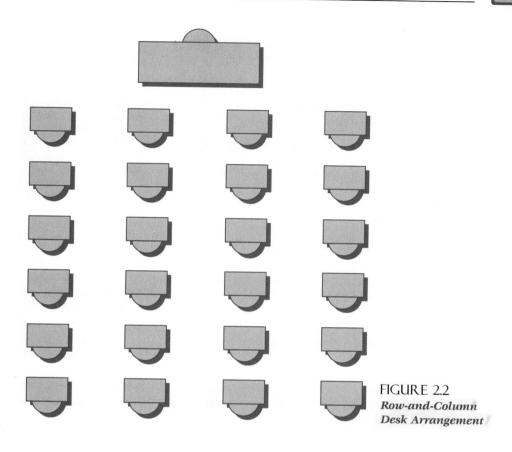

FIGURE 2.2
Row-and-Column
Desk Arrangement

such as cooperative learning or discussion, both of which depend on student-to-student interaction.

Interactive Tasks

As was outlined in Table 2.2, a direct instruction lesson proceeds through five phases: (1) provide objectives and establish set; (2) demonstrate the skill or understanding that is the focus of the lesson; (3) provide guided practice; (4) check for understanding and provide feedback, and (4) assign independent practice. These phases are described below.

Provide Objectives and Establish Set

Regardless of the instructional model being used, good teachers always begin their lessons by explaining their objectives and establishing a learning set. The intent of these initial steps is to get students' attention and to motivate them to participate in the lesson.

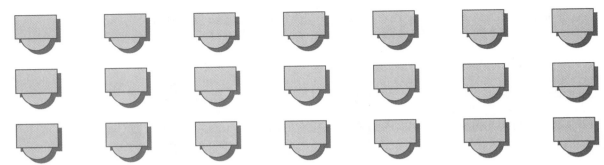

FIGURE 2.3
Horizontal Desk Arrangement

Explaining goals and objectives to students gives them a reason to participate and helps them know what is expected of them.

Explaining Goals and Objectives. Students need a reason for participating in a particular lesson, and they need to know what is expected of them. Effective teachers telegraph their goals and expectations by providing abbreviated versions of their lesson plans on the blackboard or on charts made from newsprint or butcher paper. Some teachers prefer newsprint charts because they can be made up the night before. They can be posted on the wall, leaving the blackboard free for other use, and they can be stored for future use. Effective teachers also outline the phases or steps of a particular lesson and the time required for each step. This allows the students to see the overall flow of a lesson and how the various parts fit together. Sharing the time parameters for the lesson also encourages students to help keep the lesson on schedule. Figure 2.4 provides an example of a lesson overview.

Making students aware of what they are going to learn helps them make connections between a particular lesson and its relevance to their own lives, motivating them to exert more effort. It also helps students draw relevant prior learning from long-term memory to working memory, where it can be used to integrate the new information provided in a demonstration or presentation.

FIGURE 2.4
Aims and Overview of Today's Lesson on Microscopes

Today's objective: The objective of today's lesson is to learn how to bring into focus the lens on a compound light microscope so you can make an accurate observation of plant cells.

Agenda:

5 minutes	Introduction, review, and objectives
5 minutes	Rationale
10 minutes	Demonstration of how to adjust lens on microscope—questions and answers
20 minutes	Practice with your microscope (I'll come around and help)
10 minutes	Wrap-up and assignment for tomorrow

Establishing Set. To get runners ready and off to an even start in a foot-race, the command from the starter is "Get ready . . . Get set . . . Go!" The "get set" alerts runners to settle into their blocks, focus their attention on the track ahead, and anticipate a smooth and fast start.

Establishing set for a lesson in school works in very much the same way. Effective teachers have found that a brief review which gets students to recall yesterday's lesson or perhaps a question or anecdote that ties in to students' prior knowledge is a good way to get started. Figure 2.5 shows a teacher establishing set with his students by reviewing the previous day's lesson.

Set activities also help students get their minds off other things they have been doing (changing classes in secondary schools; changing subjects in elementary schools; lunch and recess) and begin the process of focusing on the subject of the forthcoming lesson.

These activities also serve as motivators for lesson participation. Each teacher develops his or her own style for establishing set, but no effective teacher eliminates this important element from any lesson.

In sum, giving the rationale and overviews for any lesson is important, but particularly so for skill-oriented lessons. Such lessons typically focus on discrete skills that students may not perceive as important but that require substantial motivation and commitment to practice on the part of students. Knowing why a particular skill is being taught generally helps to motivate and bring the desired commitment from students better than

Establishing set means planning an introductory activity that will capture students' attention, help them see the relevance of the lesson, and motivate them to participate.

Remember yesterday we learned to identify the theme of a story by finding adjectives, verbs, and adverbs that evoked a certain mood. Today we will continue to identify themes, but we will learn to identify them by looking for symbols.

Theme

Mood Symbols

FIGURE 2.5
Establishing Set through Review
SOURCE: From E. D. Gagné. *The cognitive psychology of school learning*, p. 45. Copyright © 1985 by Ellen D. Gagné. Reprinted by permission of Little, Brown and Company.

such general statements as "It's good for you."; "You'll need it to find a job."; or "It's required in the curriculum guide."

Present and Demonstrate

The second phase of a direct instruction lesson is presenting or demonstrating the learning materials. The key to successful lessons is to present information as clearly as possible and to follow guidelines of effective demonstrations.

Achieving Clarity. A teaching behavior that research has consistently shown to have an impact on student learning is the teacher's ability to be clear and specific. Common sense also tells us that students will learn more when teachers are clear and specific than when they are vague. Nonetheless, researchers and observers of both beginning and experienced teachers find many instances of explanations that are vague and confusing. This generally occurs when a teacher does not have sufficient command of the topic to explain it to others. A taped example of a vague presentation is presented below.

> And this, of course, means, ah, many factors in terms of standard of living. Ah, I think in an effort to do this, however, many of the underdeveloped areas of Yugoslavia have been kind of helped equally, equality. And, ah, much of the effort and expense that's been going into underdeveloped areas, and this has served in almost a negative fashion. (Hiller, Gisher, & Kaess, 1969, p. 672)

It is not surprising that students with a teacher like this, who either does not understand the subject or cannot communicate it clearly, will not learn very much. Clarity of presentation is achieved through planning and organization as has already been explained. Practicing the suggestions provided by Rosenshine and Stevens (1986) and shown in Figure 2.6 will also help you learn how to achieve clarity.

Conducting Demonstrations. Direct instruction relies heavily on the proposition that much of what is learned comes from observing others. As described earlier, Bandura's behavioral modeling theory specifically demonstrates that it is from watching others model particular behaviors that students learn to perform these same behaviors and to anticipate their consequences. The behavior of others, both good and bad, thus becomes a guide for the learner's own behavior. Needless to say, learning by imitation saves students much needless trial and error. However, it can also allow them to learn inappropriate or incorrect behaviors.

To effectively demonstrate a particular concept or skill requires teachers to acquire a thorough understanding or *mastery* of the concept or skills prior to the demonstration and to carefully *rehearse* all aspects of the demonstration prior to the actual classroom event.

1. Clarity of goals and main points
   a. State the goals or objectives of the presentation
   b. Focus on one thought (point, direction) at a time
   c. Avoid digressions
   d. Avoid ambiguous phrases and pronouns

2. Step-by-step presentations
   a. Present the material in small steps
   b. Organize and present the material so that one point is mastered before the next point is given
   c. Give explicit, step-by-step directions (when possible)
   d. Present an outline when the material is complex

3. Specific and concrete procedures
   a. Model the skill or process (when appropriate)
   b. Give detailed and redundant explanations for difficult points
   c. Provide students with concrete and varied examples

4. Checking for students' understanding
   a. Be sure that students understand one point before proceeding to the next point
   b. Ask students questions to monitor their comprehension of what has been presented
   c. Have students summarize the main points in their own words
   d. Reteach the parts of the presentation that the students have difficulty comprehending, either by further teacher explanation or by students tutoring other students

FIGURE 2.6
Aspects of Clear Presentation
SOURCE: From B. Rosenshine and R. Stevens, Teaching functions. Reprinted with the permission of Macmillan Publishing Company from *Handbook of research on teaching*, 3d ed., M. C. Wittrock, ed. Copyright © 1986 by the American Educational Research Association.

◆ *Acquire understanding and mastery.* To ensure that students will observe correct rather than incorrect behaviors, teachers must attend to exactly what goes into their demonstrations. The old adage often given to children by parents, "do as I say, not as I do," is not sufficient for teachers trying to teach precise basic information or skills. Examples abound in every aspect of human endeavor in which people unknowingly perform a skill incorrectly because they observed and learned the skill from someone who was doing it wrong. The important point here is that if teachers want students to do something right, they must ensure that it is demonstrated correctly.

◆ *Attend to rehearsal.* It is exceedingly difficult to demonstrate anything with complete accuracy. The more complex the information or skill, the more difficult it is to be precise in classroom demonstrations. To ensure correct demonstration and modeling requires practice ahead of time. It also necessitates that the teacher think through the critical attributes of the skill or concept clearly and distinctly. For example, suppose you want to teach your students how to use a computerized system for locating information in the library, and you are going to demonstrate how call numbers correspond to a book's loca-

Effective demonstration requires a thorough mastery of what is being taught and careful rehearsal prior to the classroom event.

tion. It is important to check out the system you will use in your demonstration and rehearse, so the numbering system demonstrated is consistent with what students will find in their particular library. If the demonstration consists of such steps as turning on the computer, punching in identifying information on the book, writing down the call number, and then proceeding to the stacks, it is important that these steps be rehearsed to the point that none (such as writing down the call number) is forgotten during your demonstration.

Provide Guided Practice

Common sense says that "practice makes perfect." In reality, this principle does not always hold up. Everyone knows people who drive their cars every day but who are still poor drivers, or people who have children to raise but who are poor parents. Unfortunately, you also know of teachers who have taught for many years but are no better than the day they stepped in front of their first class. Also, all too often the assignments teachers give students do not really provide the type of practice that is needed. Writing out answers to questions at the end of a chapter, doing 20 mathematics problems, or writing an essay does not always help students master important understandings and skills.

Guided practice increases retention, makes skills more automatic, and promotes transfer to new situations.

A critical step in the direct instruction model is the way the teacher approaches **guided practice.** Fortunately for teachers, a considerable amount of research evidence now exists that can guide efforts to provide practice. For example, it is known that active practice can increase retention, make learning more automatic, and make it possible for the learner to transfer learning to new or stressful situations. The following principles can guide the way teachers provide for practice.

◆ *Assign short, meaningful amounts of practice.* In most instances, particularly with a new skill, it is important to ask students to perform the desired skill for short periods of time and, if the skill is complex, to simplify the task at the beginning. Brevity and simplification, however, should not distort the pattern of the whole skill. Look again at the example of a teacher using the direct instruction model to help students learn how to locate a book in the library. After sufficient explanation and demonstration, the teacher wants students to practice the skill. One approach would be to send students to the library to locate 20 books listed on a worksheet. Probably a more efficient and controlled plan would be to have sample sets of catalog cards in the room, simplifying the complexity of the whole catalog system, and have students look up one book at a time in the card or computer index (shortening the practice).

◆ *Assign practice to increase overlearning.* For skills that are critical to later performance, practice must continue well beyond the stage of initial mastery. Many skills associated with the performing arts, athletics, reading, and typing have to be overlearned so they become automatic. It is only through **overlearning** and complete mastery that a skill can be used effectively in new and novel situations or under stress. This ability to *automatically* perform a skill or combination of skills is what separates an expert from a novice in all fields. Teachers must be careful, however, because efforts to produce overlearning can become monotonous. If they do, they may actually decrease students' motivation to learn.

Overlearning a skill produces the automaticity needed to use it in various combinations and in both novel and stressful situations.

◆ *Be aware of the advantages and disadvantages of massed and distributed practice.* Many schools in the United States have homework policies, stipulating usually about 30 minutes per night per subject for older students and at least a few minutes a night for younger students. Although homework can be valuable for extending student learning, a required amount of time each night can be harmful. The amount and timing of practice depends on several factors. Generally, psychologists have defined this issue as **massed practice** (continuous) versus **distributed practice** (divided into segments). Although the research literature does not give direct principles that can be followed in every instance, massed practice is usually recommended for learning new skills, with the caution that long periods of practice can lead to boredom and fatigue. Distributed practice is most effective for refining an already familiar skill if you keep in mind the caution that the interval of time between practice segments should not be so long that students forget or regress and have to start over again.

Generally speaking, massed practice is recommended when learning new skills and distributed practice when refining existing skills.

◆ *Attend to the initial stages of practice.* The initial stages of practice are particularly critical because it is during this period that the learner can unknowingly start using incorrect techniques which later must be unlearned. It is also during the initial stages of practice that the learner will want to measure success in terms of his or her performance as contrasted to the demonstrated technique.

Check Understanding and Provide Feedback

This is the phase of a direct instruction lesson that most closely resembles what is sometimes called *recitation.* It is often characterized by a teacher's asking students questions and students' providing answers they think are correct. The teacher then responds to the students' answers. This is a very important aspect of a direct instruction lesson, because without knowledge of results, practice is of little value to students. In fact, the most important task for teachers using the direct instruction model is to provide students with meaningful **feedback** and **knowledge of results.** Teachers can provide feedback in many ways, such as through verbal feedback, video or audio taping of performance, tests, and written comments. Without specific feedback, students will not learn to write well by writing, read well by reading, or run well by running.

Without knowledge of results (feedback), practice is of little value to students.

The critical question for teachers is how to provide effective feedback for large classes of students. Guidelines deemed important include the following.

Guideline 1   Provide feedback as soon as possible after the practice.

It is not necessary to provide feedback instantaneously, but it should be soon enough after the actual practice that students can remember clearly their own performance. This means that teachers who provide written comments on essays should be prompt in returning corrected papers. It means that tests gauged to measure mathematics or other performance should be corrected immediately and errors discussed with students. Similarly, feedback of performance requiring the use of video or audio devices should be scheduled so that delay is kept to a minimum.

Guideline 2   Make feedback specific.

For best results, feedback should be as specific as possible, be provided immediately following practice, and fit the developmental level of the learner.

In general, feedback should be as specific as possible to be most helpful to students. For example, "Your use of the word *domicile* is pretentious; *house* would do nicely." instead of, "You are using too many big words." Or, "Your hand was placed exactly right for an effective backhand." instead of, "Good backhand." Or, "Three words were spelled incorrectly on your paper: *Pleistocene, penal,* and *recommendation.*" instead of, "Too many misspelled words."

Guideline 3   Concentrate on behaviors and not intent.

Feedback is most helpful to students and raises less defensiveness if it is aimed directly at some behavior as contrasted to one's interpretation of the intent behind the behavior. For example, "I cannot read your handwriting. You do not provide enough blank space between words and you make your O's and A's identical." instead of, "You do not work on making your handwriting neat." Or, "When you faced the class in your last speech, you spoke so softly that most students could not hear what you were saying." instead of, "You should try to overcome your shyness."

Guideline 4   Keep feedback appropriate to the developmental stage of the learner.

As important as knowledge of results is, feedback must be administered carefully to be helpful. Sometimes, students can be given too much feedback or feedback that is too sophisticated for them to handle. For example, a person trying to drive a car for the first time can appreciate hearing that he or she let the clutch out too quickly, causing the car to jerk. A beginning driver, however, is not ready for explanations about how to drop the brake and use the clutch to keep the car from rolling on a steep hill. A young student being taught the "i before e" rule in spelling probably will respond favorably to being told that he or she spelled *brief* correctly but may not be ready to consider why *recieve* was incorrect.

Guideline 5   Emphasize praise and feedback on correct performance.

Everyone prefers to receive positive rather than negative feedback. In general, praise will be accepted whereas negative feedback may be denied. Teachers, therefore, should strive to provide praise and positive feedback particularly when students are learning new concepts and skills. When incorrect performance is observed, of course it must be corrected. Madeline Hunter (1982) provided a sensible way to approach the problem of dealing with incorrect responses and performance. She recommended the following teacher behaviors:

Although incorrect performance must be corrected, teachers should try to provide positive feedback when students are learning new skills.

1. Dignify the student's incorrect response or performance by giving a question for which the response would have been correct. For example, "George Washington would have been the right answer if I had asked you who was the first President of the United States."

2. Provide the student with an assist, hint, or prompt. For example, "Remember the President in 1828 had also been a hero in the War of 1812."

3. Hold the student accountable. For example, "You didn't know President Jackson today, but I bet you will tomorrow when I ask you again." (pp. 85–90)

A combination of positive and negative feedback is best in most instances. For example, "You did a perfect job of matching subjects and verbs in this paragraph except in the instance where you used a collective subject." Or, "You were holding the racket correctly as you approached the ball, but you had too much of your weight on your left foot." Or, "I like the way you speak up in class, but during our last class discussion you interrupted Ron three different times when he was trying to give us his point of view."

Guideline 6   When giving negative feedback, show how to perform correctly.

Knowing that something has been done incorrectly does not help students do it correctly. Negative feedback should always be accompanied by teacher actions that demonstrate the correct performance. If a student is shooting a basketball with the palm of the hand, the teacher should point that out and demonstrate how to place the ball on the fingertips. If a writing sample is splattered with incorrectly used words, the teacher should pencil in words that would be more appropriate. If students are holding their hands incorrectly on the computer keyboard, the correct placement should be modeled.

Negative feedback should be accompanied by demonstrations of how to correctly perform a skill.

Guideline 7   Help students to focus on "process" rather than on outcomes.

Many times, beginners want to focus their attention on measurable performance. "I just typed 35 words per minute without any errors." "I wrote
my essay in an hour." "I drove the golf ball 175 yards." "I cleared the bar at
4 feet 6 inches." It is the teacher's responsibility to get students to look at
the *process* or technique behind the performance and to help students
understand that incorrect techniques may achieve immediate objectives
but will probably prohibit later growth. For example, a student may type
35 words per minute using only two fingers, but that student will probably
never reach 100 words per minute using this technique. Starting the
approach on the wrong foot may be fine for clearing the high jump bar at
4 feet 6 inches but will prevent ever reaching 5 feet 6 inches.

Guideline 8   Teach students how to provide themselves with feedback
and how to judge their own performance.

Students should be taught to assess and judge their own performance.

It is important for students to learn how to assess and judge their own
performance. Teachers can help students judge their own performance in
many ways. They can explain the criteria used by experts in judging performance. They can give students opportunities to judge peers and to
assess their own progress in relation to that of others. They can emphasize
the importance of self-monitoring and goal setting and of not being satis-
fied with only "extrinsic" feedback from the teacher.

The process of assigning practice and providing feedback to students is
very important for teachers and requires learning a complex set of behaviors. Learning Aid 2.3 at the end of this chapter has been designed to
observe how experienced teachers use practice and provide feedback.

Provide Independent Practice

Homework is most often a continuation of practice and should involve activities that students can perform successfully.

Most **independent practice** assigned to students as the final phase of a
direct instruction lesson is homework. Homework, or independent practice, is an opportunity for students to perform newly acquired skills on
their own and, as such, should be viewed as a continuation of practice, not
a continuation of instruction. Also, homework and independent practice
can be used as a way of extending learning time for students. But homework should not be assigned carelessly or frivolously. If the teacher
doesn't value it, neither will the students. Here are three general guidelines for independent practice given as homework.

1. Teachers should give students homework that they can perform successfully. Homework should not involve the continuation of instruction, but the continuation of practice or preparation for the next
day's content.

2. Teachers should inform parents about the level of involvement expected of them. Are parents expected to help their sons or daughters with answers to difficult questions or simply to provide a quiet atmosphere in which the students can complete their homework assignments? Are they supposed to check over assignments? Do they know the approximate frequency and duration of homework assignments?

3. Teachers should provide feedback on the homework. Many teachers simply check to determine whether the homework was performed. What this says to the students is that it doesn't matter how it is done as long as it is done. Students soon figure out that the task is to get something—anything—on paper. One method of providing feedback is to involve other students in correcting the homework.

LEARNING ENVIRONMENT AND MANAGEMENT TASKS

Research of the 1970s and 1980s produced some very good classroom management guidelines that apply to virtually all classrooms and all teaching models. These involve the way teachers strive to gain student cooperation, the means they use to motivate students, the way they establish and teach clear rules and procedures, and the actions taken at the beginning of the school year that lead to smooth-running classrooms later on. Although these general aspects of classroom management are extremely important, it is equally important for teachers to recognize that management behavior varies depending on the instructional approach a teacher uses and the type of learning tasks that derive from that approach. What might be considered "out of control" in one instance might be "in order" in another. For instance, when a teacher is talking to the whole class during a direct instruction lesson, it is not appropriate for students to talk to each other. Talk, however, is appropriate, even required, during a lesson using small-group discussion. This section describes the unique management requirements for direct instruction.

In a direct instruction lesson, the teacher normally structures the learning environment very tightly. In the early stages of the lesson, the teacher is an active presenter or demonstrator and expects students to be active listeners. Successful use of the model requires good conditions for presenting and listening: a quiet area with good visibility including appropriate facilities for use of audio and visual aides. The success of the model also depends on students' being sufficiently motivated to watch what the teacher is doing and to listen to what the teacher is saying. It is not a time for students to be sharpening pencils, talking to neighbors, or working on other tasks. Later, when students are asked to recite or to practice what they have just observed, different management concerns will surface. In essence, direct instruction requires rules governing student talk, procedures to insure good **pacing,** particular strategies for **distributing participation,** and for dealing with misbehavior.

Managing Student Talk

Management of direct instruction requires rules governing student talk and procedures that ensure good pacing, student participation, and prompt handling of misbehavior.

Students talking at inappropriate times or asking questions that slow down the pace of a lesson are among the most troublesome management concerns during a direct instruction lesson. This problem can vary in severity from a loud, generalized classroom clamor that disturbs the teacher next door to a single student talking to a neighbor when the teacher is explaining or demonstrating an important idea. As described in Chapter 1, teachers must have a rule that prescribes "no talking" when the teacher is explaining things, and this rule must be consistently reinforced. During the practice or recitation phase of the lesson, students must be taught to listen to other students' ideas and to take turns when participating in the recitation or discussion.

Pacing

Students sometimes deliberately slow the pace of instruction by asking unnecessary questions or requesting unneeded directions.

Direct instruction lessons break down when appropriate momentum is not maintained and the instructional events become sluggish. In an interesting study Walter Doyle and Kathy Carter showed how students can sometimes deliberately break up the pace of instruction. Initially, Doyle and Carter (1984) were interested in how specific academic tasks are connected to student involvement and classroom management. To explore this topic, they observed one junior high school English teacher and her students in a middle-class suburban school for a period of almost three months. The teacher, Mrs. Dee, was selected for study because she was an experienced teacher who was considered to have considerable expertise in teaching writing to students.

In the study researchers found that students had considerable influence over the task demands of the classroom. For instance, over a period of time, Mrs. Dee assigned students a variety of major and minor writing tasks. Examples included writing an essay comparing Christmas in Truman Capote's story "A Christmas Memory" with Christmas today; writing a short story report; and writing descriptive paragraphs with illustrations. In some of the writing tasks, Mrs. Dee tried to encourage student creativity and self-direction by leaving the assignments somewhat open-ended. From detailed observations of Mrs. Dee's classroom, however, Doyle and Carter found that students pressed to reduce the amount of self-direction and independent judgment in some of the writing assignments. Students, even those considered very bright, used tactics such as asking questions or feigning confusion to force Mrs. Dee to become more and more concise and explicit. In other words, the students influenced the teacher to do more and more of their thinking.

Doyle and Carter also found that by asking questions about content and procedures, students could not only change the nature of the assignment but could also slow down the pace of classroom activities. This was sometimes done to get an assignment postponed or just to use up class time. When Mrs. Dee refused to answer some of the students' delaying questions, the classroom situation degenerated further. Here is a direct quote from a report of what the researchers observed:

> Some students became quite adamant in their demands. . . . On such occasions, order began to break down and the normal smoothness and momentum of the classes were reinstated only when the teacher provided the prompts and resources the students were requesting. The teacher was pushed, in other words, to choose between conditions for students' self-direction and preserving order in the classroom." (p. 146)

Mrs. Dee was an experienced enough teacher to know that order had to come first or everything else was lost.

Kounin's research, introduced in Chapter 1, described how teachers sometimes do things themselves that interfere with the flow of lesson activities. For example, sometimes a teacher might start an activity and then leave it "in midair." Kounin labeled this type of behavior a *dangle*. An example of a **dangle** occurs when a teacher asks students to respond to a question and then suddenly decides that he or she needs to explain or demonstrate one more point. Teachers also slow down lessons by doing what Kounin labeled *flip-flops*. A **flip-flop** happens when an activity is started, then stopped while another is begun, and then the original started again. An example of a flip-flop would be when a teacher tells students to get out their books and start practicing, then interrupts the practice to explain a point, and then resumes the practice again. Dangles and flip-flops interfere with a smooth progression of classroom activities, cause for some students confusion, and most important, present opportunities for uninvolved students to misbehave.

Good lesson momentum reduces the opportunity for uninvolved students to misbehave.

Teachers also do things that slow down the momentum of lessons. Kounin described two types of important slow-down behaviors—*fragmentation* and *overdwelling*. A teacher who goes on and on after explanations are clear to students is **overdwelling.** A teacher who breaks activities into overly small units is **fragmenting.** Slowing down momentum disrupts a smooth lesson pace and gives uninvolved students opportunities to interrupt classroom activities. Minimizing disruptive and slow-down behaviors is a difficult skill for teachers to learn, because students become very skilled in performing these behaviors and masking them under the pretense of wanting to understand. Smoothness and momentum definitely vary with the nature of individual classes. Teachers need to learn that what may be a dangle in one classroom may not be so in another. They need to be alert for signs that what may be overdwelling with one group of students may be an appropriate pace for another group.

Dealing with Misbehavior

Direct instruction lessons are taught mainly to whole groups of students. In any large-group situation, there is opportunity for some students to be involved while others are not only uninvolved but perhaps misbehaving. Rather than attempting to uncover and deal with the causes of student misbehavior, a most difficult and time-consuming task that does not necessarily lead to better management, we recommend that teachers focus on the misbehavior itself and find ways to change it, at least while the misbehaving student is in the classroom. This approach emphasizes the importance of teachers' accurately spotting misbehavior and making quick, precise interventions. Kounin's concepts of teacher *with-it-ness, overlappingness,* and *desist behavior* are all helpful strategies in this regard.

The skills of with-it-ness and overlappingness are difficult for teachers to master because they call for a quick, accurate reading of classroom situations and the ability to perform several different teaching behaviors simultaneously. Once learned, however, they do much to ensure more smoothly running lessons and classrooms.

Being With It

With-it-ness refers to a teacher's ability to accurately monitor all that is happening in the classroom, including misbehavior.

You can all remember a teacher from your own school days who seemed to have "eyes in the back of her head." This skill has been labeled by Kounin (1970) as **with-it-ness.** Teachers who are "with it" spot deviant behavior right away and are almost always accurate in identifying the student who is responsible. Teachers who lack this skill normally do not spot misbehavior early, and they often make mistakes when assigning blame.

Overlappingness

A teacher's ability to deal with more than one classroom situation at a time is known as overlappingness.

This term refers to a teacher's ability to deal with more than one classroom activity or episode at a time. In terms of student misbehavior, **overlapping** refers to a teacher's ability to inconspicuously deal with a particular misbehavior so the lesson is not interrupted. Moving close to an offender is one overlapping tactic effective classroom managers use. Putting a hand on the shoulder of a student who is talking to his neighbor while continuing with instructions about how to do a lab project is another. Integrating into the lesson a "smart" remark or a question intended to delay instruction is a third example of overlappingness.

Desist Behaviors

In classrooms, just as in any social setting, some participants are likely to commit deviant acts. An example of deviant behavior on the freeway would be driving several miles an hour above the speed limit; in church, it might be falling asleep during the sermon; in a library, it is talking while others are trying to study. Those charged with the responsibility of enforcing rules and procedures may or may not choose to respond to each deviant incident. For example, most highway patrol officers will not stop a motorist traveling a few miles over the speed limit on the freeway; most ministers will not choose to confront a single sleeping parishioner; and those who talk very softly in libraries will probably not elicit a response from the librarian. There are times, however, when those in charge will choose to respond to deviant behaviors. Kounin calls this a **desist incident,** meaning an incident serious enough that, if not dealt with, is likely to lead to further, widening management problems. The way that desist incidents are identified and dealt with is the business of classroom management.

When deviant behavior is judged serious enough to warrant a teacher response, it is known as a desist incident.

Teachers respond to desist incidents in various ways. Kounin (1970) identified several teacher **desist behaviors.** Three of these behaviors are illustrated in Figure 2.7. Clear as compared to fuzzy desist actions by teachers communicate to students exactly what they are doing wrong. A teacher's use of firm language likewise communicates to students that he or she means business. Using anger to handle desist incidents has to be controlled carefully. As the example in Figure 2.7 illustrates, it does not harm students to know that what they are doing makes the teacher angry. At the same time, teacher anger should not be expressed in an uncontrolled, negative, or punishing fashion.

Clarity
The degree to which a teacher specifies what is wrong.
  Unclear desist: "Stop that!"
  Clear desist: "Do not sharpen your pencil while I am talking."

Firmness
The degree to which a teacher communicates "I mean it."
  Unfirm desist: "Please don't do that."
  Firm desist: "I absolutely will not tolerate that from you!"

Roughness
The degree to which a teacher expresses anger.
  Unrough desist: "You shouldn't do that anymore."
  Rough desist: "When you do that I get angry."

FIGURE 2.7
Examples of Teacher Desist Behaviors

FIGURE 2.8
*Guidelines for
Managing
Inappropriate
Behavior*
SOURCE: From C. Evertson
and E. Emmer (1982),
Preventive classroom
management. In D. Duke
(ed.), *Helping teachers
manage classrooms.*
Alexandria, Va.:
Association for
Supervision and
Curriculum Development,
p. 27. Reprinted with
permission.

1. Ask the student to stop the inappropriate behavior. Maintain contact with the child until the appropriate behavior is correctly performed.

2. Make eye-contact with the student until appropriate behavior returns. This is suitable when the teacher is certain the student knows what the correct response is.

3. Restate or remind the student of the correct rule or procedure.

4. Ask the student to identify the correct procedure. Give feedback if the student does not understand it.

5. Impose the consequence or penalty of the rule or procedure violation. Usually, the consequence for violating a procedure is simply to perform the procedure until it is correctly done. When the student understands the procedure and is not complying in order to receive attention or for other inappropriate reasons, the teacher can use a mild penalty, such as withholding a privilege.

6. Change the activity. Frequently, off-task behavior occurs when students are engaged too long in repetitive, boring tasks or in aimless recitations. Injecting variety in seatwork, refocusing the discussion, or changing the activity to one requiring another type of student response, is appropriate when off-task behavior spreads throughout a class.

Drawing on the research of Kounin's and their own work, Carolyn Evertson and Edmund Emmer provided guidelines for the management of inappropriate behavior. Their guidelines are shown in Figure 2.8. Teachers can expect some students to misbehave during direct instruction lessons that require extended attention. The best way to deal with this misbehavior is to have well-planned lessons that move along smoothly, to spot deviant incidents accurately, and to deal with them promptly and firmly.

Distributing Participation

One of the most serious criticisms of direct instruction is the teacher's dominant role and the large majority of students' rather passive roles. In many cases, the lack of student participation during a direct instruction lesson can be partially attributed to the way space is used. Using the row-and-column formation described in Figure 2.2 tends to influence student interaction. In what is now considered a classic study, Adams and Biddle (1970) found that during most lessons and at all grade levels, there was a central group of students who dominated the lesson. Teachers talked to them and asked them questions; students responded and also asked their own questions. The other students in the classroom—a large majority—did not actively participate and were likely either to withdraw or to talk with neighbors.

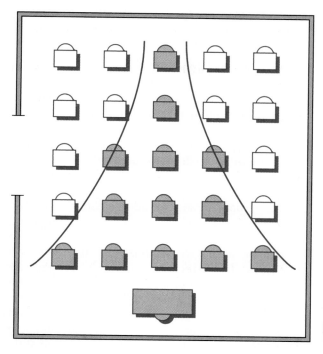

FIGURE 2.9
Action Zone in the Classroom

The study found that the active students were always located in one section of the classroom, which Adams and Biddle labeled the *action zone* (see Figure 2.9).

The **action zone** consists of the students in the middle of the front rows and those down the middle aisle. Sixty-four percent of the teacher's questions were directed toward students in this area. This phenomenon is partially due to the position of the teacher, who remained front and center. But researchers have been curious to seek other explanations as well. For example, do the more motivated students *choose* action zone seats? Some evidence supports the theory that sitting in the action zone does affect participation regardless of motivation. It has also been hypothesized that the important ingredient in the action zone phenomena is the teacher's eye contact. Teachers establish better eye contact with those students in the action zone, which, in turn, causes them to participate more in classroom recitations. Later chapters will describe how teachers can influence participation rates by changing the seating arrangements and the basic discourse patterns found in most classrooms. For instance, the issue of student participation in small groups will be described in Chapter 3 on cooperative learning. Many suggestions are provided on how to increase participation, to give all students broader opportunities to carry on dialogue with each other, and to engage in higher-level thinking in Chapter 5 on classroom discussion.

An action zone *is that section of the classroom where most student-teacher interaction occurs.*

ASSESSMENT AND EVALUATION

Teachers using direct instruction often use paper-and-pencil tests to measure students' declarative knowledge and performance assessments to measure their procedural knowledge.

Chapter 1 emphasized the importance of matching testing and evaluation strategies to the goals and objectives for particular lessons and to the inherent purposes of a particular model. Despite complaints about it, direct instruction remains the most popular teaching model in American schools, especially in the higher grade levels, and it is the most appropriate model for teaching knowledge and skills that lend themselves to step-by-step instruction. Assessment of goals associated with this model focuses on paper-and-pencil tests to measure declarative knowledge and a variety of performance tests to measure skill development. For example, a paper-and-pencil test can be used to see if students can identify the characters on the typewriter's keyboard; a timed typing test can be used to see how well they can type. Students can be asked to identify verbs in a column of nouns. They can be asked to demonstrate that they can write a complete sentence. Writing the correct steps in any of the teacher models described in this book is a measure of straightforward declarative knowledge, whereas one's ability to use a particular model can be demonstrated only in a classroom. In most instances, mastering certain declarative knowledge (keyboard knowledge, verb recognition, steps in teaching model) is a necessary prerequisite to performing a targeted skill. Thus, teachers using direct instruction often use both paper-and-pencil and performance tests. General principles for these types of tests are described in the following sections.

General Principles of Test Construction

The most important aspect of student evaluation in most classrooms is the tests teachers make and give to students. Good test construction requires both skill and a commitment to this aspect of teaching. The general principles that follow offer teachers some much needed guidelines for constructing their own tests. Gronlund (1982) provided five basic principles that should guide teachers as they design an assessment system and create their own tests. These five principles are summarized here.

♦ *Harmony with instructional objectives.* An often heard student complaint is, "But the test didn't cover what we covered in class." For whatever reasons, students who say this believe they have been unfairly judged. Gronlund's first principle is that teachers should construct a test so it measures clearly the learning objectives they have communicated to students. In short, the test should be in harmony with the teacher's instructional objectives. For example, if a teacher has just completed a unit of work on the American colonial period and wants students to understand all aspects of this era, then the test should cover more than just the religious leaders of the period.

◆ *Cover all learning tasks.* Most lessons and units of instruction contain a variety of learning objectives ranging from the recall of factual information to the understanding, analysis, and creative application of specific principles. A good test does not focus entirely on one type of objective, such as factual recall; rather, it measures a representative sample of a teacher's learning objectives.

◆ *Use appropriate test items.* There are, as you know from your own experience, many different kinds of test items and testing formats available to teachers. Some types of test items, such as matching or fill-in-the-blanks, are better suited for measuring recall of specific information; others, such as essay items, are better for tapping higher-level thinking processes and skills. A good test includes items that are most appropriate for a particular objective.

◆ *Make tests as valid and reliable as possible and interpret with care.* A test is said to be reliable when it produces dependable, consistent scores for people who take it more than once over a period of time. A test is said to be valid when it measures what it claims to measure. For example, a test that claims to measure students' attitudes toward mathematics would be invalid if it really measured their attitude toward their current mathematics teacher. Teacher-made tests that are clearly written and minimize guessing are generally more reliable than are ambiguous ones that encourage guessing. Likewise, tests containing a fairly large number of items are generally more reliable than those with just a few items. No single test, however, can ever give a completely accurate picture of what a student knows or can do. Thus, there is always the need to interpret results with caution and to rely on multiple sources of evaluation information before making final judgments about students' work.

◆ *Use tests to improve learning.* This final principle is meant to remind teachers that although tests are used primarily to diagnose or assess student achievement, they can also be learning experiences for students. Going over test results, for instance, provides teachers opportunities to reteach important information students have missed. Debate and discussion over correct answers can stimulate further study about a topic. Effective teachers integrate their testing processes into their total instructional programs for the purpose of guiding and enhancing student learning.

REFLECTION BOX   CONSIDERING USE OF DIRECT INSTRUCTION

Direct instruction, including lecture or recitation teaching, comprise a large proportion of classroom time in American classrooms. The amount of time devoted to explaining information, demonstrating, and conducting recitations increases at the higher grade levels of elementary school, in middle schools, and in high schools. It is prevalent everywhere, and remains the most popular teaching model. However, the model is not without its critics, and it will be important for you to be aware of the complaints that have been lodged against direct instruction and to explore your own views and values about the model and its use in your classroom.

The primary criticism of direct instruction is its emphasis on teacher talk. Most observers claim that teacher talk accounts for between one-half and three-fourths of every class period, and according to Cuban (1982, 1984), this phenomenon has remained constant during most of the twentieth century. Some educators argue that too much time is devoted to direct instruction, and over the past two decades, considerable effort has gone into creating other teaching models aimed at decreasing the amount of teacher talk. Others argue that the model is limited to teaching basic skills and low-level information and that it is not useful for accomplishing higher-level objectives. Still others criticize the model because of the behavioral theory underlying it. They argue that the model unavoidably supports the view that students are empty vessels to be filled with carefully segmented information rather than active learners with an innate need to acquire information and skills. Finally, there are those, including some of the model's early creators, who criticize direct instruction because of abuses in the way in which the

SUMMARY

◆ Acquiring basic information and skills is an important goal of every subject taught in schools. In almost any field, students must learn the basics before they can go on to more advanced learning.

◆ Teachers use direct instruction to help students learn basic skills and knowledge. The direct instruction model draws its empirical and theoretical support from systems analysis, behavioral modeling theory, and the teacher effectiveness research. It has been widely used and tested in school and nonschool settings.

◆ The instructional effects of the direct instruction model are to promote mastery of simple and complex skills and declarative knowledge that can be carefully defined and taught in a step-by-step fashion.

◆ The general flow or syntax of a direct instruction lesson consists usually of five phases: providing objectives and establishing set; demonstrating or explaining the materials to be learned; providing guided practice; checking for student understanding and providing feedback; and providing for extended practice and transfer.

model was implemented in many classrooms. For example, in one large public school system on the East Coast, every teacher was expected to give a direct instruction lesson every day. If other approaches were used while a teacher was being observed by a supervisor, the teacher received a negative evaluation. In another instance, teachers were required to write their objectives in behavioral format on the chalkboard every day, something never envisioned by the model's developers.

The continued popularity of explaining and demonstrating is not surprising, since the most widely held educational objectives are those associated with the acquisition of skills and the retention of basic information. Curricula in schools have been structured around bodies of information from the various academic disciplines—science, mathematics, English, and the social sciences. Consequently, curriculum guides, textbooks, and tests are similarly organized and are routinely used by teachers. Experienced teachers know that direct instruction is an effective way to help students acquire the array of basic information and skills believed by society as important for students to know.

This book takes a balanced view toward direct instruction. As repeatedly stressed throughout the book, direct instruction is just one of several approaches used by effective teachers. The real key to effective instruction is a teacher's ability to call on a varied repertoire of instructional approaches that permit the teacher to match instructional approaches to particular learning goals and to the needs of particular students.

What do you think? If you had your own classroom today, what uses would you make of direct instruction? How would you guard against abuses?

◆ The direct instruction model requires a highly structured learning environment and careful orchestration by the teacher. That tight structure does not mean the environment has to be authoritarian or uncaring.

◆ Preinstructional planning tasks associated with the model put emphasis on carefully preparing objectives and performing task analysis.

◆ Conducting a direct instruction lesson requires a teacher to explain things clearly; to demonstrate and model precise behaviors; and to provide for practice, monitoring of performance, and feedback.

◆ Practice should be guided by several principles: assign short, meaningful amounts of practice, assign practice to increase overlearning, and make appropriate use of massed and distributed practice.

◆ Direct instruction lessons require the unique classroom management needs of gaining student attention in a whole-group setting and sustaining this attention for extended periods of time.

◆ Particular classroom management concerns include organizing the classroom setting for maximum effect; maintaining appropriate pace, flow, and momentum; sustaining engagement, involvement, and participation; and dealing with student misbehavior quickly and firmly.

◆ Assessment tasks associated with the direct instruction model emphasize practice and developing and using appropriate basic knowledge and performance tests that accurately measure simple and complex skills and provide feedback to students.

◆ Despite the variety of complaints launched against direct instruction, it remains the most popular teaching model.

LESSON PLAN FORMAT
FOR A DIRECT INSTRUCTION MODEL LESSON

PURPOSE: This is a lesson plan format suggested for use with the model. As with the formats suggested for other teaching models, experiment with this format to determine if it meets your requirements. Be flexible, and modify it as the need arises.

DIRECTIONS: Use the following suggested format as a model for writing a direct instruction lesson.

Planning Tasks

Content or Skill to Be Taught _____

_____

Objectives

1. Given _____, the student will be able to
   (situation)
   _____ with
   (target behavior)
   _____
   (level of performance)

2. Given _____, the student will be able to
   (situation)
   _____, with
   (target behavior)
   _____
   (level of performance)

Conducting the Lesson

Time	Phase and Activities	Materials
_____	Lesson objectives and set _____	
_____	Lesson demonstration _____	
_____	Initial guided practice _____	
_____	Checking for understanding and providing feedback _____	
_____	Independent practice activities _____	

Pitfalls to Avoid

During Introduction   During Transitions   During Ending

OBSERVING DIRECT INSTRUCTION IN MICROTEACHING OR CLASSROOMS

DIRECTIONS: This form highlights the key aspects of the direct instruction model. It can be used to observe a peer in a microteaching laboratory or an experienced classroom teacher. It can also be used to assess a lesson you have taught and videotaped. As you observe the lesson, check the category you believe describes the level of performance of the teacher you are observing. Also answer the general questions about the lesson at the bottom of the form.

Teacher Behavior	Excellent	Acceptable	Needs Improvement	Not Needed
Planning				
How appropriate was the skill selected to teach?	_____	_____	_____	_____
How well prepared was the teacher overall?	_____	_____	_____	_____
How well had the teacher performed task analysis?	_____	_____	_____	_____
Execution				
How well did the teacher				
Explain goals and purposes?	_____	_____	_____	_____
Establish set?	_____	_____	_____	_____
Demonstrate the skill or material?	_____	_____	_____	_____
Provide for initial practice?	_____	_____	_____	_____
Check for student understanding?	_____	_____	_____	_____
Provide feedback to students?	_____	_____	_____	_____
Provide for independent practice?	_____	_____	_____	_____

Level of Performance

Overall Planning

What did you like best about the way the lesson was planned and organized?

_____

_____

What could be improved? _____

_____

_____

Lesson Execution

Think about teaching style and delivery. What did you like best about the way the lesson was presented? _____

_____

_____

What could be improved? _____

_____

_____

If you are a student in peer microteaching, how did you feel about the teacher's interaction with you? _____

_____

_____

L   E   A   R   N   I   N   G   A   I   D   2.3

OBSERVING TEACHER USE OF PRACTICE

PURPOSE: As emphasized in this chapter, practice is an important element in the direct instruction model and requires finesse to manage properly. Use this aid in the field to help refine your understanding of the use of practice.

DIRECTIONS: During skill lessons, observe a teacher each day for several days. Stay in the same subject area, and try to observe from the first day a skill is introduced to the last day it is covered. For example, you may watch a teacher introduce, develop, and review the skill of writing a business letter, or multiplying by 5s, or cleaning a carburetor. Whatever the skill, pay close attention to how the teacher handles student practice. Use the questions below to guide your observation and reflection.

1. On the first day the skill was introduced, what type of practice assignment did the teacher make: guided practice, independent practice, or both? _____

   _____

   How much time was devoted to the practice segment in class? _____

   As homework? _____

   What proportion of the total lesson was devoted to practice? _____

   Describe the teacher's behavior during the practice segment. _____

   _____

   Describe the students' behavior during the practice segment. _____

   _____

2. As the skill was developed over one or a few days, what type of practice assignment did the teacher make: guided practice, independent practice, or both? _____

   How much time was devoted to the practice segment in class? _____

   As homework? _____

   What proportion of the total lesson was devoted to practice? _____

   Describe the teacher's behavior during the practice segment. _____

   _____

   Describe the students' behavior during the practice segment. _____

   _____

3. As the skill was reviewed, what type of practice assignment did the teacher make: guided practice, independent practice, or both? _____

How much time was devoted to the practice segment in class? _____

As homework? _____

What proportion of the total lesson was devoted to practice? _____

Describe the teacher's behavior during the practice segment. _____
_____

Describe the students' behavior during the practice segment. _____
_____

Analysis and Reflection: How did the teacher portion out practice? In other words, did you see massed or distributed practice, or both? _____ At what points in the development of the skill were these observed: early on, during the development phase, or during review? _____
_____

Did the teacher give an indication that practice assignments were being matched to students' developing ability to perform the skill? _____ If so, how did the teacher gauge student performance? _____
_____

What kinds of teacher behavior characterized earlier skill lessons? Later skill lessons? _____
_____

What kinds of student behavior characterized earlier skill lessons? Later skill lessons? _____
_____

Do you think this teacher made wise decisions in providing for student practice? Why or why not? _____
_____
_____
_____

TASK ANALYSIS AND DEMONSTRATION

PURPOSE: To help you gain skill in performing task analysis and conducting demonstrations and to develop products of this work for your portfolio.

DIRECTIONS: Following the steps below, perform a task analysis, conduct a demonstration of some specific skill, and find a means to visually document your work in the portfolio.

Step 1: Choose a topic from your teaching field that consists of a number of skills. Do a task analysis identifying all the subskills associated with the topic. For example, if you choose ice hockey, some of the subskills associated with that sport are: dressing with proper equipment, ability to stand on ice, gliding forward, gliding backward, and passing while moving.

Step 2: Put the subskills in some logical order showing how they relate to one another or how some are prerequisite to others. Do this with some type of flowchart or diagram. This diagram should be done carefully so it can be included in your portfolio.

Step 3: Select one skill and prepare a 5- to 10-minute lesson to demonstrate it to a particular audience. The audience may be a group of students, peers in your college classroom, or family members. Your lesson should also be placed in your portfolio.

Step 4: Conduct the demonstration after making arrangements to record it visually. This can be done with a camcorder or a 35 mm camera. This visual record of the lesson should be placed in your portfolio.

Step 5: Critique your task analysis and demonstration. How appropriate was the skill you selected to demonstrate? Did the demonstration work as you planned? What would you do differently next time?

Step 6: Arrange the following in your portfolio: the task analysis, the demonstration lesson, pictures of you conducting the demonstration, and your critique.

BOOKS FOR THE PROFESSIONAL

Cruickshank, D. R., Bainer, D., & Metcalf, K. (1995). *The act of teaching.* New York: McGraw-Hill. This book has a good chapter that describes the variations of the direct instruction model.

Gagné, R. M., & Briggs, L. J. (1979). *Principles of instructional design.* New York: Holt, Rinehart & Winston. This book contains very good chapters on designing instruction, particularly in understanding task analysis and assessing student performance.

Good, T. L., Grouws, D., & Ebmeier H. (1983). *Active mathematics teaching.* New York: Longman. This is one of the original descriptions of direct instruction and the research that supports its use.

Hunter, M. (1982). *Mastery teaching.* El Segundo, Calif.: TIP Publications. This book presents a brief account of specific strategies developed by the late Madeline Hunter, many of which are consistent with the focus of the direct instruction model.

COOPERATIVE LEARNING

I n the previous chapter, the teaching model called *direct instruction* was described. Direct instruction is used primarily when teachers want students to learn important skills or academic content. Although academic learning is extremely important, it is not the only objective of student learning. This chapter presents a model of instruction called *cooperative learning* that goes beyond helping students learn academic content and skills to address important social and human relation goals and objectives.

As with the previous chapter, we begin with an overview of the teaching model and then present its theoretical and empirical underpinnings. This is followed by a section that describes the specific procedures used by teachers as they plan, conduct, and manage the learning environment during cooperative learning lessons. The final section highlights the assessment and evaluation tasks associated with cooperative learning.

OVERVIEW OF COOPERATIVE LEARNING

The term task structures *refers to the kinds of cognitive and social tasks that different teaching models and lessons require of students.*

All teaching models are characterized, in part, by their task structures, their goal structures, and their reward structures. **Task structures** refers to the way lessons are organized and to the kind of work students carry out in the classroom. It encompasses whether the teacher is working with the whole class or small groups, what students are expected to accomplish as well as the cognitive and social demands placed on them as they work to accomplish assigned learning tasks. Task structures differ according to the various activities involved in particular teaching approaches. For example, some lessons require students to sit passively while receiving information from a teacher's talk; other lessons require students to complete work sheets and still others to discuss and debate.

A lesson's **goal structure** is the amount of interdependence required of students as they perform their work. Three types of goal structures have been identified. Goal structures are **individualistic** if achievement of the instructional goal requires no interaction with others and is unrelated to how well others do. **Competitive** goal structures exist when students perceive they can obtain their goals if the other students fail to obtain theirs. **Cooperative** goal structures exist when students can obtain their goal only when other students with whom they are linked can obtain theirs.

The terms goal structure *and* reward structure *both refer to the degree of cooperation or competition required of students in order to achieve their goals and rewards.*

The **reward structure** for various instructional models can also vary. Just as goal structures can be individualistic, competitive, or cooperative, so too can reward structures. Individualistic reward structures exist when a reward can be achieved regardless of what anyone else does. The satisfaction of running a 4-minute mile is an example of an individualistic reward structure. Competitive reward structures are those in which rewards are obtained for individual effort in comparison to others. Grading on a curve is an example of a competitive reward structure as is the way winners are defined in many track and field events. In contrast, situations in which individual effort helps others to be rewarded use cooperative reward structures. Winning at team sports, such as in football, is an example of a cooperative reward system in place, even though teams may compete with each other.

Lessons organized around direct instruction and most other teaching models are characterized by task structures where teachers work mainly with a whole class of students or where students are working individually to master academic content. The goal and reward structures for direct instruction are based on individual competition and effort. On the other hand, as its name implies, the cooperative learning model is characterized by cooperative task, goal, and reward structures. Students working in cooperative learning situations are encouraged and/or required to work together on a common task, and they must coordinate their efforts to complete the task. Using cooperative learning, two or more individuals are interdependent for a reward they will share if they are to be successful as a group. Most cooperative learning lessons can be characterized by the following features:

The cooperative learning model requires student cooperation and interdependence in its task, goal, and reward structures.

- ◆ Students work cooperatively in teams to master academic materials
- ◆ Teams are made up of high, average, and low achievers
- ◆ Whenever possible, teams include a racial, cultural, and sexual mix of students
- ◆ Reward systems are group oriented rather than individually oriented.

All these features are explained more fully later in the chapter.

Instructional Goals and Learner Outcomes

The cooperative learning model was developed to achieve at least three important instructional goals: academic achievement, acceptance of diversity, and social skill development.

The three instructional goals of cooperative learning are academic achievement, acceptance of diversity, and development of social skills.

Academic Achievement

Although cooperative learning encompasses a variety of social objectives, it also aims at improving student performance on important academic tasks. Its developers have demonstrated that the model's cooperative reward structure raises the value students place on academic learning and changes the norms associated with achievement. For instance, it has been well documented for over three decades that many young people in the United States place low value on academic achievement (see Coleman,

1961). In most cases, the norms of youth culture actually punish those students who want to excel academically. Robert Slavin and others have sought to change these norms through the use of cooperative learning. For example, Slavin (1984) noted:

> Students often do not value their peers who do well academically, while they do value their peers who excel in sports. . . . This is so because sports success brings benefits to groups (the team, the school, the town), while academic success benefits only the individual. In fact, in a class using grading on the curve or any competitive grading or incentive system, any individual's success reduces the chances that any other individual will succeed." (p. 54)

Slavin and others believe that the group focus of cooperative learning can change the norms of youth culture and make it more acceptable to excel in academic learning tasks.

In addition to changing norms associated with achievement, cooperative learning can benefit both low- and high-achieving students who work together on academic tasks. Higher achievers tutor lower achievers, thus providing special help from someone who shares their youth-oriented interests and language. In the process, higher achievers gain academically because serving as a tutor requires thinking more deeply about the relationship of ideas within a particular subject.

Acceptance of Diversity

Cooperative reward structure increases the value students place on academic learning and decreases their racial and cultural biases.

A second important effect of the cooperative learning model is wider acceptance of people who are different by virtue of their race, culture, social class, ability, or disability. Following the premises outlined by Gordon Allport (1954), it is known that mere physical contact among different racial or ethnic groups or mainstreamed children is insufficient to reduce prejudice and stereotyping. Cooperative learning presents opportunities for students of varying backgrounds and conditions to work interdependently on common tasks, and through the use of cooperative reward structures, learn to appreciate each other.

Social Skill Development

A third and important goal of cooperative learning is to teach students skills of cooperation and collaboration. These are important skills to have in a society in which much adult work is carried out in large, interdependent organizations and in which communities are becoming more culturally diverse. Yet, many youth and adults lack effective social skills. This situation is evidenced by how often minor disagreements between individuals can lead to violent acts or how often people express dissatisfaction when asked to work in cooperative situations.

TABLE 3.1   SYNTAX OF THE COOPERATIVE LEARNING MODEL

Phases	Teacher Behavior
Phase 1 Present goals and set	Teacher goes over objectives for the lesson and establishes learning set.
Phase 2 Present information	Teacher presents information to students with either demonstration or text.
Phase 3 Organize students into learning teams	Teacher explains to students how to form learning teams and helps groups make efficient transition.
Phase 4 Assist team work and study	Teacher assists learning teams as they do their work.
Phase 5 Test over materials	Teacher tests over learning materials or groups present results of their work.
Phase 6 Provide recognition	Teacher finds ways to recognize both individual and group efforts and achievement.

Syntax

There are six major phases or steps involved in a cooperative learning lesson. The lesson begins with the teacher's going over the goals of the lesson and getting students motivated to learn. This phase is followed by the presentation of information, often in the form of text rather than verbally. Students are then organized into study teams. This step is followed by one in which students, assisted by the teacher, work together to accomplish interdependent tasks. Final phases of a cooperative learning lesson include presentation of the group's end product or testing what students have learned and recognition of group and individual efforts. The six phases of a cooperative lesson are summarized in Table 3.1. There are several different approaches to cooperative learning, and the syntax varies slightly depending on the approach being used. Four approaches and their differences are described in later sections of this chapter.

Learning Environment and Management System

The learning environment for cooperative learning is characterized by democratic processes and active roles for students in deciding what should be studied and how. The teacher provides a high degree of structure in forming groups and defining overall procedures, but students are left in control of the minute-to-minute interactions within their groups. If cooperative learning lessons are to be successful, extensive resource materials must be available in the teacher's room or in the school's library or media center. Success also requires avoiding the traditional hazards associated with group work by carefully managing student behavior.

THEORETICAL AND EMPIRICAL SUPPORT

The cooperative learning model did not evolve from the thinking of any one individual or a single approach to learning. Its roots go back to the early Greeks, but its contemporary development can be traced to the work of educational psychologists and pedagogical theorists at the beginning of the twentieth century.

John Dewey, Herbert Thelan, and Democratic Classrooms

In 1916, John Dewey, then at the University of Chicago, wrote a book called *Democracy and Education.* In that book, he set forth a concept of education contending that classrooms should mirror the larger society and function as a laboratory for real life learning. Dewey's pedagogy necessitated that teachers create within their learning environments a social system characterized by democratic procedures and scientific processes. Their primary responsibility was to motivate students to work cooperatively and to consider the important social problems of the day. In addition to their small-group problem-solving efforts, students learned democratic principles through day-to-day interaction with one another.

Many years after Dewey popularized his pedagogy, Herbert Thelan (1954, 1960), also at the University of Chicago, developed more precise procedures for helping students work in groups. Like Dewey, Thelan argued that the classroom should be a laboratory or miniature democracy the purpose of which was to inquire into important social and interpersonal problems. Thelan, who was interested in group dynamics, developed a more detailed and structured form of group investigation and, as further described later, provided the conceptual basis for contemporary developments in cooperative learning.

Cooperative behavior was viewed by Dewey and Thelan as the foundation of democracy, and schools were seen as laboratories for developing democratic behavior.

Cooperative group work as conceived by both Dewey and Thelan went beyond improving academic learning. They viewed cooperative behavior and processes as an indispensable part of human endeavor, the foundation on which strong democratic communities could be built and maintained. The logical way to accomplish these important educational objectives according to Dewey and Thelan was to structure classrooms and students' learning activities in ways that would model the desired outcomes.

Gordon Allport and Intergroup Relations

In 1954, the Supreme Court issued its historic *Brown v. Board of Education of Topeka* decision, which held that public schools in the United States could no longer operate under a "separate but equal" policy but must become racially integrated. This ruling led to subsequent decisions and actions by judicial and legislative bodies across the country calling for public school authorities to submit plans for desegregation.

At the time, thoughtful theorists and observers warned that putting people of different ethnic or racial backgrounds in the same location, of itself, would not counteract the effects of prejudice or promote better intergroup acceptance. They knew, for example, that an integrated school's cafeteria might still be characterized by African-American students sitting on one side of the room and white students on the other. They also knew that a community might be highly integrated but still have restaurants or churches patronized by an all white or an all black clientele.

A leading sociologist of the time, Gordon Allport, argued that laws alone would not reduce intergroup prejudice and promote better acceptance and understanding. Shlomo Sharan and his colleagues summarized three basic conditions formulated by Allport to counteract racial and ethnic prejudice: "(1) unmediated interethnic contact, (2) occurring under conditions of equal status between members of the various groups participating in a given setting, (3) where the setting officially sanctions interethnic cooperation" (1984, p. 2).

Sociologist Gordon Allport argued that unmediated, interethnic contact occurring under conditions of equal status was needed to reduce racial and ethnic prejudice.

Some of the recent interest in the cooperative learning model has grown out of attempts to structure classrooms and teaching processes according to Allport's three conditions. Some of Robert Slavin's work, which is described later, has been conducted in the inner cities on the eastern seaboard as part of integration efforts. The work of David and Roger Johnson at the University of Minnesota has explored how cooperative classroom environments lead to better learning and more positive regard toward handicapped students mainstreamed (integrated) into regular classrooms. The work of Sharan and his colleagues in Israel, which is highlighted in this chapter's research box, was prompted by that country's need to find ways to promote better ethnic understanding between Jewish immigrants with European backgrounds and those with Middle Eastern backgrounds.

RESEARCH BOX   THE RESEARCH, DEVELOPMENT, EVALUATION CYCLE: DISCOVERING THE EFFECTS OF INNOVATION

The research box in Chapter 2 described how researchers in the process-product tradition sought ways to find relationships between what teachers do in their classrooms (the processes of teaching) and what happens to their students (the product of teaching). Researchers in this traditions were content to study practices already employed by regular teachers and seldom tried to introduce innovative methods or practices.

Some educational researchers are not content to accept teaching practices as they currently exist but want to invent and to test new models of instruction. Their work proceeds much differently than does the work of a researcher in the process-product tradition. Sometimes this approach is referred to as the research, development, and evaluation model. Scientific research in this tradition proceeds as *developers* (researchers, teachers, and others interested in inventing new approaches) use the results of *basic research* to develop innovative practices and subsequently test these innovations through *evaluation* and comparison of the effects of the new approach with more traditional ones. The knowledge base on cooperative learning is the product of this type of research.

Basic Research

The fields of social psychology and group dynamics that emerged in the early part of the twentieth century provided an important scientific knowledge base that was subsequently used by cooperative learning theorists and developers. For example, in the early twentieth century, social psychologists began research on a topic commonly referred to as *social facilitation*. Classic studies in this tradition, such as Allport (1924) and Dashiell (1935), compared the performance of individuals doing physical and intellectual tasks alone with individuals doing the same tasks with others present. This research showed that having others present in some instances had important effects on performance. Developers used this knowledge at a later time to plan specific cooperative learning strategies and procedures.

Research comparing the effects that cooperative versus competitive situations have on individual and group performance also dates back to the early part of the twentieth century. Experiments conducted in laboratories, in work organizations, and in classrooms consistently showed that cooperative goal structures (activities in which individuals are working together toward common group goals) were more effective than were competitive goal structures.

Obviously, research on cooperative behavior has become increasingly important as twentieth-century living has become characterized by global, interdependent communities and complex social institutions that require a high degree of cooperation among members. Consequently, most people, including many educators, prize cooperative behavior and believe it to be an important goal for education. Many of schools' extracurricular activities, such as team sports and dramatic and musical productions, are justified on this basis. But what about activities within the academic classroom? Do certain types of activities, such as those associated with cooperative learning, have effects on students' social skills, particularly on their cooperative attitudes and behaviors? Does the basic research on group facilitation and cooperative behavior transfer to the classroom?

Developing and Testing Cooperative Learning: An Example

The past 20 years have seen the application of basic research on cooperation and the development of methods aimed at introducing cooperative learning into classrooms. One particularly interesting project took place in Israel.

For over a decade, Sharan and his colleagues (1984) at Tel Aviv University worked on developing and testing cooperative learning models, particularly the group investigation approach to cooperative learning called Group Investigation (GI). The research team was interested in the ability of cooperative learning to improve social relations among different Jewish subgroups in Israel, particularly between those who had western European and those who had Middle Eastern ethnic background. In one study, researchers randomly assigned 33 English and literature teachers to three training groups. Teachers in group 1 were taught how to "fine-tune" their whole-class teaching skills. Those in group 2 were taught how to use Slavin's STAD and those in group 3 were taught Sharan's group investigation approach to cooperative learning. Students taught by the teachers were from junior high schools that had a mixed Western and Eastern Jewish ethnic composition. The investigators collected massive amounts of information before, during, and after the experiment, including data from achievement tests, classroom observations, and cooperative behavior of students. The summary of the research presented here concentrates only on the measurement of and effects on *cooperative behavior.*

For the test of cooperative behavior, students were selected from classrooms using each of the three instructional approaches and were asked to engage in a task called "Lego Man." In six-member teams (each with three western European and three Middle Eastern members), students were asked to plan how they would carry out a joint task that consisted of constructing a human figure from 48 Lego pieces. Trained observers (naive as to the instructional approach that had been used) recorded students' cooperative, competitive, and individualistic behaviors as they worked on the Lego man task.

The study showed clearly that the instructional methods influenced the students' cooperative and competitive behavior. Group investigation generated more cooperative behavior, both verbal and nonverbal, than whole-class teaching or STAD did. STAD, however, produced more cooperative behavior than did whole-class teaching. Students from both cooperative learning classrooms displayed less competitive behavior than those who came from whole-class teaching classrooms. In other analyses done on these data, Sharan and his colleagues (1984) showed that the cooperative learning approaches also increased the cross-ethnic cooperation during the Lego task more than whole-class teaching.

Experiential Learning

Experiential learning, where individuals are personally involved in the learning, provides theoretical support for the cooperative learning model.

A final theoretical perspective that provides intellectual support for cooperative learning comes from theorists and researchers who are interested in how individuals learn from experience. Experience accounts for much of what people learn. For example, most people learn to ride their first bicycle by riding one, and they learn about being a sister by being one. Conversely, even though everyone can read books about marriage and child rearing, those who have married and raised children know that these experiences are never quite the same as described in books. Experience provides insights, understandings, and techniques that are difficult to describe to anyone who has not had similar experiences. Johnson and Johnson (1994), preeminent cooperative learning theorists, described experiential learning this way:

> Experiential learning is based upon three assumptions: that you learn best when you are personally involved in the learning experience, that knowledge has to be discovered by yourself if it is to mean anything to you or make a difference in your behavior, and that a commitment to learning is highest when you are free to set your own learning goals and actively pursue them within a given framework. (p. 7)

The concept of experiential learning is discussed further in subsequent chapters.

Effects on Academic Achievement

One of the important aspects of cooperative learning is that while it is helping promote cooperative behavior and better group relations among students, it is simultaneously helping students with their academic learning. Slavin (1986) reviewed the research and reported that 45 studies had been done between 1972 and 1986 investigating the effects of cooperative learning on achievement. These studies were done at all grade levels and included the following subject areas: language arts, spelling, geography, social studies, science, mathematics, English as a second language, reading, and writing. Studies he reviewed were conducted in urban, rural, and suburban schools in the United States and in Israel, Nigeria, and Germany. Out of the 45 studies, 37 of them showed that cooperative learning classes have significantly outperformed control group classes in academic achievement. Eight studies found no differences. None of the studies showed negative effects for cooperative learning.

The majority of studies done on the effects of cooperative learning show that it produces both academic and social benefits.

To summarize, a strong theoretical and empirical framework for cooperative learning reflects the perspective that humans learn from their experiences, and that active participation in small groups helps students learn important social skills while simultaneously developing democratic attitudes and logical thinking skills.

CONDUCTING COOPERATIVE LEARNING LESSONS

Planning Tasks

Many functions of teacher planning described in previous chapters can be applied to cooperative learning. But cooperative learning requires some unique planning tasks as well. For example, time spent organizing or analyzing specific skills required for a direct instruction lesson may instead be spent gathering resource materials, text, or work sheets so that small groups of students can work on their own. Instead of planning for the smooth flow and sequencing of major ideas, the teacher may plan how to make smooth transitions from whole-class to small-group instruction. Following are some of the unique planning tasks and decisions required of teachers preparing to teach a cooperative learning lesson.

Choose an Approach

Although the basic principles of cooperative learning do not change, there are several variations of the model. Four approaches that should be part of the beginning teacher's repertoire are described here.

Student Teams Achievement Divisions (STAD). STAD was developed by Robert Slavin and his colleagues at the Johns Hopkins University and is perhaps the simplest and most straightforward of the cooperative learning approaches. Teachers employing STAD, also referred to as student team learning, present new academic information to students each week using verbal presentation or text. Students within a given class are divided into four- or five-member learning teams, each of which has representatives of both sexes, various racial or ethnic groups, and high, average, and low achievers. Team members use work sheets or other study devices to master the academic materials and then help each other learn the materials through tutoring, quizzing one another, and/or carrying on team discussions. Individually, students take weekly or biweekly quizzes on the academic materials. These quizzes are scored, and each individual is given an *improvement score*. This improvement score (explained in more detail later in the chapter) is based not on a student's absolute score, but instead on the degree to which the score exceeds a student's past averages.

In the STAD model of cooperative learning, heterogeneous teams help each other learn by using a variety of cooperative study methods and quizzing procedures.

Each week a short (generally one page) newsletter or some other device, announces teams with the highest scores and students who have high improvement scores or who have perfect scores on the quizzes. Sometimes all teams who reach a certain criterion are recognized, as is explained later.

In the Jigsaw model, each team member is responsible for mastering part of the learning material and then teaching that part to the other team members.

Jigsaw. Jigsaw was developed and tested by Elliot Aronson and his colleagues at the University of Texas and then adapted by Slavin and his Johns Hopkins colleagues. Using Jigsaw, students are assigned to five- or six-member heterogeneous study teams. Academic materials are presented to the students in text form, and each student has the responsibility to learn a portion of the material. For example, if the textual material is on cooperative learning, one student on the team would be responsible for STAD, another for Jigsaw, another for group investigation, and perhaps the other two would become experts in the research base and history of cooperative learning. Members from different teams with the same topic (sometimes called the expert group) meet to study and help each other learn their topic. Then students return to their home team and teach other members what they have learned. Figure 3.1 illustrates the relationship between home and expert teams. Following home team meetings and discussions, students take quizzes individually about the learning materials. In the Slavin version of Jigsaw, team scores use the same scoring procedures used in STAD. High-scoring teams and individuals are recognized in the weekly class newsletter or by some other means.

In the group investigation model, students not only work together but help plan both the topics for study and the investigative procedures used.

Group Investigation (GI). Many of the key features of the group investigation approach were designed originally by Thelan. More recently, this approach has been extended and refined by Sharan and his colleagues at Tel Aviv University. The group investigation approach is perhaps the most complex of the cooperative learning approaches and the most difficult to implement. In contrast to STAD and Jigsaw, students are involved in planning both the topics for study and how to proceed with their investiga-

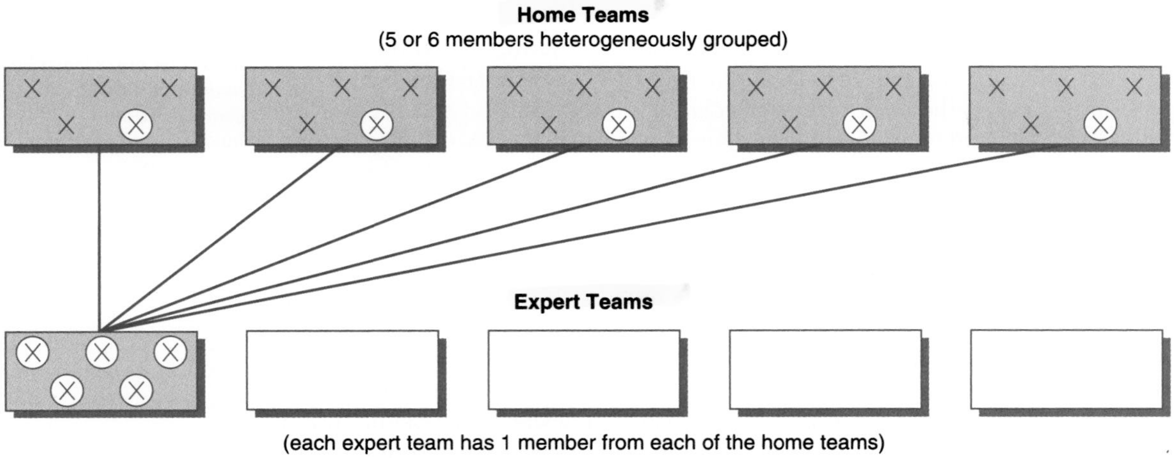

Home Teams
(5 or 6 members heterogeneously grouped)

Expert Teams

(each expert team has 1 member from each of the home teams)

FIGURE 3.1
Illustration of Jigsaw Teams

tions. This approach necessitates more sophisticated classroom norms and structures than approaches that are more teacher-centered do. It also requires teaching students good communication and group process skills.

Teachers who use the GI approach usually divide their classes into five- or six-member heterogeneous groups. In some instances, however, groups may form around friendships or an interest in a particular topic. Students select topics for study, pursue in-depth investigation of chosen subtopics, and then prepare and present a report to the whole class. Sharan and colleagues (1984) have described the following six steps of the GI approach:

1. *Topic selection.* Students choose specific subtopics within a general problem area usually delineated by the teacher. Students then organize into two- to six-member task-oriented groups. Group composition is academically and ethnically heterogeneous.

2. *Cooperative planning.* Students and teacher plan specific learning procedures, tasks, and goals consistent with the subtopics of the problem selected in step 1.

3. *Implementation.* Pupils carry out their plan formulated in step 2. Learning should involve a wide variety of activities and skills and should lead students to different kinds of sources both inside and outside the school. The teacher closely follows the progress of each group and offers assistance when needed.

4. *Analysis and synthesis.* Pupils analyze and evaluate information obtained during step 3 and plan how it can be summarized in some interesting fashion for possible display or presentation to classmates.

5. *Presentation of final product.* Some or all groups in the class give an interesting presentation of the topics studied in order to get classmates involved in each other's work and to achieve a broad perspective on the topic. Group presentations are coordinated by the teacher.

6. *Evaluation.* In cases where groups pursued different aspects of the same topic, pupils and teachers evaluate each group's contribution to the work of the class as a whole. Evaluation can include either individual or group assessment, or both. (pp. 4–5)

The Structural Approach. A final approach to cooperative learning has been developed over the past decade mainly by Spencer Kagen and his colleagues (see Kagen, 1993). Although it has much in common with other approaches, the structural approach emphasizes the use of particular structures designed to influence student **interaction patterns.** The structures developed by Kagen are intended to be alternatives to more traditional classroom structures, such as the recitation, where the teacher poses questions to the whole class and students provide answers after rais-

In the structural approach, teams may vary from two to six members and the task structure may emphasize either social or academic goals.

ing their hands and being called on. Kagen's structures call for students to work interdependently in small groups and are characterized by cooperative rather than individual rewards. Some structures have the goal of increasing student acquisition of academic content; other structures are designed to teach social or group skills. *Think-pair-share* and *numbered heads together,* described here, are two examples of structures teachers can use to teach academic content or to check on student understanding of particular content. *Active listening* and *time tokens* are examples of structures to teach social skills and are described later in the chapter.

Think-pair-share. The think-pair-share strategy has grown out of the cooperative learning and wait-time research. The particular approach described here, initially developed by Frank Lyman and his colleagues at the University of Maryland (1985), is an effective way to change the discourse pattern in a classroom. It challenges the assumption that all recitations or discussions need to be held in whole-group settings, and it has built-in procedures for giving students more time to think, to respond, and to help each other. Suppose a teacher has just completed a short presentation, or students have read an assignment, or a puzzling situation has been described. The teacher now wants students to consider more fully what has been explained or experienced. She chooses to use the think-pair-share strategy as contrasted to whole-group question and answer. She employs the following steps:

Step 1: Thinking The teacher poses a question or issue associated with the lesson and asks students to spend a minute thinking alone about the answer or the issue. Students need to be taught that talking or walking about is not part of think time.

Step 2: Pairing Next the teacher asks students to pair off and discuss what they have been thinking about. Interaction during this period could be sharing answers if a question was posed or sharing ideas if a specific issue was identified. Normally, teachers would allow no more than 4 or 5 minutes for pairing.

Step 3: Sharing In the final step, the teacher asks the pairs to share with the whole class what they have been talking about. It is effective to simply go around the room from pair to pair and continue until about a fourth or a half of the pairs have had a chance to report.

Numbered heads together. Numbered heads together is an approach developed by Spencer Kagen (1993) to involve more students in the review of

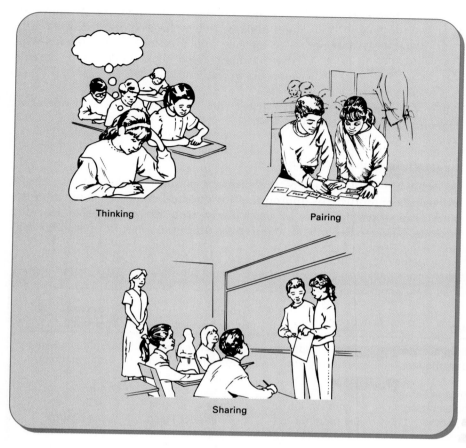

Thinking

Pairing

Sharing

FIGURE 3.2
Illustration of Think-Pair-Share

materials covered in a lesson and to check their understanding of a lesson's content. Instead of directing questions to the whole class, teachers use the following four-step structure:

Step 1: Numbering Teachers divide students into three- to five-member teams and has them number off so each student on a team has a number between one and five.

Step 2: Questioning Teachers ask students a question. Questions can vary. They can be very specific and in question form. "How many states in the Union?" Or they can be directives, such as, "Make sure everyone knows the capitals of the five states that border on the Pacific Ocean."

Step 3: Head Together Students put their head together to figure out and make sure everyone knows the answer.

Step 4: Answering The teacher calls a number and students with that number raise their hands and provide answers to the whole class.

Table 3.2 summarizes and compares the four approaches to cooperative learning described above.

Choose Appropriate Content

Because cooperative learning requires self-direction and initiative, teachers must be careful to choose content that interests students.

As with any lesson, one of the primary planning tasks for teachers is choosing content that is appropriate for the students given their interests and prior learning. This is particularly true for cooperative learning lessons, because the model requires a substantial amount of student self-

TABLE 3.2   COMPARISON OF FOUR APPROACHES TO COOPERATIVE LEARNING

	STAD	Jigsaw	Group Investigation	Structural Approach
Cognitive Goals	Simple academic information	Simple academic information	Complex academic information and inquiry skills	Simple academic information
Social Goals	Group work and cooperation	Group work and cooperation	Cooperation in complex groups	Group and social skills
Team Structure	4–5 member heterogeneous learning teams	5–6 member heterogeneous learning teams—use of home and expert teams	5–6 member learning groups—may be homogeneous	Varies—pairs, trios, 4–6 member groups
Lesson Topic Selection	Usually teacher	Usually teacher	Usually students	Usually teacher
Primary Task	Students may use work sheets and help each other master learning materials	Students investigate materials in expert groups—help members of home group learn materials	Students complete complex inquiries	Students do assigned tasks—social and cognitive
Assessment	Weekly tests	Varies—can be weekly tests	Completed projects and reports—can use essay tests	Varies
Recognition	Newsletters and other publicity	Newsletters and other publicity	Written and oral presentations	Varies

direction and initiative. Without interesting and appropriately challenging content, a cooperative lesson can quickly break down.

Veteran teachers know from experience which topics are best suited for cooperative learning just as they know the approximate developmental levels and the interests of students in their classes. Inexperienced teachers must depend more on curriculum guides and textbooks for appropriate subject matter. However, there are several questions that all teachers can ask themselves to determine the appropriateness of subject matter:

◆ Have the students had some previous contact with the subject matter, or will it require extended explanation by the teacher?

◆ Is the content likely to interest the group of students for which it is being planned?

◆ If the teacher plans to use text, does it provide sufficient information on the topic?

◆ For STAD or Jigsaw lessons, does the content lend itself to objective quizzes that can be administered and scored quickly?

◆ For a Jigsaw lesson, does the content allow itself to be divided into several natural subtopics?

◆ For a group investigation lesson, does the teacher have sufficient command of the topic to guide students into various subtopics and direct them to relevant resources? Are relevant resources available?

Form Student Teams

Another important planning task for cooperative learning is deciding how student learning teams are to be formed. Obviously, this task will vary according to the goals teachers have for a particular lesson and the racial and ethnic mix and the ability levels of students within their classes. Following are some examples of how teachers might decide to form student teams:

How student teams are to be formed is an important planning task for teachers.

◆ A fifth-grade teacher in an integrated school might use cooperative learning for the purpose of helping students to better understand peers from different ethnic or racial backgrounds. The teacher might take great care to have racially or ethnically mixed teams in addition to matching for ability levels.

◆ A seventh-grade English teacher in a mostly middle-class white school might form student teams according to students' achievement levels in English.

◆ A tenth-grade social studies teacher with a homogeneous group of students might decide to use group investigation and form teams according to student interest in a particular subtopic but also keep in mind a mix of different ability levels of the students.

◆ A fourth-grade teacher with several withdrawn students in her class may decide to form cooperative teams based on ability but also find ways to integrate the isolates with more popular and outgoing class members.

◆ Early in the year a teacher with several students new to the school might form learning teams on a random basis, thus ensuring opportunities for new students to meet and work with students they don't already know. Later, students' abilities could be used to form learning teams.

Obviously, the composition of teams holds almost infinite possibilities. During the planning phase, teachers must delineate clearly their academic and social objectives. They also need to collect adequate information about their students' abilities so that if heterogeneous ability teams are desired, they have the needed information. Finally, teachers should recognize that some features of group composition may have to be sacrificed in order to meet others.

Develop Materials and Objectives

When teachers prepare for a direct instruction lesson, a major task is to gather materials that can be translated into meaningful verbal messages or into a demonstration that illustrates a particular skill. Although teachers provide students with verbal information in a cooperative learning lesson, this information is normally accompanied by text, work sheets, and study guides.

Providing interesting and developmentally appropriate study materials is important if student teams are to work independently.

If students are to be given text, it is important that it be both interesting and at an appropriate reading level for the particular class of students. Using materials from a college textbook or other advanced text is generally inappropriate for school-aged students except perhaps for those in advanced high school classes. If study guides are to be developed by teachers, these should be designed to highlight the content deemed most important. Good study guides and materials take time to develop. They cannot be done well the night before a particular lesson is to begin.

Getting maximum assistance from school support staff when planning a cooperative learning lesson takes time and careful planning.

If teachers are using the group investigation method, an adequate supply of materials must be collected for use by student learning teams. In some schools, a beginning teacher can rely on the school librarian and media specialists for gathering materials. This procedure usually requires the teacher to communicate clearly the goals and objectives of a particular lesson and to be precise about how many students will be involved. For librarians and media specialists to be of maximum assistance, they need enough lead time for them to do their work. Again, teachers are cautioned about making last-minute requests. The following guidelines are offered to get maximum assistance from school support staff when planning a cooperative learning lesson:

◆ Meet with the school librarian and media specialists at least two weeks prior to the lesson and go over your lesson objectives. Ask for their ideas and assistance.

◆ Follow up this meeting with a brief memo summarizing ideas, time-lines, and agreements.

◆ Check back a few days before materials are needed to see if things are coming along as you expect and offer your assistance if that is needed.

◆ If the materials are to be used in your room, ask the specialist to help you design a system for keeping track of them. You may also ask the specialist to come into your room and explain the system to your students.

Orient Students to Tasks and Roles

It is important to plan so students have a clear understanding about their roles and the teacher's expectations as they participate in a cooperative learning lesson. If other teachers in the school are using cooperative learning, this task will be easier, because students will already be aware of the model and their role in it. In schools where few teachers use cooperative learning, teachers will have to spend time describing the model to students and working with them on requisite skills. Procedures to teach communication and other social skills are described later in this chapter.

If students have not had previous experience with cooperative learning, it is vital that the teacher orient them to its unique task, goal, and reward structures.

An important thing to remember for teachers who have not used cooperative learning before, and who are using it with students who are not familiar with the model, is that at first it may appear not to be working. Students will be confused about the cooperative reward structure. Parents may also object. Also, students at first may not be very enthusiastic about the possibilities of small-group interactions on academic topics with their peers.

Finally, special written directions about the goals and activities of a particular cooperative learning lesson should be given to students—on tagboard displays for younger children and as handouts for older students. Included in these directions would be information about:

◆ The goals of the lesson
◆ What students are expected to do while working in learning teams
◆ Timelines for completion of particular work or activities
◆ Dates for quizzes when using STAD or Jigsaw
◆ Dates for major presentations when using group investigation
◆ Grading procedures—both individual and group rewards
◆ Format for presentations of reports

Using the cooperative learning model can be difficult for an inexperienced teacher because it requires the simultaneous coordination of a variety of activities. On the other hand, this model can achieve some important educational goals that other models cannot, and the rewards of this type of teaching can be enormous for the teacher who plans carefully.

Plan for Time and Space

Cooperative learning lessons take more time than most other instructional models because of its reliance on small-group interaction.

An additional important planning task for cooperative learning is deciding how time and space will be used. As described in Chapter 1, time is a scarcer commodity than most teachers realize, and cooperative learning, with its reliance on small-group interaction, makes stronger demands on time resources than do some other models of instruction. Most teachers underestimate the amount of time for cooperative learning lessons. It simply takes longer for students to interact around important ideas than it does for a teacher to present the ideas directly to students. Making transitions from whole class to small groups can also take up valuable instructional time. Careful planning can help teachers become more realistic about time requirements, and it can minimize the amount of noninstructional time.

Cooperative learning requires special attention to the use of classroom space, and it requires moveable furniture. The *cluster* and *swing* arrangements illustrated here are two examples of how experienced teachers use space during cooperative learning.

Cluster-seating and swing-seating arrangements lend themselves to cooperative learning because of their flexibility.

Cluster-Seating Arrangement.   Seating clusters of four or six, such as those illustrated in Figure 3.3, are useful for cooperative learning and other small-group tasks. If a cluster arrangement is used, teachers may have to ask students to move their chairs for lectures and demonstrations so that all students will be facing the teacher. If not carefully planned, this movement, as described in Chapter 1, can lead to disruption and cause management problems.

Swing-Seating Arrangement.   A particularly inventive approach for flexibility was developed by Lynn Newsome, a reading teacher in Howard County, Maryland (MAACIE, 1990). For cooperative learning, she uses a seating arrangement that allows her to "swing" from a direct instruction lesson to cooperative learning lessons. In her classroom, desks are arranged in a wing formation as shown at the top of Figure 3.4. On cue, students in the "wing" desks (shaded) move them to form groups of four, as shown at the bottom of Figure 3.4. Newsome reports that both formations allow her to "maintain eye contact with all students, and the room appears spacious" (MAACIE, 1990, p. 5).

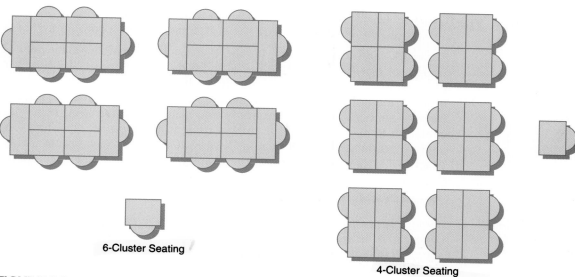

6-Cluster Seating

4-Cluster Seating

FIGURE 3.3
Four- and Six-Cluster Seating Arrangements

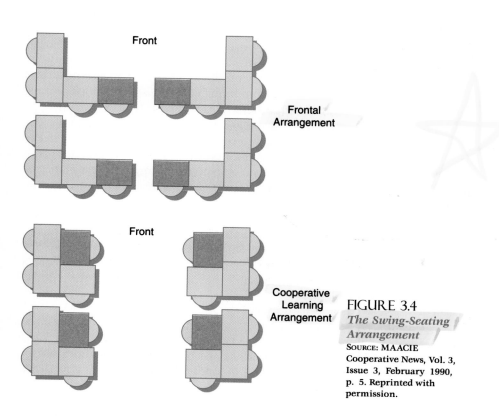

Front

Frontal
Arrangement

Front

Cooperative
Learning
Arrangement

FIGURE 3.4
The Swing-Seating Arrangement
SOURCE: MAACIE
Cooperative News, Vol. 3,
Issue 3, February 1990,
p. 5. Reprinted with
permission.

Interactive Tasks

Table 3.1 showed the syntax for the cooperative learning model divided into six phases: (1) presenting the goals for the lesson and establishing set; (2) presenting information to students with verbal demonstration, text, or other forms; (3) organizing students into learning teams; (4) managing and helping students during team study and seatwork; (5) testing team presentation of materials; (6) recognizing student achievement. The first four steps are discussed in this section. Testing and student recognition will be described in the final section of the chapter, Assessment and Evaluation.

Present Goals and Establish Set

Cooperative learning teachers should devote special attention to explaining lesson objectives and establishing set, since their lessons often extend over several days.

Some aspects of presenting goals and establishing set are no different for cooperative learning than they are for other models. Effective teachers begin all lessons by reviewing, by explaining their objectives in understandable language, and by showing how the lesson ties in to previous learning. Because many cooperative learning lessons extend beyond a particular day or week and because the goals and objectives are multifaceted, the teacher usually puts special emphasis on this phase of instruction.

For example, when teachers are introducing a group investigation lesson for the first time, they will want to spend sufficient time with students to make sure specific steps and roles are clearly understood. At this point, the teacher may want to discuss how students can take responsibility for their own learning and not rely solely on the teacher. It may also be a time to discuss how knowledge comes from many sources, such as books, films, and one's own interactions with others.

If a teacher is about to introduce Jigsaw, he or she may want to discuss how people are required to work interdependently with others in many aspects of life and how Jigsaw gives students an opportunity to practice cooperative behaviors. If the teacher's main objective is to improve acceptance of students from other ethnic backgrounds or races, for instance, he or she may want to explain this idea to students and discuss how working with people different from us will provide opportunities to know one another better.

The important point of these examples is that students are more likely to work toward important goals and objectives if the rationale for the lesson has been explicitly discussed. It is difficult for students to perform a task well if they are unclear about why they are doing it or if the criteria for success are kept secret.

Present Information

Chapter 2 provided an extended discussion concerning the importance of presenting verbal information clearly to students and described guidelines for doing so. These guidelines will not be repeated here. It is important, however, to point out a brief caution about the use of text.

Teachers of young children know that relying on text to transmit content involves helping the children learn to read the assigned materials. Teachers in the upper grades and secondary schools (and in college, for that matter) often assume their students can read and comprehend the assigned materials. Many times this is an incorrect assumption. If a cooperative learning lesson requires students to read text, then effective teachers, regardless of the age level of their students or the subject being taught, should assume responsibility for helping students become better readers.

Organize and Assist Study Teams

Organizing students into learning teams and getting them started on their work is one of the most difficult steps for teachers using cooperative learning. This is the phase in a cooperative learning lesson during which bedlam can result unless the transition is carefully planned and managed. There is nothing more frustrating to teachers than transitional situations in which 30 students are moving into small groups and no one is sure of what they are to do. Equally frustrating is having students from different groups simultaneously demanding the teacher's attention and help. The next section presents guidelines for managing transitions and for helping students during group work.

The transition from whole-class instruction to small-group work must be carefully orchestrated.

LEARNING ENVIRONMENT AND MANAGEMENT TASKS

The cooperative learning environment presents special management hazards for teachers, and it compels teachers to attend to a unique set of management tasks. For example, describing to students how to accomplish a complex group project is clearly more difficult than assigning them problems at the end of a textbook chapter. Similarly, it is more difficult to organize students into study teams and cooperate effectively than it is to get them to line up for recess or to sit and listen to their teacher. Consider, for example, the problems faced by Ken when he tried to use cooperative learning as a student teacher.*

*Ken's story is a true one. It was experienced by Ken while he was doing his student teaching and was described by Weinstein & Mignano (1992).

Ken's Story

I couldn't wait to get my students into small groups. I didn't want to be like my cooperating teacher—she does all the talking and students are never allowed to work together. They seem so passive and so isolated from one another. Although she wasn't particularly enthusiastic about small-group work, she gave me her blessing. I was really excited. I was sure that the kids would respond well if they were given the chance to be active and to interact.

I decided to use small groups in science, since my cooperating teacher has given me the most freedom in this area. (I think she doesn't like science and doesn't think it's all that important, so she lets me do whatever I want.) I told the kids that they could choose their own groups. I figured that being allowed to work with friends would be really motivating.

Well, just getting into groups was chaotic. First, we had to move the desks from rows into clusters. Then there was lots of shouting and arguing about who was going to be in which group. The whole process took about 10 minutes and was really noisy. My cooperating teacher was *not* pleased, and I was really upset when I saw what happened. My class is real heterogeneous—I've got blacks, whites, Hispanics, Asian-Americans. Well, the groups turned out really segregated. They also tended to be just about all-boy or all-girl. Even worse—I have one mainstreamed girl in my class (she's learning disabled and really hyperactive), and nobody wanted to work with her at all. I ended up *making* a group take her, and they were pretty nasty about it. And there's another kid who's real shy and quiet; I had to get him into a group, too. It was really embarrassing for both of them.

Finally, I got everyone settled down and they started to work on the assignment. We've been talking about seeds and plants, and each group was supposed to plan an experiment that they would actually carry out to demonstrate what plants needed in order to grow. I emphasized that they were supposed to work together and make sure everyone contributed to the plan.

Well, it was a real mess. A couple of the groups worked out okay, but one group argued the whole time and never got anything written. In another group—all boys—they decided to just let the kid who was smartest in science plan the experiment. He kept coming up and complaining that no one else would do any work. And it was true. The rest just sat and fooled around the whole time. Another group had three girls and one boy. The boy immediately took charge. He dominated the whole thing; the girls just sat there and let him tell them what to do.

I had pictured everyone cooperating, helping one another, contributing ideas. But it didn't work out that way at all. And the noise—it just kept getting louder and louder. I kept turning off the lights and reminding them to use their "indoor voices." For a few minutes, they'd get quieter, but then it would get loud again. Finally, my cooperating teacher stepped in and yelled at everybody. I was really humiliated. I just couldn't control them. Right now, I'm pretty turned off to using cooperative groups. I think maybe she's right. Maybe these kids just can't handle working together. Maybe I should just go back to having everyone sit and listen to me explain the lesson. (pp. 176–177)

Many of the general management guidelines described in Chapter 1 as well as those related to direct instruction (see Chapter 2) also apply to cooperative learning lessons and could assist Ken with his management problems. When using any teaching model, it is important have a small set of rules and routines that govern student talk and movement, to keep lessons moving smoothly, to maintain a general level of decorum in the classroom, and to deal quickly and firmly with student misbehavior when it occurs. Management tasks unique to cooperative learning are: helping students make the transition from whole class to cooperative learning groups; assisting students as they work in groups; and teaching students social skills and gaining cooperative behavior.

Helping with Transitions

As described previously, the process of getting students into learning groups and started on their work is difficult. As you can see from Ken's story, this process can cause serious problems for a beginning teacher. Several simple but important strategies can be used by teachers to make transitions go smoothly.

1. **Write key steps on the chalkboard or on charts.** Visual cues assist large groups of students as they move from one place in the room to another. Think of these as signs similar to those provided for people lining up to purchase theater tickets to a popular play or posted queuing procedures used at public events such as football games. Here is an example of such a display:

   Step 1   Move quickly to the location where your team's name has been posted on the wall.
   Step 2   Choose one team member to come up to my desk to gather needed learning materials.
   Step 3   Spend 10 minutes reading your particular assignment.
   Step 4   At my signal, begin your discussions.
   Step 5   At my signal, return to your learning team and start pre-senting your information.

2. **State directions clearly and ask two or three students to paraphrase the directions.** Getting several students to repeat the directions helps everyone to pay attention and also gives the teacher feedback on whether or not the directions are understood.

3. **Identify a location for each learning team and have that clearly marked.** Left to their own devices, students at any age (even adults) will not evenly distribute themselves around a room. They will tend to cluster in areas of the room that are most easily accessible. For effective small-group work, teachers should clearly designate those parts of the room they want each team to occupy and insist that teams go to that particular location.

Transition into small groups is helped by writing directions on the chalkboard, having students repeat them, and assigning each team a specific space.

These procedures are highly prescriptive and structured. Once teachers and students become accustomed to working in cooperative learning groups, more flexibility can be allowed. However, for inexperienced teachers in the earlier stages of using cooperative learning, tightly structured directions and procedures can make lessons move much more smoothly and prevent the frustration and discouragement experienced by Ken.

Managing and Assisting Group Work

Cooperative learning teachers need to be available to student teams, but students must also learn to depend on each other rather than on their teacher.

Uncomplicated cooperative learning activities allow students to complete their work with minimum interruption or assistance from a teacher. With other activities, the teacher may need to work closely with each of the learning teams, reminding them of the tasks they are to perform and of the time allocated for each step. For example, when using the group investigation approach, the teacher must remain constantly available to assist with resource identification. There is a fine line for the teacher to follow during this phase of a cooperative learning lesson. Too much interference and unrequested assistance can be annoying to students. It can also take away opportunities for student initiative and self-direction. At the same time, if the teacher finds that students are unclear about the directions or that they cannot complete required group tasks, then they must intervene and offer assistance. In short, teachers need to provide students with assistance when they need it but must recognize how important it is for students to depend on each other, not on the teacher.

Teaching Cooperation

In many schools, students get few opportunities to work on common tasks, and subsequently, many do not know how to work cooperatively. To help students cooperate necessitates attention to the kinds of tasks assigned to small groups; it also requires teachers to teach their students important social and group skills, such as the ones described below.

Task Interdependence

As described earlier in this chapter, cooperative learning task and activity structures must be interdependent rather than independent. An example of an **independent task** is when a teacher gives each student a math work sheet, divides students into groups and tells them they can help each other, but then requires each student to complete his or her own work sheet, which will be graded individually. Although students may help one another, they are not interdependent to accomplish the task. This same lesson would become an **interdependent task** if the teacher divided the class into groups and required each group to complete one math work sheet with all member's names on it. Many teachers using cooperative learning for the first time fail to structure tasks so that they are interdependent, and they become frustrated when their students do not cooperate or choose to work alone.

Having group members share materials, as is the case in the example above, is one way to structure task interdependence; having pairs of students work on assignments together is another. A third way to structure interdependence around materials is to give some students the problems and others the answers and ask them to find a match between the two through discussion. Following the procedures in the Jigsaw cooperative learning lesson described earlier is another way to create interdependence.

The Jigsaw lesson requires group members to be dependent on each other for information. One student, you may remember, studied in expert groups to become an expert on STAD while another student was responsible for group investigation. Each student in the group was then responsible for teaching what he or she learned to others in their home group.

Role differentiation is another way to structure interdependence. During a group investigation project, for instance, one student might be responsible for typing the report on her word processor, another for creating transparencies to use in the presentation, and still another for delivering the actual presentation. Each group member performs a specific task, but the success of the group as a whole depends on the cooperative actions of all members.

Social Skills and Group Skills

Teachers should not assume that students have the requisite social or group skills to work cooperatively. Students may not know how to interact with one another, how to develop cooperative plans of action, how to coordinate the contributions of various group members, or how to assess group progress toward particular goals. To make cooperative learning work, teachers will have to teach needed social and group skills.

Social Skills. Social skills involve those behaviors that promote successful social relationships and enable a person to work effectively with others. Social skills are taught to children by many different individuals: parents, child providers, neighbors, and teachers. Ideally, children progress from infants who possess few social skills to adults who have a rich repertoire of skills. However, many children and young people (and adults as well) never learned requisite social skills to live and work effectively together. Skills found lacking in many children and youth include sharing, participation, and communication. It is important that teachers help students master these skills.

The sharing, participation, and communication skills needed for cooperative learning will have to be taught to students.

Sharing skills. Many students have difficulty sharing time and materials. This complication can lead to serious management problems during a cooperative learning lesson. Being bossy toward other students, talking incessantly, and doing all the work for the group are examples of students' inabilities to share. Domineering students are often well intentioned and just do not understand the effects of their behavior on others or on their group's work. These students need to learn the value of sharing and how to rein in their controlling behaviors. *Round robin* and *pair checks,* two examples of lessons teachers can use to teach sharing skills, are described here.

- ◆ *Round robin.* Round robin is an activity that teaches students how to take turns when working in a group. The process is quite simple. The teacher introduces an idea or asks a question that has many possible answers. Students are then asked to make their contributions. One student starts, makes his or her contribution, and passes the turn to the next person, who does the same. Turn taking continues until every person in the group has had a chance to talk.
- ◆ *Pair checks.* A way to help domineering students learn sharing skills is to have them work in pairs and employ the pair checks structure. The version of pair checks described below includes the eight steps recommended by Spencer Kagen (1993).

Step 1: Pair work	Teams divide into pairs. One student in the pair works on a work sheet or problem while the other student helps and coaches.
Step 2: Coach checks	The student who was the coach checks the partner's work. If coach and worker disagree on an answer or idea, they may ask the advice of other pairs.
Step 3: Coach praises	If partners agree, coach provides praise.
Steps 4–6: Partners switch	All partners change roles and repeat steps 1–3.
Step 7: Pairs check	All team pairs come back together and compare answers.
Step 8: Team celebrates	If all agree on answers, team members do team handshake or cheer.

Participation skills. Whereas some students dominate group activity, other students may be unwilling or unable to participate. Sometimes students who avoid group work are shy. Often shy students are very bright and they may work well alone or with one other person. However, they find it very difficult to participate in a group. The rejected student is another type of student who may have difficulty participating in group activity. Finally, there is the otherwise typical student who chooses, for whatever reason, to work alone and refuses to participate in cooperative group endeavors.

Making sure that shy or rejected students get into groups with students who have good social skill is one way teachers can involve these students. Structuring task interdependence, described previously, is another means to discourage students' wanting to work alone. Using planning sheets where various group tasks are listed along with the students responsible for completing each task is a third way to teach and ensure balanced participation among group members. *Time tokens* and *high talker tap out* described here are special activities that teach participation skills.

◆ **Time tokens.** If a teacher has cooperative learning groups in which a few people dominate the conversation and a few are shy and never say anything, time tokens can help distribute participation more equitably. Each student is given several tokens worth 10 or 15 seconds of talk time. A student monitors interaction and asks talkers to give up a token whenever they have used up the designated time. When a student uses up all his or her tokens, the student can say nothing more. This, of course, necessitates that those still holding tokens enter into the discussion.

◆ **High talker tap out.** It is not uncommon to find only a small percentage of students participating in group work or discussions. One way to produce more balanced participation is to assign one student to keep track of each student's participation. If the monitor observes a particular student talking repeatedly, he or she can pass a note asking that student to refrain from further comments until everyone has had a turn. The monitor can also encourage shy students to take a turn in the same manner.

Communication Skills. It is quite common to find both younger and older students (adults also) lacking in important communication skills. We all have experienced difficulty describing our own ideas and feelings so they are accurately perceived by listeners and in accurately hearing and interpreting what others say to us. Cooperative learning groups cannot function effectively if the work of the group is characterized by miscommunication. The four communication skills—paraphrasing, describing behavior, describing feelings, and checking impressions—described in Chapter 5 are important and should be taught to students to ease communication in group settings.

Often during classroom interaction, students are not listening to one another. Instead, they sit in whole group with a hand in the air waiting for their turn to speak or in small groups, talking or interrupting incessantly. One way to promote active listening is during some classroom discussions (those where the main objective is learning to listen) to insist that before a student can speak, he or she must first paraphrase what was said by the student who just finished speaking. More on teaching active listening and paraphrasing can be found in Chapter 5.

Group Skills.   Most people have had experiences working in groups in which individual members were nice people and had good social skills. Yet the group as a whole did not work well. Members may have been pulling in different directions, and consequently, work was not getting done. Just as individuals must learn social skills to interact successfully in group or community setting, groups as an entity must learn group skills and processes if they are to be effective. Before students can work effectively in cooperative learning groups, they must also learn about one another and respect each other's differences.

Before students can work effectively in cooperative learning groups, they must learn about each other and respect individual differences.

Team building.   Helping build team identity and member caring are important tasks for teachers who use cooperative learning groups. Simple tasks include making sure everyone knows one another's name and having members decide on a team name. Having teams make a banner or create a logo can also build *esprit de corps* among members. The following activities can be used to teach group skills and to build a positive team identity.

- ◆ *Team interviews.* Have students in the cooperative learning teams interview one another. They can find out other members' names; places they have traveled; special interests or a favorite sport, holiday, color, book, movie. Each student can be asked to interview every other student in the group and then share with the total group what they learned about group members and the group as a whole. A variation on this procedure is to have each student interview one other student in the team (or class) and then prepare an introduction for that person to be presented to the whole group (class).
- ◆ *Team murals.* Using a variety of materials such as magic markers, crayons, chalk, paints, and pictures from magazines, teachers can ask students to work together to make a mural illustrating how they would like their team to work together. Encourage all members to participate in the mural. After it has been completed, have members discuss their contributions and explain their mural to members of other teams.
- ◆ *Magic number 11.* Kagen (1993) described a team project in which students sit in a circle and hold out a clenched hand. They shake their hand up and down and say, "One, two, three." On the count of three, each student puts out so many fingers. The goal is to have all the fingers showing add up to 11. No talking is allowed. After success, teams cheer.

Teaching Social and Group Skills. Teaching specific social skills is no different than teaching specific content skills such as map reading or how to use a microscope. Chapter 2 described the direct instruction model, which requires teachers to demonstrate and model the skill being taught and to provide time for students to practice the skill and receive feedback on how they are doing. In general, this is the model that teachers should use when teaching important social and group skills. The topic of teaching social skills and study skills to students will be described in more detail in Chapters 5 and 6.

The direct instruction model, which focuses on skill instruction, is useful in teaching the social and group skills needed for successful cooperative learning.

ASSESSMENT AND EVALUATION

It is important to use assessment and evaluation strategies that are consistent not only with the goals and objectives of a particular lesson but also with the particular model of instruction being used. For example, if a teacher is using direct instruction to teach a specific skill, a performance test is required to measure student mastery of the skill and to provide corrective feedback. Similarly, if the goal is for students to acquire straightforward declarative knowledge, then teacher-made paper-and-pencil tests are often the best means to measure whether or not the goal has been accomplished.

In Chapter 2, considerable explanation was provided about how to measure simple skills and basic declarative knowledge. The evaluation and assessment procedures described were based, for the most part, on the assumption that the teacher was using a competitive or an individualistic reward system. Because the cooperative learning model operates under a cooperative reward structure and because many cooperative learning lessons aim at accomplishing complex cognitive and social learning, different approaches to assessment and evaluation are required. Some of these are described here.

Because of its cooperative task, goal, and reward structures, cooperative learning requires testing procedures different from those for a model built on competitive learning.

Testing in Cooperative Learning

For STAD and the Slavin version of Jigsaw, teachers have students take quizzes on the learning materials. Test items on these quizzes, in most instances, must be of an objective paper-and-pencil type, so they can be scored in class or soon after. Figure 3.5 illustrates how individual scores are determined, and Figure 3.6 shows how a quiz scoring sheet might look. Slavin (1986), the developer of this scoring system, described it this way:

Step 1
Establish base line

Each student is given a base score based on averages on past quizzes.

Step 2
Find current quiz score

Students receive points for the quiz associated with the current lesson.

Step 3
Find improvement score

Students earn improvement points to the degree to which their current quiz score matches or exceeds their base score, using the scale provided below.

More than 10 points below base _____ 0 points
10 points below to 1 point below base _____ 10 points
Base score to 10 points above base _____ 20 points
More than 10 points above base _____ 30 points
Perfect paper (regardless of base) _____ 30 points

FIGURE 3.5
Scoring Procedures for STAD and Jigsaw
SOURCE: From R. Slavin (1986), *Student team learning* (3d ed.), Center for Research on Elementary and Middle Schools, p. 19. © Johns Hopkins. Reprinted with permission.

The amount that each student contributes to his or her team is determined by the amount the student's quiz score exceeds the student's own past quiz average. . . . Students with perfect papers always receive the . . . maximum, regardless of their base scores. This individual improvement system gives every student a good chance to contribute maximum points to the team if (and only if) the student does his or her best, and thereby shows substantial improvement or gets a perfect paper. This improvement point system has been shown to increase student academic performance even without teams . . . but it is especially important as a component of STAD since it avoids the possibility that low performing students will not be fully accepted as group members because they do not contribute many points. (p. 24)

A special scoring system does not exist for the group investigation approach. The group report or presentation serves as one basis for evaluation, and students should be rewarded for both individual contributions and the collective product.

Grading in Cooperative Learning

A special challenge for cooperative learning teachers is how to grade students for both team and individual achievement.

In cooperative learning, the teacher has to be careful with the way grades are assigned beyond the weekly point system just described. Consistent with the concept of cooperative reward structure, it is important for the teacher to reward the group product—both the end result and the cooperative behavior that produced it. Teachers also want to assess each member's contribution to the final product. These dual assessment tasks, however, can prove troublesome for teachers when they try to determine how to assign individual grades for a group product. For instance, sometimes a few ambitious students may take on a larger portion of the responsibility for completing the group project and then be resentful toward classmates who made only minor con-

Student	Date: May 23 Quiz: Addition with Regrouping Base Score	Quiz Score	Improvement Points	Date: Quiz: Base Score	Quiz Score	Improvement Points	Date: Quiz: Base Score	Quiz Score	Improvement Points
Sara A.	90	100	30						
Tom B.	90	100	30						
Ursula C.	90	82	10						
Danielle D.	85	74	0						
Eddie E.	85	98	30						
Natasha F.	85	82	10						
Travis G.	80	67	0						
Tammy H.	80	91	30						
Edgar I.	75	79	20						
Andy J.	75	76	20						
Mary K.	70	91	30						
Stan L.	65	82	30						
Alvin M.	65	70	20						
Carol N.	60	62	20						
Harold S.	55	46	10						
Jack E.	55	40	0						

FIGURE 3.6

Quiz Score Sheet for STAD and Jigsaw

SOURCE: From R. Slavin (1986), *Student team learning* (3d ed.), p. 20. Center for Research on Elementary and Middle Schools. © Johns Hopkins. Reprinted with permission.

tributions yet receive the same evaluation. Similarly, students who have neglected their responsibilities to the group effort may develop cynicism toward a system that rewards them for work they did not accomplish.

Some experienced teachers have found a solution to this dilemma by providing two evaluations for students, one for the group's effort and one for each person's individual contribution.

Recognition of Cooperative Effort

A final important assessment and evaluation task unique to cooperative learning is recognizing student effort and achievement. Slavin and the Johns Hopkins' developers created the concept of a weekly class newsletter for use with STAD and Jigsaw. The teacher (sometimes the class itself) reports and publishes the results of team and individual learning in this newsletter. An example of a weekly newsletter is shown in Figure 3.7.

THE LITTLE LEOPARD

Issue No. 5

March 21, 1994

CALCULATORS OUTFIGURE CLASS!

The Calculators (Charlene, Alfredo, Laura, and Carl) calculated their way into first place this week, with big ten-point scores by Charlene, Alfredo, and Carl, and a near-perfect team score of 38! Their score jumped them from sixth to third in cumulative rank. Way to go Calcs! The Fantastic Four (Frank, Otis, Ursula, and Rebecca) also did a fantastic job, with Ursula and Rebecca turning in ten pointers, but the Tigers (Cissy, Lindsay, Arthur, and Willy) clawed their way from last place last week to a tie with the red-hot Four, who were second the first week, and first last week. The Fantastic Four stayed in first place in cumulative rank. The Tigers were helped out by ten-point scores from Lindsay and Arthur. The Math Monsters (Gary, Helen, Octavia, Ulysses, and Luis) held on to fourth place this week, but due to their big first-place score in the first week they're still in second place in overall rank. Helen and Luis got ten points to help the M.M.'s. Just behind the Math Monsters were the Five Alive (Carlos, Irene, Nancy, Charles, and Oliver), with ten-point scores by Carlos and Charles, and then in order the Little Professors, Fractions, and Brains. Susan turned in ten points for the L.P.'s, as did Linda for the Brains.

This Week's Rank	This Week's Score	Overall Score	Overall Rank
1st – Calculators	38	81	3
2nd – Fantastic Four	35	89	1
2nd – Tigers	35	73	6
3rd – Math Monsters	40/32	85	2
5th – Five Alive	37/30	74	5
6th – Little Professors	26	70	8
7th – Fractions	23	78	4
8th – Brains	22	71	7

(2nd – Fantastic Four and 2nd – Tigers → Tie)

TEN-POINT SCORERS

Charlene	(Calculators)	Helen	(Math Monsters)
Alfredo	(Calculators)	Luis	(Math Monsters)
Carl	(Calculators)	Carlos	(Five Alive)
Ursula	(Fantastic Four)	Charles	(Five Alive)
Rebecca	(Fantastic Four)	Susan	(Little Professors)
Lindsay	(Tigers)	Linda	(Brains)
Arthur	(Tigers)		

* * * * * *

FIGURE 3.7

Sample Weekly Newsletter

SOURCE: From R. Slavin (1986), *Student team learning* (3d ed.), p. 25. Center for Research on Elementary and Middle Schools. © Johns Hopkins. Reprinted with permission.

More recently, the Johns Hopkins group has tended to play down the competition among teams. Instead of determining winning teams, they recommend pitting teams against preestablished criteria to evaluate team achievement. Figure 3.8 shows the criteria used by some teachers and an example of a team summary sheet.

The developers of the group investigation approach recognize team efforts by highlighting group presentations and by displaying the results of group investigations prominently in the room. This form of recognition can be emphasized even more by inviting guests (parents, students from another class, or the principal) to hear final reports. Newsletters summarizing the results of a class's group investigation can also be produced and sent to parents and others in the school and community. More is said about the topic of recognition in the following chapter on problem-based instruction.

FIGURE 3.8

Determining and Rewarding Team Scores and Team Summary Sheet

SOURCE: From R. Slavin (1986), *Student team learning* (3d ed.), p. 19. Center for Research on Elementary and Middle Schools. © Johns Hopkins. Used with permission.

Step 1:
Determining team scores

Team scores are figured by adding each member's individual improvement points and dividing by the number of members on the team.

Step 2:
Recognizing team accomplishments

Each team receives a particular certificate based on the following point system.

Team Average	Award
15 points	Good Team
20 points	Great Team
25 points	Super Team

Team name   *Fantastic Four*

Team members	1	2	3	4	5	6	7	8	9	10	11	12	13	14
Sara A.	30													
Eddie E.	30													
Edgar I.	20													
Carol N.	20													
Total team score	100													
Team average*	25													
Team award	*Super Team*													

* Team average = a total team score ÷ number of team members

REFLECTION BOX   REFLECTIONS ON COOPERATIVE
LEARNING

Cooperative learning should be a part of every beginning teacher's repertoire. Careful developmental work and empirical research have produced a
model that helps to promote greater tolerance for differences, to teach
important social and group skills, and to increase academic achievement.
Inexperienced teachers, however, should be careful and should know
about the difficulties involved in implementing cooperative learning in
some settings.

     In some communities, for instance, teachers may find strong resis-
tance to the idea of cooperative reward structures. Many parents and
community members value independent effort and believe these norms
should be emphasized in schools preparing youth for an adult world
characterized by competition. Many students, particularly those who
excel in the more traditional, individualistic reward structures, will like-

SUMMARY

◆ Cooperative learning is unique among the models of teaching, because it uses a
different task and reward structure to promote student learning. The task structure requires students to work together in small groups. The reward structure
recognizes collective as well as individual effort.

◆ The cooperative learning model grows out of an educational tradition emphasizing democratic thought and practice, active learning, cooperative behavior, and
respect for diversity in multicultural societies.

◆ The cooperative learning model aims at instructional effects beyond academic
learning, specifically, promoting intergroup acceptance and social and group
skills.

◆ The syntax for cooperative learning models relies on small-group work as contrasted to whole-class teaching and includes six major phases: providing objectives and set; giving students information through presentation or text; organizing students in learning teams; providing time and assisting team study; testing
for results or assessing group products; and recognizing both individual and
group achievements.

◆ The model's learning environment requires cooperative rather than competitive
task and reward structures.

◆ A strong theoretical and empirical base supports the use of cooperative learning
for the following educational objectives: cooperative behavior, academic learning, and improved diversity relationships.

◆ Planning tasks associated with cooperative learning put less emphasis on organizing academic content and more emphasis on organizing students for small-
group work and collecting a variety of learning materials to be used during
group work.

◆ Four variations of the basic approaches to cooperative learning can be used: student team learning, Jigsaw, group investigation, and the structural approach.

wise object to approaches in which interdependent activities are valued and rewards are shared.

Some educators hold high expectations for cooperative learning as an effective means to increase positive student social behavior and to correct many of the social injustices that exist in our society. The model has demonstrated success in helping to accomplish these types of goals. However, educators should be careful not to overstate the benefits of the model and to educate citizens to recognize that no approach to teaching can solve long-standing social ills overnight.

What do you think? Will you be a teacher who will want to use cooperative learning in your classroom? What steps will you take to help parents and students understand the importance of cooperation in today's world? How will you react to negative attitudes by parents or students or by fellow teachers or the principal?

Regardless of the approach, the lesson is characterized by students working in groups and by group-oriented rewards.

♦ Conducting a cooperative learning lesson changes a teacher's role from one of center-stage performer to one of choreographer of small-group activity.

♦ Small-group work presents special management challenges to teachers. Teachers must help students make transitions to their small groups, manage their group work, and teach important social and group skills.

♦ Assessment and, particularly, evaluation tasks replace the traditional competitive approaches of other models of teaching with individual and group rewards, along with new forms of recognition.

♦ A variety of ways (e.g., newsletters and group presentations) exist to provide recognition of student cooperative accomplishments.

LESSON PLAN FORMAT
FOR COOPERATIVE LEARNING

PURPOSE: This is a suggested format for making a lesson plan tailored specifically to planning requirements of the cooperative learning model. You can try it out as you plan for teaching or microteaching. Revise the format as you see the need.

DIRECTIONS: Follow the guidelines below as you plan a cooperative learning lesson.

Planning Tasks

Content That Is Focus of Lesson _____

_____

Lesson Objectives

    Academic objectives _____

_____

    Social objectives _____

_____

Composition of Learning Teams

    Number and size of groups _____

_____

    Criteria for membership _____

_____

Material Requirements

    Materials needed _____

_____

    Supplies and equipment needed _____

_____

Conducting the Lesson

Procedures for introducing and explaining lesson _____

_____

Directions for helping transition to learning teams _____

_____

Notes/hints to remember as students work _____

_____

Important dates to remember _____   _____

_____   _____

Student Recognition

Means for recognition _____

Pitfalls to Avoid

During Introduction of the Lesson	As Students Work in Teams	As Work Is Reported and Recognized

OBSERVING COOPERATIVE LEARNING IN MICROTEACHING OR CLASSROOMS

DIRECTIONS: This form highlights the key aspects of a cooperative learning lesson. It can be used to observe a peer in a microteaching laboratory or an experienced classroom teacher. It can also be used to assess a lesson you have taught and videotaped. As you observe the lesson, check the category you believe describes the level of performance of the teacher you are observing. Also answer the general questions about the lesson at the bottom of the form.

	Level of Performance			
Teacher Behavior	Excellent	Acceptable	Needs Improvement	Not Needed
Planning				
How appropriate was the content for the lesson?	_____	_____	_____	_____
How appropriate were plans for team formation?	_____	_____	_____	_____
How appropriate were materials gathered to support the lesson?	_____	_____	_____	_____
How well prepared was the teacher overall?	_____	_____	_____	_____
Execution				
How well did the teacher				
Explain goals and purposes?	_____	_____	_____	_____
Establish set?	_____	_____	_____	_____
Explain small-group activities?	_____	_____	_____	_____
Make transition to learning teams?	_____	_____	_____	_____
Help students during team study?	_____	_____	_____	_____
Recognize individual effort?	_____	_____	_____	_____
Recognize team effort?	_____	_____	_____	_____

Overall Planning

What did you like best about the way the lesson was planned and organized?

_____

_____

What could be improved?_____

_____

Lesson Execution

Think about teaching style and delivery. What did you like best about the way the lesson was presented?_____

_____

What could be improved?_____

_____

If you were a student in peer microteaching, how did you feel about the teacher's interaction with you?_____

_____

INTERVIEWING TEACHERS ABOUT CLASSROOM GOAL AND REWARD STRUCTURES

PURPOSE: Goal and reward structures can have a significant impact on the learning environment. This aid is to help you examine how goal and reward structures are exhibited in classrooms.

DIRECTIONS: Use these questions as a guide in interviewing teachers about how they use classroom goal and reward structures.

(Remember that goal structures can be individualistic, competitive, or cooperative; that is, students' attainment of a goal can be unrelated to others' attainment, dependent on the failure of others, or dependent on the success of others. Reward structures are distinct from goal structures in that they refer to the rewards students receive for attaining their goals. Reward structures can also be individualistic, competitive, or cooperative. As in goal structures, if rewards are given individually and independently of the rewards others receive, then the reward structure is individualistic. If one's reward is dependent on the failure of others to receive the reward, the reward structure is competitive. A reward structure in which one's reward is dependent on the success of another is cooperative. Think about a track meet as an example. If the goal is to win the race, then one person's winning means others fail. This is a competitive goal structure. The ribbon or trophy is the reward. If only the winner receives a ribbon, then the reward structure is competitive. If everyone receives a ribbon, say, for participation, then the reward structure is individualistic.)

1. What activities do you have students do in which their ability to complete the activity or attain the goal of the activity is unrelated to whether other students complete it?

   _____

   _____

   _____

2. What activities do you have students do in which their ability to complete the activity or to attain the goal of the activity depends on other students not completing it or attaining the goal?

   _____

   _____

   _____

3. What activities do you have students do in which they must work together and one student's ability to complete the activity to attain the goal depends on other students also being able to complete it or attain the goal?

_____

_____

_____

4. In what ways do you reward students so that one student's reward is unrelated to rewards for any other student?

_____

_____

_____

5. In what ways do you reward students so that one student's reward depends on another student's not receiving the reward?

_____

_____

_____

6. In what ways do you reward students so that one student's reward depends on whether other students also receive the reward?

_____

_____

_____

Analysis and Reflection: What are the predominant goal and reward structures in these teachers' classes? Are all three types of structures represented? Is the mix of structures appropriate? What would be a better mix?

CREATING YOUR OWN LESSON FOR TEACHING SOCIAL SKILLS

PURPOSE: Teaching social skills is an important and sometimes difficult aspect of a teacher's work. The purpose of this aid is to help you gain skill in designing a social skill's lesson and to develop products of this work that can become part of your teaching portfolio.

DIRECTIONS: Follow the steps below to design a social skills lesson, teach that lesson, and display it in words and pictures in your portfolio.

Step 1: Choose a social skill such as cooperation, listening to others, or helping others with their work, and design a short lesson to introduce students to that skill. Do a task analysis of the skill (as described in Chapter 2) identifying all the subskills associated with the overall skill.

Step 2: Put the subskills in some logical order showing how they relate to one another and those that might be prerequisite to others. Do this with some type of flowchart or web.

Step 3: Select one of the subskills, and prepare a short lesson to demonstrate the skill to a particular audience. It may be a group of students, peers in your college classroom, or family members. The lesson plan you create should also be placed in your portfolio.

Step 4: Teach the social skill, and capture what you do with a camcorder or a 35 mm camera. This visual record of the lesson should be placed in your portfolio.

Step 5: Critique your social skill lesson. How appropriate was the selected social skill for your audience? Did the lesson turn out as you planned it? What would you do differently next time?

Step 6: Arrange the following in your portfolio: the task analysis of the social skill, your lesson plan, pictures of you conducting the lesson, and your critique.

BOOKS FOR THE PROFESSIONAL

Aronson, E., Blaney, S. C., Sikes, J., & Snapp, M. (1978). *The Jigsaw classroom.* Beverly Hills, Calif.: Sage Publications. The book presents an in-depth discussion of the Jigsaw procedure including results of research and detailed directions for teachers.

Hertz-Lazarowith, R., & Miller, N. (1992). *Interaction in cooperative groups.* Cambridge, UK: University of Cambridge Press. This is a major collection of essays on cooperative learning with special attention paid to the theory behind the model and research that support its use.

Johnson, D. W., & Johnson, R. T. (1986). *Learning together and alone: Cooperation, competition, and individualization* (2d ed.). Englewood Cliffs, N.J.: Prentice-Hall. This book gives a detailed rationale for the goal and reward structures required of cooperative learning and also provides many good ideas for teachers who want to implement cooperative learning in their classrooms.

Kagen, S. (1993). *Cooperative learning.* San Juan Capistrano, Calif.: Resources for Teachers. A resource manual to assist teachers with using cooperative learning in their classrooms, this book is filled with lesson ideas and aids.

Slavin, R. (1983). *Cooperative learning.* New York: Longman. This book provides a detailed rationale behind cooperative learning along with summaries of Slavin's early research on the topic.

CHAPTER 4

PROBLEM-BASED INSTRUCTION

155

T his chapter is about problem-based instruction (PBI) and its use in promoting higher-level thinking in problem-oriented situations, including learning how to learn. The model has also been referred to by other names, such as project-based teaching, **experienced-based education, authentic learning,** and **anchored instruction.** Unlike the direct instruction model described in Chapter 2, in which the emphasis was on teachers presenting ideas or demonstrating skills, a teacher's role in problem-based instruction is to pose problems, to ask questions, and to facilitate investigation and dialogue. Most important, the teacher provides scaffolding—a supportive framework—that enhances inquiry and intellectual growth. Problem-based instruction cannot occur unless teachers create classroom environments in which an open and honest exchange of ideas can occur. In this respect, many parallels exist between problem-based instruction and classroom discussion, which will be described in Chapter 5.

A teacher's role in PBI is to pose authentic problems, facilitate student investigation and dialogue, and support student learning.

As with previous chapters, we begin with an overview of problem-based instruction and a presentation of its theoretical and empirical underpinnings. A brief discussion of the model's historical traditions is also provided. This will be followed by sections that describe the specific procedures involved in planning, conducting, and evaluating problem-based learning. The chapter will conclude with a discussion of the learning environment and management system requirements of problem-based learning and its assessment tasks.

OVERVIEW OF PROBLEM-BASED INSTRUCTION

The essence of problem-based instruction (PBI) consists of presenting students with authentic and meaningful problem situations that can serve as springboards for investigations and inquiry. To illustrate this concept, consider the following scenario at an elementary school in a small town near Maryland's Chesapeake Bay.

> 10-year old Jamel rises to speak. "The chair recognizes the delegate from Ridge School," says the chair, a student from the local high school.
>
> "I'd like to speak in favor of House Bill R130," Jamel begins. "This bill would tell farmers that they can't use fertilizer on land that is within 200 feet of the Chesapeake Bay because it pollutes the bay and kills fish. Farmers can still grow enough crops even if they don't plant close to water. We all will have a better life if we can stop pollution in the bay. I yield to questions."
>
> A hand goes up. The chair recognizes a delegate from Carver School. "How does fertilizer harm the bay?" she asks. Jamel explains how the fertilizer sup-

plies nutrients to algae, and when too much algae grows it deprives oysters, crabs, clams, and other marine life of oxygen.

A delegate from Green Holly School offers another viewpoint: "I'm a farmer," says 11-year old Maria. "I can hardly pay all my bills as it is, and I've got three kids to feed. I'll go broke if I can't fertilize my whole field." (Slavin, Madden, Dolan, & Wasik, 1994, pp. 3–4)

This debate continues for over an hour as students consider the problem of pollution and its relationship to the economy from the perspectives of farmers, commercial crabbers, business owners, and citizens who see pollution ruining the local tourist industry and the value of homes in the Chesapeake region.

These students are participating in "Roots and Wings," a PBI project developed at Johns Hopkins University. The purpose of "Roots and Wings" is to help students learn academic content and problem-solving skills by engaging them in real life problem situations. This particular program, like other PBI projects, has certain characteristics that distinguish it from other teaching approaches.

Special Features of Problem-Based Instruction

Various developers of problem-based instruction have described the instructional model as having the following features (Krajcik, Blumenfeld, Marx, & Soloway, 1994; Slavin, Madden, Dolan, & Wasik, 1992, 1994; Cognition & Technology Group at Vanderbilt, 1990).

The main features of PBI include a driving question or problem, an interdisciplinary focus, authentic investigations, collaboration, and the production of artifacts and exhibits.

◆ *Driving question or problem.* Rather than organizing lessons around particular academic principles or skills, problem-based learning organizes instruction around questions and problems that are both socially important and personally meaningful to students. They address authentic, real life situations that evade simple answers and for which competing solutions exist.

◆ *Interdisciplinary focus.* Although a problem-based lesson may be centered in a particular subject (science, math, social studies), the actual problem under investigation has been chosen because its solution requires students to delve into many subjects. For example, the pollution problem raised in the Chesapeake Bay lesson cuts across several academic and applied subjects—biology, economics, sociology, tourism, and government.

◆ *Authentic investigation.* Problem-based instruction necessitates that students pursue *authentic* investigations that seek real solutions to real problems. They must analyze and define the problem, develop hypotheses and make predictions, collect and analyze information, conduct experiments (if appropriate), make inferences, and draw

PBI lessons are organized around authentic, real life situations that evade simple answers and invite competing solutions.

conclusions. The particular investigative methods used, of course, depend on the nature of the problem being studied.

◆ *Production of artifacts and exhibits.* Problem-based instruction requires students to construct products in the form of *artifacts* and *exhibits* that explain or represent their solutions. A product could be a mock debate like the one in the "Roots and Wings" lesson. It could be a report, a physical model, a video, or a computer program. Artifacts and exhibits, as will be described later, are planned by students to demonstrate to others what they have learned and to provide a refreshing alternative to the traditional report or term paper.

◆ *Collaboration.* Like the cooperative learning model described in Chapter 3, problem-based instruction is characterized by students working with one another most often in pairs or small groups. Working together provides motivation for sustained involvement in complex tasks and enhances opportunities for shared inquiry and dialogue and for the development of thinking and social skills.

Student collaboration in PBI encourages shared inquiry and dialogue and the development of thinking and social skills.

Instructional Goals and Learner Outcomes

PBI helps students develop their thinking and problem-solving skills, learn authentic adult roles, and become independent learners.

Problem-based instruction was not designed to help teachers convey huge quantities of information to students. Direct instruction and lecture are better suited to this purpose. Rather, problem-based instruction was developed primarily to help students develop their thinking, problem-solving, and intellectual skills; learn adult roles by experiencing them through real or simulated situations; and become independent, autonomous learners. A brief discussion of these three goals follows.

Thinking and Problem-Solving Skills

A bewildering array of ideas and words are used to describe the way people think. But what does thinking really involve? What are thinking skills and particularly what are **higher-order thinking** skills? Most of the definitions that have been provided describe abstract **intellectual processes** such as the following:

◆ Thinking is a process involving mental operations such as induction, deduction, classification, and reasoning.

◆ Thinking is a process of symbolically representing (through language) real objects and events and of using those symbolic representations to discover the essential principles of those objects and events. Such symbolic (abstract) representation is usually contrasted with mental operations that are based on the concrete level of facts and specific cases.

◆ Thinking is the ability to analyze, criticize, and reach conclusions based on sound inference or judgment.

Most contemporary statements about thinking recognize that higher-level thinking skills are not the same as skills associated with more routine patterns of behavior. They emphasize that even though precise definitions of higher-order thinking cannot always be found, we recognize such thinking when we see it in operation. Furthermore, higher-order thinking, unlike more concrete behaviors, is complex and not easily reduced to fixed routines. Consider the following statements provided by Lauren Resnick (1987) about what she designates as higher-order thinking:

◆ Higher-order thinking is *nonalgorithmic.* That is, the path of action is not fully specified in advance.

◆ Higher-order thinking tends to be *complex.* The total path is not "visible" (mentally speaking) from any single vantage point.

◆ Higher-order thinking often yields *multiple solutions,* each with costs and benefits, rather than unique solutions.

◆ Higher-order thinking involves *nuanced judgment* and interpretation.

◆ Higher-order thinking involves the application of *multiple criteria,* which sometime conflict with one another.

◆ Higher-order thinking often involves *uncertainty.* Not everything that bears on the task at hand is known.

◆ Higher-order thinking involves *self-regulation* of the thinking process. We do not recognize higher-order thinking in an individual when someone else "calls the plays" at every step.

◆ Higher-order thinking involves *imposing meaning,* finding structure in apparent disorder.

◆ Higher-order thinking is *effortful.* There is considerable mental work involved in the kinds of elaborations and judgments required. (pp. 2–3)

Notice that Resnick used words and phrases such as *nuanced judgment, self-regulation, imposing meaning,* and *uncertainty.* Obviously, thinking processes and the skills people need to activate them are highly complex. Resnick also pointed out the importance of context when *thinking about thinking.* That is, although thinking processes have some similarities across situations, they also vary according to what one is thinking about. For instance, the processes we use to think about mathematics differ from those we use to think about poetry. The processes for thinking about abstract ideas differ from those used to think about real life situations. Because of the complex and contextual nature of higher-order thinking skills, they cannot be taught using approaches suitable for teaching more concrete ideas and skills. Higher-order thinking skills and processes are, however, clearly teachable, and most programs and curricula developed for this purpose rely heavily on approaches similar to problem-based instruction.

Higher-order thinking skills cannot be taught by using approaches designed for teaching concrete ideas and skills.

Adult Role Modeling

Resnick also provided the rationale for how problem-based instruction helps students to perform in real life situations and to learn important adult roles. In a speech entitled "Learning in School and Out," Resnick (1987b) described how school learning, as traditionally conceived, differs in four important ways from mental activity and learning that occurs outside schools. Her four comparisons are paraphrased here.

1. School learning focuses on the individual's performance, whereas out-of-school mental work involves collaboration with others.
2. School learning focuses on unaided thought processes, whereas mental activity outside school usually involves cognitive tools such as computers, calculators, and other scientific instruments.
3. School learning cultivates symbolic thinking regarding hypothetical situations, whereas mental activity outside school engages individuals directly with concrete and real objects and situations.
4. School learning focuses on general skills (reading, writing, and computing) and general knowledge (world history, chemical elements), whereas situation-specific thinking such as whether to buy or lease a new car dominates out-of-school mental activity.

PBI projects resemble out-of-school learning situations more closely than they do the academic lessons that characterize most school learning.

Resnick's perspective provides a strong rationale for problem-based instruction. She argues that this form of instruction is essential to bridge the gap between formal school learning and the more practical mental activity found outside school. Note how the features of problem-based instruction correspond to out-of-school mental activity.

◆ Problem-based instruction encourages collaboration and the joint accomplishment of tasks.
◆ Problem-based instruction has elements of an apprenticeship. It encourages observation and dialogue with others so that a student can gradually assume the observed role (scientist, teacher, doctor, artist, or historian, etc.).
◆ Problem-based learning engages students in self-selected investigations that enable them to interpret and explain real world phenomena and to construct their own understanding about these phenomena.

Independent and Autonomous Learners

Finally, problem-based learning strives to help students become independent and **autonomous learners.** Guided by teachers who repeatedly encourage and reward them for asking questions and seeking solutions to real problems on their own, students learn to perform these tasks independently later in life.

Syntax

Problem-based instruction usually consists of five major phases that begin with a teacher's orienting students to a problem situation and culminate with the presentation and analysis of student work and artifacts. When the problem is modest in scope, all five phases of the model may be covered in a few class periods. However, more complex problems may take a full school year to accomplish. The five phases of the model are described in Table 4.1.

Learning Environment and Management System

Unlike the tightly structured learning environment required for direct instruction or the careful use of small groups in cooperative learning, the learning environment and management system for problem-based instruction is characterized by open, democratic processes and by active student roles. In fact, the whole process of helping students become independent, autonomous learners who are confident of their own intellectual skills necessitates active involvement in an intellectually safe, inquiry-oriented environment. Although the teacher and students proceed through the phases of a problem-based learning lesson in a somewhat structured and predictable fashion, the norms surrounding the lesson are those of open inquiry and freedom of thought. The learning environment emphasizes the central role of the learner, not of the teacher.

The classroom environment of PBI is student centered and encourages open inquiry and freedom of thought.

TABLE 4.1 SYNTAX FOR PROBLEM-BASED LEARNING	
Phase	**Teacher Behavior**
Phase 1 Orient students to the problem	Teacher goes over the objectives of the lesson, describes important logistical requirements, and motivates students to engage in self-selected problem-solving activity.
Phase 2 Organize students for study	Teacher helps students define and organize study tasks related to the problem.
Phase 3 Assist independent and group investigation	Teacher encourages students to gather appropriate information, conduct experiments, and search for explanations and solutions.
Phase 4 Develop and present artifacts and exhibits	Teacher assists students in planning and preparing appropriate artifacts such as reports, videos, and models and helps them share their work with others.
Phase 5 Analyze and evaluate the problem-solving process	Teacher helps students to reflect on their investigations and the processes they used.

THEORETICAL AND EMPIRICAL SUPPORT

Direct instruction, as you read in Chapter 2, draws its theoretical support from behavioral psychology and social learning theory. Teachers using direct instruction rely mainly on external stimuli, such as reinforcement, to maintain student cooperation and to keep them engaged in academic tasks. The teacher's role in a direct instruction lesson consists mainly of presenting information to students and modeling particular skills in a clear and efficient manner. Problem-based teaching, on the other hand, draws on **cognitive psychology** for its theoretical support. The focus is not so much on what students are doing (their behavior) but what they are thinking (their cognitions) while they are doing it. Although the role of a teacher in problem-based lessons sometimes involves presenting and explaining things to students, it more usually involves serving as a guide and facilitator so that students learn to think and to solve problems on their own.

Getting students to think, to solve problems, and to become autonomous learners are not new goals for education. Teaching strategies, such as **discovery learning, inquiry training,** and **inductive teaching** have long and prestigious histories. The **Socratic method,** dating back to the early Greeks, emphasized the importance of inductive reasoning and of dialogue in the teaching-learning process. John Dewey (1933) described in some detail the importance of what he labeled *reflective thinking* and the processes teachers should use to help students acquire productive thinking skills and processes. Jerome Bruner (1962) emphasized the importance of discovery learning and how teachers should help learners become "constructionists" of their own knowledge. For our purposes, problem-based instruction will be traced through three main streams of twentieth-century thought.

Dewey and the Democratic Classroom

Dewey's view that schools should be laboratories for real life problem solving provides the philosophical underpinning for PBI.

As with cooperative learning, problem-based instruction finds its intellectual roots in the work of John Dewey. In *Democracy and Education* (1916), Dewey described a view of education in which schools would mirror the larger society and in which classrooms would be laboratories for real life problem solving. Dewey's pedagogy encouraged teachers to engage students in problem-oriented projects and help them inquire into important social and intellectual problems. Dewey and his disciples, such as Kilpatrick (1918), argued that learning in school should be purposeful rather than abstract and that purposeful learning could best be accomplished by having children in small groups pursue projects of their own interest and choosing. This vision of purposeful or problem-centered learning fueled by students' innate desire to explore personally meaningful situations clearly links contemporary problem-based instruction with the educational philosophy and pedagogy of Dewey.

Piaget, Vygotsky, and Constructivism

Whereas Dewey provided the philosophical underpinnings for problem-based instruction, twentieth-century psychology has provided much of its theoretical support. The European psychologists Jean Piaget and Lev Vygotsky were instrumental in developing the concept of **constructivism** on which much of contemporary problem-based instruction rests.

Constructivist theories of learning, which stress the learner's need to investigate one's environment and construct personally meaningful knowledge, provide the scientific basis for PBI.

Jean Piaget (1886–1980), a Swiss psychologist, spent over 50 years studying how children think and the processes associated with intellectual development. In explaining how the intellect develops in young children, Piaget confirmed that children are innately curious and are constantly striving to understand the world around them. This curiosity, according to Piaget, motivates them to actively *construct* representations in their minds about the environment they are experiencing. As they grow older and acquire more language and memory capacity, their mental representations of the world become more elaborate and abstract. At all stages of development, however, children's need to understand their environment motivates them to investigate and to construct theories that explain it.

The **cognitive-constructivist perspective** on which problem-based instruction rests borrows heavily from Piaget. It posits, as did he, that learners of any age are actively involved in the process of acquiring information and constructing their own knowledge. Knowledge does not remain static but instead is constantly evolving and changing as learners confront new experiences that force them to build on and modify prior knowledge. In the words of Piaget, good pedagogy

must involve presenting the child with situations in which he himself experiments, in the broadest sense of that term—trying things out to see what happens, manipulating things, manipulating symbols, posing questions and seeking his own answers, reconciling what he finds one time with what he finds at another, comparing his finding with those of other children. (Duckworth, 1964, p. 2)

Lev Vygotsky (1896–1934) was a Russian psychologist whose work, because of communist censorship, was not known by most Europeans and Americans until recently. Like Piaget, Vygotsky believed that the intellect develops as individuals confront new and puzzling experiences and as they strive to resolve discrepancies posed by these experiences. In the quest for understanding, individuals link new knowledge to prior knowledge and construct new meaning. Vygotsky's beliefs differed from those of Piaget, however, in some important ways. Whereas Piaget focused on the stages of intellectual development that all individuals go through regardless of social or cultural context, Vygotsky placed more importance on the *social aspect of learning*. Vygotsky believed that **social interaction** with others spurred the construction of new ideas and enhanced the learner's intellectual development.

The zone of proximal development *is the label given by Vygotsky to the zone between a learner's actual level of development and his/her level of potential development.*

A key idea stemming from Vygotsky's interest in the social aspect of learning was his concept of the *zone of proximal development*. According to Vygotsky, learners have two different levels of development: the level of actual development and the level of potential development. The **level of actual development** defines an individual's current intellectual functioning and the ability to learn particular things on one's own. Individuals also have a **level of potential development,** which Vygotsky defined as the level an individual can function at or achieve with the assistance of other people, such as a teacher, parent, or more advanced peer. The zone between the learner's actual level of development and the level of potential development was labeled by Vygotsky as the **zone of proximal development.**

The importance to education of Vygotsky's ideas is clear. Learning occurs through social interaction with teachers and peers. With appropriate challenges and assistance from teachers or more capable peers, students are moved forward into their zone of proximal development where new learning occurs.

Bruner and Discovery Learning

The era of the 1950s and 1960s saw significant curriculum reform in the United States that began in mathematics and the sciences, but extended to history, the humanities, and the social sciences. Reformers, mainly university scholars, strived to shift elementary and secondary curricula from a near-total focus on the transmission of established academic content to a focus on investigative processes. Pedagogy of the new curricula included activity-based instruction in which students were expected to use their own direct experiences and observations to gain information and to solve scientific problems. Textbooks were often abandoned in favor of lab manuals. Teachers were encouraged to be facilitators and question askers rather than presenters and demonstrators of information.

Discovery learning *emphasizes active, student-centered learning experiences from which students discover their own ideas and derive their own meaning.*

Jerome Bruner, a Harvard psychologist, was one of the leaders in the curriculum reform of this era. He and his colleagues provided important theoretical support for what became known as **discovery learning,** a model of teaching that emphasized the importance of helping students understand the structure or key ideas of a discipline, the need for active student involvement in the learning process, and a belief that true learning comes through personal discovery. The goal of education was not only to increase the size of a student's knowledge base but also to create possibilities for student invention and discovery.

When discovery learning was applied in the sciences and social sciences, it emphasized the **inductive reasoning** and **inquiry processes** characteristic of the scientific method. Richard Suchman (1962) developed an approach he called **inquiry training.** When using Suchman's approach, teachers present students with puzzling situations or **discrepant events** that are intended to spark curiosity and motivate inquiry. An example of one of Suchman's inquiry lessons with a discrepant event is described here.

> The teacher holds up a pulse glass. The pulse glass consists of two small globes connected by a glass tube. It is partially filled with a red liquid. When the teacher holds one hand over the right bulb, the red liquid begins to bubble and move to the other side. If the teacher holds one hand over the left bulb, the red liquid continues to bubble but moves to the other side.
>
> The teacher asks students, "Why does the red liquid move?"
>
> As students seek answers to this question, the teacher encourages them to ask for data about the pulse glass and the moving liquid, to generate hypotheses or theories that help explain the red liquid's movement, and to think of ways they can test their hypotheses or theories.

Suchman worked mainly in the field of elementary science. Somewhat similar programs, however, were developed to use in high school science classes (Schwab, 1965). When discovery approaches were used in other fields, such as the humanities or history, the processes of inquiry used in those fields guided the lessons. For example, Edwin Fenton (1967) developed what he called an *inductive approach* to use in history classrooms. Fenton emphasized the importance of getting students to ask the same kinds of questions historians might ask, to participate in historical analysis, and to test inferences and theories against real artifacts from the historical record.

Contemporary problem-based instruction also relies on another concept from Bruner, his idea of **scaffolding.** Bruner described scaffolding as a process in which a learner is helped to master a particular problem beyond his or her developmental capacity through the assistance (scaffolding) of a teacher or more accomplished person. Note how similar Bruner's scaffolding concept is to Vygotsky's zone of proximal development concept.

Scaffolding is the process whereby a more knowledgeable person (teacher) helps a less knowledgeable person to master a problem beyond his/her current level of functioning.

The role of social dialogue in the learning process was also important to Bruner. He believed that social interactions within and outside the school accounted for much of a child's acquisition of language and problem-solving behaviors. The type of dialogue required, however, was not typically found in most classrooms. Many of the small-group strategies described in this text have grown out of the need to change the discourse structures in classrooms.

The intellectual links between discovery learning and problem-based instruction are clear. In both models, teachers emphasize active student

RESEARCH BOX   META-ANALYSIS: COMBINING THE RESULTS OF MANY STUDIES

The results of a single study testing the effects of an innovative practice were described in Chapter 3. However, no single study on any topic or in any field provides definitive conclusions about the effects of a particular approach. The way to have confidence in conclusions is to combine the results of many studies. The process of combining results across several studies is called **meta-analysis.** Meta-analysis is a relatively new research methodology. Its development is generally attributed to Gene Glass (1976). Essentially meta-analysis is a method of reviewing all experimental studies that have been performed over a period of time on a particular topic and then synthesizing the results of these studies. The mathematics of meta-analysis is beyond the scope of this discussion, but it involves computing what statisticians refer to as *effect size,* defined as a score that represents the strength of a treatment in an experiment or how much effect a particular approach has had. Researchers using meta-analysis examine the effect sizes from several experiments and, through this analysis, draw conclusions about particular teaching practices. Two important meta-analyses are described here to illustrate this type of research and to provide a partial picture about what kinds of instructional effects to expect from problem-based instruction.

Bredderman's Meta-Analysis

Several process- and activity-based curricula were developed during the 1960s. Three such curricula involved science instruction for elementary students: Elementary Science Study (ESS), Science—A Process Approach (SAPA), and the Science Curriculum Improvement Project (SCIS). All three of these curricula were process oriented, meaning that the emphasis was on how to discover and construct knowledge rather than on understanding predetermined content. All three were activity based, meaning students used their own direct experience, observation, and experimentation to gain information and to solve scientific problems. In the early 1980s, Ted Bredderman studied the effects of the elementary science projects listed here by using meta-analysis techniques.

Bredderman (1983) began his study by identifying 57 studies conducted between 1967 and 1978 that compared the effects of the new process and activity-oriented curricula with the effects of more traditional (content-

involvement, an inductive rather than a deductive orientation, and student discovery or construction of their own knowledge. Instead of giving students ideas or theories about the world, which is what teachers do when using direct instruction, teachers using discovery or problem-based learning approaches pose questions to students and allow students to based) science curricula. Over 900 classrooms and 13,000 students partici-pated in these studies. Most of the studies were conducted after teachers were given special training on the new curricula. Studies analyzed by Bred-derman (1983) typically compared the trained teachers with teachers in the same school or neighboring schools where the new curricula were not being used and who had received no special training. Bredderman was able to identify nine outcome variables across the 57 studies:

results

- *science content*
- *scientific method*
- *intelligence*
- *creativity*
- *perception*
- *logical development*
- *language development*
- *mathematics*

Bredderman's meta-analysis provided some interesting results. The use of process- and activity-oriented science programs increased student achievement in all the outcome variables except logical development. The largest effects were found in three areas: understanding of scientific meth-ods, intelligence, and creativity. Finally, when the process- and activity-based programs were compared to traditional programs in regard to student acquisition of science content, Bredderman noted that the activity-based curriculum produced only modest increases, but did not produce negative effects. This led Bredderman to conclude that "the accumulating evidence on the science curriculum reform efforts . . . . consistently suggests that the more activity-process-based approaches to teaching science result in gains over traditional methods in a wide range of student outcomes" (p. 513).

Meta-Analysis of Studies in Medical Education

Since the early part of the twentieth century, medical education consisted of students spending a good portion of their early years in lecture-based instruction to learn the biological foundations of medicine. During the past two decades, however, medical education has undergone some major changes. The focus of reform has been on the methods used to teach the basic sciences and the manner in which clinical education is provided. Sev-eral medical schools in the United States and Canada have experimented with problem-based instruction as an alternative to the more conventional methods. The approach to problem-based instruction in medical education is similar to the model employed in K–12 education. It involves confronting medical students with an ill-defined problem and asking them to find work-

(continued)

arrive at their own ideas and theories. This approach has proven to be effective, as demonstrated in this chapter's research box.

Discovery learning and problem-based instruction differ, however, in important ways. Discovery learning lessons, for the most part, emanate from discipline-based questions, and student inquiry proceeds under the

RESEARCH BOX (Continued) META-ANALYSIS: COMBINING
THE RESULTS OF MANY STUDIES

able solutions. Problem solving occurs through self-study and discussion in small groups often led by a faculty facilitator. Particular problems are presented to students prior to formal instruction on foundational science concepts. Thus, students are required to seek and construct their own knowledge through self-study and small-group interaction. Many medical educators believe that problem-based instruction makes students take greater responsibility for their own learning and results in greater mastery of important foundational content.

In 1993, two medical researchers, Mark Albanese and Susan Mitchell, completed a meta-analysis of studies that compared the outcomes of problem-based instruction to outcomes of convention practices. They sought studies that had investigated such outcomes as student acquisition of basic science information, clinical abilities, thought processes (thinking ability), and student and faculty satisfaction. The researchers identified slightly over 100 studies that compared problem-based instruction in medical education with conventional methods between 1972 and 1992.

The Albanese and Mitchell meta-analysis produced some interesting findings about the effects of problem-based instruction. Medical students trained with problem-based instruction methods performed better on clinical examinations than students trained with conventional methods. They were better at problem formation and tended to engaged in more productive reasoning processes. On the other hand, students trained with problem-based instruction methods scored lower on basic science examinations and viewed themselves less prepared in the basic sciences as compared to students receiving the more conventional, lecture-based instruction. This latter finding led Albanese and Mitchell to conclude that although medical students prepared with problem-based methods may be better thinkers and more clinically adept than students prepared with conventional methods, they may have deficits in basic science knowledge. They also concluded that perhaps the best approach to use in medical education is to have a balance between lecture-based, teacher-directed approaches and student-centered, problem-based approaches. Note the similarity between the conclusion reached by Albanese and Mitchell and the one expounded in this text, that is, that different models of instruction are designed to accomplish different instructional goals. Good education proceeds when teachers have a rich repertoire of teaching models that can be used in a multifaceted instructional program.

PBI differs from discovery learning in that it focuses on real life problems as contrasted to academic problems and those that are meaningful to students.

direct guidance of the teacher within the confines of the classroom. Problem-based instruction, on the other hand, starts with meaningful, real life problems that students have a hand in selecting and proceeds with whatever in-school and out-of-school investigations are needed to solve the problem. Also, because they are real life problems, their solution requires interdisciplinary investigation.

CONDUCTING PROBLEM-BASED LESSONS

The concept of problem-based instruction is quite straightforward. It is not difficult to grasp the basic ideas associated with the model. Effective execution of the model, however, is more difficult. It requires considerable practice and necessitates making specific decisions during its planning, interactive, and postinstructional phases. Some of the teaching principles are similar to those already described for direct instruction and cooperative learning, but others are unique to problem-based instruction. In the discussion that follows, emphasis is given to the unique features of the model.

Planning Tasks

At its most fundamental level, problem-based instruction is characterized by students working in pairs or small groups to investigate ill-defined real life problems. Since this type of instruction is highly interactive, some believe that detailed planning is not necessary and perhaps not even possible. This simply is not true. Planning for problem-based instruction, as with other interactive, student-centered approaches to teaching, requires as much, if not more, planning effort. It is the teacher's planning that facilitates smooth movement through the various phases of problem-based lessons and the accomplishment of desired instructional goals.

Because of its interactive nature, PBI requires as much planning as, if not more than, the more teacher-centered models.

Decide on Objectives

Deciding on specific goals and objectives for a problem-based lesson is one of three important planning considerations. Previously, we described how problem-based instruction was designed to help achieve such goals as enhancing intellectual and investigative skills, understanding adult roles, and helping students to become autonomous learners. Some problem-based learning lessons may be aimed at achieving all these goals simultaneously. It is more likely, however, that teachers will emphasize one or two goals in particular lessons. For instance, a teacher may design a problem-based lesson on environmental issues. However, instead of having students simulate adult roles or seek solutions to environmental problems, as was the case in the "Roots and Wings" lesson, the teacher may instead ask students to conduct an on-line computer search of the topic, in order to develop this type of investigative skill. Regardless of whether a lesson is focused on a single objective or has a broad array of goals, it is important to decide on objectives ahead of time so they can be communicated clearly to students.

Design Appropriate Problem Situations

Some PBI teachers like to give students a strong hand in selecting the problem to be investigated because this increases their motivation.

Problem-based instruction is based on the premise that puzzling and ill-defined problem situations will arouse students' curiosity and thus engage them in inquiry. Designing appropriate problem situations or planning ways to facilitate the planning process is a critical planning task for teachers. Some developers of problem-based instruction believe that students should have a big hand in defining the problem to be studied, because this process will foster ownership of the problem (Krajcik, 1994). Others, however, move students toward helping refine preselected problems that emanate from the school's curricula and for which the teacher has sufficient materials and equipment.

A good problem situation should be authentic, puzzling, and ill defined, allow collaboration, be meaningful to the students, and be consistent with the teacher's curriculum goals.

A good problem situation must meet at least five important criteria. First, it should be *authentic*. This means that the problem should be anchored in students' real world experiences rather than in the principles of particular academic disciplines. How to deal with pollution in the Chesapeake Bay is an example of a real life problem. Learning about the effects of sunlight on nutrients and algae in warm water is an example of an academic (scientific) problem in biology. Second, the problem should be somewhat ill defined and pose a sense of mystery or puzzlement. Ill-defined problems resist simple answers and require alternative solutions, each of which has strengths and weaknesses. This, of course, provides the fodder for dialogue and debate. Third, the problem should be meaningful to students and appropriate for their level of intellectual development. Fourth, problems should be sufficiently broad to allow teachers to accomplish their instructional goals yet sufficiently confined to make lessons feasible within available time, space, and resource limitations. Finally, a good problem should benefit from group effort, not be hindered by it.

Most puzzling situations either explore the cause-and-effect relationships within a particular topic or pose "why" or "what if" questions. The number of puzzling situations in any field is endless. As you approach choosing a particular situation for a lesson consider the following points.

- ◆ Think about a situation involving a particular problem or topic that has been puzzling to you. The situation must pose a question or problem that requires explanation through cause-and-effect analyses and/or provides opportunities for students to hypothesize and speculate.
- ◆ Decide if a particular situation is naturally interesting to the particular group of students with whom you are working, and decide if it is appropriate for their stage of intellectual development.
- ◆ Consider whether or not you can present the problem situation in a fashion that is understandable to your particular group of students and that highlights the "puzzling" aspect of the problem.
- ◆ Consider whether working on the problem is feasible. Can students conduct fruitful investigations given the time frame and resources available to them?

Obviously there are many problem situations that can be defined and posed to students. Indeed, the list is almost limitless. Following are several examples that have been reported by teachers. Some of these are tightly focused and can be completed in rather short periods of time. Others are more complex and require a whole course of study to complete.

Roots and Wings. Sometimes simulated problem situations are used rather than real life problems. In "Roots and Wings," developers created an integrated problem-based approach to learning elementary science, social studies, reading, writing, and mathematics. Here are two examples of the types of problems posed to students in this program.

◆ *World Lab.* For 90 minutes each day, students assume the roles of various historical figures or contemporary occupational groups. They may be asked to solve the pollution problem in the Chesapeake Bay, to serve as advisors to the pharaohs of ancient Egypt, or to frame solutions to unfair taxes such as the American colonies did prior to the Declaration of Independence and the Revolutionary War.

◆ *Mathematics.* Mathematics for elementary students is moved from an abstract to a problem-solving focus. Students are asked to solve real life math problems such as how to measure the depth of a pond or to estimate the time it would take for a ship to cross the Chesapeake Bay and are given many hands-on mathematics activities. The curriculum is also characterized by extensive use of calculators, computers, and math manipulatives.

Learning Expeditions. Several school systems across the United States have been experimenting with a problem-based learning project called "Learning Expeditions" (see Rugen & Hart, 1994). This project is one of several "break-the-mold" projects. Designed initially by Outward Bound educators, it is now being used in five cities: Boston; Denver; New York; Dubuque, Iowa; and Portland, Maine. Students involved in expeditionary learning are asked to inquire into stimulating problems and to find solutions through purposeful investigations and fieldwork. Some of the learning expeditions projects can be completed in three or four weeks; others last several months. Students are presented with ill-defined and open-ended themes or topics that cut across the traditional school subjects. Examples include such topics as urban renewal, pond life, or endangered species. From these more general topics, specific questions are posed. Examples of questions reported by teachers include the following:

◆ How can we tell when a community is thriving?
◆ What are the complex factors that influence pond life?
◆ How endangered are various species? How are endangered species affected by the complex interaction between humans and the environment?

As with other problem-based curricula, expeditionary learning strives to spark student interest by addressing authentic problem situations, helping students engage in field-oriented investigations, and helping them arrive at their own solutions.

Rogue Eco-System Project. Teachers interested in environmental problems have been among the leaders in problem-based instruction. This is illustrated by the problem-based learning approach used by Hans Smith, a biology teacher at Crater High School in Central Point, Oregon.

Smith has designed an interdisciplinary course in which students meet for 2 hours each day and receive credit for biology, government, and health. The course is centered around two environmental themes—*watersheds* and the *life cycle of the Pacific salmon* (Smith, 1995). As part of their unit on watersheds, students work on a particular project that requires them to develop a plan for a campground using their scientific knowledge about watersheds. Their plan must offer a complete environmental-impact study of campground construction, and include interaction with the governmental agencies that approve campgrounds in the state of Oregon. Smith reported that these initial projects often prompt further inquiry and even more authentic studies such as:

♦ Studying a local river by taking stream surveys, testing water, mapping habitats, and determining pool and riffle ratios
♦ Designing and building a student-operated fish hatchery in which 2,000 coho salmon are raised and released each year

Smith's use of problem-based instruction asks students to take on very large and complex problems and involves them over a rather long period of time. Smith, himself, is an example of a creative teacher willing to give students opportunities to perform numerous out-of-school adult roles such as testing water, constructing buildings, raising fish, writing reports, interacting with government agencies, and giving presentations.

Organize Resources and Plan Logistics

Problem-based instruction encourages students to work with a variety of materials and tools, some of which are in the classroom, others of which are in the school library or computer lab, and still others of which are located outside the school. Getting resources organized and planning the logistics of student investigations are major planning tasks for PBI teachers.

In almost every instance, PBI teachers will be responsible for an adequate supply of materials and other resources available for use by investigative teams. In some instances, these materials may be included in particular curriculum projects such as with the "Roots and Wings" projects. Many science classrooms contain needed supplies and equipment to support student experiments and projects. Access in many schools to on-line data bases and CD-ROM also facilitates problem-based instruction. When needed materials exist within the school, the primary planning task for teachers is to gather them and make them available to students. This normally requires working with school librarians and technology specialists. As described in Chapter 3, to obtain maximum assistance from librarians and technology specialists necessitates early notification by teachers about their plans. A series of meetings between the teacher and the specialists in which agreements are made about logistics, time lines, and rules for student conduct must be included in planning.

Sometimes students will need to do their investigative work outside the school. Students involved in the ecosystem project were encouraged to gather water samples, to present plans to local government units, and to release salmon. Some aspects of "Roots and Wings" involve interviewing local business and government leaders. Expecting students to work outside the confines of the school presents special problems for teachers and requires special planning. Teachers must plan in detail how students will be transported to desired locations and how students will be expected to behave while in nonschool settings. It also necessitates teaching students appropriate behavior for observing, interviewing, and perhaps taking photographs of people in the local community.

Projects that require out-of-school investigations or collaborations present special planning challenges for PBI teachers.

Interactive Tasks

The five phases of problem-based instruction were described in Table 4.1. Desired teacher and student behaviors associated with each of these phases are described here.

Orient Students to the Problem

At the start of a problem-based lesson, just as with all types of lessons, teachers should communicate clearly the purposes of the lesson, establish a positive attitude toward the lesson, and describe what students are expected to do. With younger students or with students who have not been involved in problem-based instruction before, the teacher must also explain the model's processes and procedures in some detail. Points that need elaborating include the following.

Students need to understand that the purpose of PBI lessons is not to acquire large amounts of new information but to investigate important problems and to become independent learners.

◆ The primary goals of the lesson are not to learn large amounts of new information but rather how to investigate important problems and how to become independent learners. For younger students, this concept might be explained as lessons where they will be asked to figure things out on their own.

◆ The problem or question under investigation has no absolute "right" answer, as most complex problems have multiple and sometimes contradictory solutions.

◆ During the investigative phase of the lesson, students will be encouraged to ask questions and to seek information. The teacher will provide assistance, but students should strive to work independently or with peers.

◆ During the analysis and explanation phase of the lesson, students should be encouraged to express their ideas openly and freely. No idea will be ridiculed by the teacher or by classmates. All students will be given an opportunity to contribute to the investigations and to express their ideas.

A good way to present the problem for a PBI lesson is to use a discrepant event that creates a sense of mystery and a desire to solve the problem.

The teacher needs to present the problem situation with care or have clear procedures for involving students in problem identification. The guidelines provided in Chapter 2 on how to conduct a classroom demonstration can be helpful here. The problem situation should be conveyed to students as interestingly and accurately as possible. Usually being able to see, feel, and touch something generates interest and motivates inquiry. Often the use of discrepant events (a situation where the outcome is unexpected and surprising) can prick students' interest. For example, demonstrations in which water runs uphill or ice melts in very cold temperatures can create a sense of mystery and a desire to solve the problem. Short videotapes of interesting events or situations illustrating real life problems such as pollution or urban blight are similarly motivational. The important point here is that the orientation to the problem situation sets the stage for the remaining investigation, so its presentation must captivate student interest and produce curiosity and excitement.

Organize Students for Study

Problem-based instruction requires developing collaboration skills among students and helping them to investigate problems together. It also requires helping them plan their investigative and reporting tasks.

Investigative teams can be formed voluntarily around friendship patterns or according to some social or cognitive arrangement.

Study Teams. Many of the suggestions for organizing students into cooperative learning groups described in Chapter 3 pertain to organizing students into problem-based teams. Obviously, how student teams are formed will vary according to the goals teachers have for particular projects. Sometimes a teacher may decide that it is important for investigative teams to represent various ability levels and racial, ethnic, or gender diversity. If diversity is important, teachers will need to make team assignments. At other times the teacher may decide to organize students according to mutual interests or to allow groups to form around existing friendship patterns. Investigative teams can thus form voluntarily. During this phase of the lesson teachers should provide students with a strong rationale for why the teams have been organized as they have.

Cooperative Planning. After students have been oriented to the problem situation and have formed study teams, teachers and students must spend considerable time defining specific subtopics, investigative tasks, and time lines. For some projects, a primary planning task will be dividing the more general problem situation into appropriate subtopics and then helping students decide which of the subtopics they would like to investigate. For example, a problem-based lesson on the overall topic of weather might be divided into subtopics involving acid rain, hurricanes, clouds, and so forth. The challenge for teachers at this stage of the lesson is seeing that all students are actively involved in some investigation and that the sum of all the subtopic investigations will produce workable solutions to the general problem situation.

For other projects, particularly those that are large and complex, an important task during this phase of instruction is to help students link the investigative tasks and activities to time lines. The Gannt Chart shown in Figure 4.1 provides an example of how one teacher helped her class plan for a problem-based learning project in history. Gannt Charts allow stu-

---

This problem-based lesson has been designed to have students work in four teams for the purpose of investigating local history. The four investigative tasks are interviewing elderly people about the community; collecting appropriate information from old newspapers in the state's historical society; studying gravestones in the local cemetery; and collecting and reading early histories written about the area.

TASK	TIME			
	Mar 10–15	Mar 18–23	Mar 26–31	April 3–7
Orient students to problem situation	xxx			
Organize study teams	xxxxxxx			
Discuss with principal when students will be gone from school	xx			
Gain permission from parents	xxxxx			
Gain permission for visits from historical society	xxx			
Have study teams plan their work		xxxxxxxx		
Go over interviewing protocol		xx		
Go over logistics for each type of visit		xx		
Have teams do preliminary visit to make sure logistics are in place		xx		
Have teams perform their investigative tasks			xxxxxxxxx	
Have teams prepare required artifacts/exhibits				xxxx
Share artifacts/exhibits with parents and others				xxxx

FIGURE 4.1

Gantt Chart: Eighth-Grade Local History Investigation

dents to plan particular tasks in relation to when each starts and ends. They are constructed by placing time across the top of the chart and then listing the tasks down the side. Xs denote the specific time assigned to accomplish particular tasks.

Assist Independent and Group Investigation

Investigative techniques common to most PBI projects include data gathering and experimentation, hypothesizing and explaining, and providing solutions.

Investigation, whether done independently, in pairs, or in small study teams is the core of problem-based instruction. Although every problem situation requires slightly different investigative techniques, most involve the processes of data gathering and experimentation, hypothesizing and explaining, and providing solutions.

Data Gathering and Experimentation.   This aspect of the investigation is critical. It is in this step that the teacher encourages students to gather data and conduct mental or actual experiments until they fully understand the dimensions of the problem situation. The aim is for students to gather sufficient information to create and construct their own ideas. This phase of the lesson should be more than simply reading about the problem in books. Teachers should assist students in collecting information from a variety of sources, and they should pose questions to get students to think about the problem and about the kinds of information needed to arrive at defensible solutions. Students will need to be taught how to be active investigators and how to use methods appropriate for the problem they are studying: interviewing, observing, measuring, following leads, or taking notes. They will also need to be taught appropriate investigative etiquette.

Hypothesizing, Explaining, and Providing Solutions.   After students have collected sufficient data and conducted experiments on the phenomena they are investigating, they will want to start offering explanations in the form of hypotheses, explanations, and solutions. During this phase of the lesson, the teacher encourages all ideas and accepts them fully. As with the data-gathering and experimentation phases, teachers continue to pose questions that make students think about the adequacy of their hypotheses and solutions and about the quality of the information they have collected. Teachers should continue to support and model free interchange of ideas and to encourage deeper probing of the problem if that is required. Questions at this stage might include "What would you need to know in order for you to feel certain that your solution is the best?" or "What could you do to test the feasibility of your solution?" or "What other solutions can you propose?"

Teacher support for the free exchange of ideas and the full acceptance of those ideas is imperative in the investigative phase.

Throughout the investigative phase, teachers should provide needed assistance without being intrusive. For some projects and with some students, teachers will need to be close at hand helping students locate materials and reminding them of tasks they are to complete. For other projects and other students, teachers may want to stay out of the way and allow students to follow their own directions and initiatives.

Develop and Present Artifacts and Exhibits

The investigative phase is followed by the creation of artifacts and exhibits. **Artifacts** are more than written reports. They include such things as videotapes that show the problem situation and proposed solutions, models that comprise a physical representation of the problem situation or its solution, and computer programs and multimedia presentations. Obviously, the sophistication of particular artifacts is tied to the students' ages and abilities. A 10-year-old's poster display of acid rain will differ significantly from a high school student's design for an instrument to measure acid rain. A second-grader's diorama of cloud formations will differ from a middle school student's computerized weather program.

PBI projects culminate in the creation and display of artifacts such as reports, posters, physical models, and videotapes.

After artifacts have been developed, teachers often organize exhibits to display students' work publicly. These exhibits should take their audiences—students, teachers, parents, and others—into account. **Exhibits** can be traditional science fairs, where each student displays his or her work for the observation and judgment of others, or verbal and/or visual presentations, where ideas are exchanged and feedback is provided. The exhibition process is heightened in status if parents, students, and community members participate. It is also heightened if the exhibit demonstrates student mastery of particular topics or processes. Newsletters, such as those described in Chapter 3, offer another means to exhibit the results of students' work and to bring closure to problem-based projects.

Analyze and Evaluate the Problem-Solving Process

The final phase of problem-based instruction involves activities aimed at helping students analyze and evaluate their own thinking processes as well as the investigative and intellectual skills they used. During this phase, teachers ask students to reconstruct their thinking and activity during the various phases of the lesson. When did they first start getting a clear understanding of the problem situation? When did they start feeling confidence in particular solutions? Why did they accept some explanations more readily than others? Why did they reject some explanations? Why did they adopt their final solutions? Did they change their thinking about the situation as the investigation progressed? What caused this change? What would they do differently next time?

LEARNING ENVIRONMENT AND MANAGEMENT TASKS

Many of the general management guidelines described in Chapter 1 apply to the management of problem-based learning. For instance, it is always important for teachers to have a clear set of rules and routines, to keep lessons moving smoothly without disruption, and to deal with misbehavior quickly and firmly. Similarly, the guidelines for how to manage group work provided in Chapter 3 on cooperative learning also apply to problem-based learning instruction. Descriptions found in Chapter 5 on how to make classroom dialogue more open and inquiry oriented should also be considered. There are, however, unique management concerns for teachers using problem-based instruction, and these are described here.

Deal with Multitask Situations

To make a multitask classroom work, students need to be taught to work both independently and together.

In classrooms where teachers are using problem-based instruction, multiple learning tasks will be occurring simultaneously. Some student groups may be working on various subtopics in the classroom, while others may be in the library, and still others out in the community. Younger students may be using interest centers where students work in pairs and small groups on problems associated with science, math, language arts, and social studies before coming together to discuss their work with the whole class. To make a multitask classroom work, students must be taught to work both independently and together. Effective teachers develop cueing systems to alert students and to assist them with the transition from one type of learning task to another. Clear rules are necessary to tell students when they are expected to talk with one another and when they are expected to listen. Charts and time lines on the chalkboard should specify tasks and deadlines associated with various projects. Teachers should establish routines and instruct students how to begin and end project activities each day or period. They should also monitor the progress being made by each student or group of students during multitask situations, a skill that requires a high degree of with-it-ness to use Kounin's term.

Adjust to Differing Finishing Rates

One of the most complex management problems faced by teachers using problem-based learning is what to do with individuals or groups who finish early or lag behind. Rules and procedures and downtime activities are needed for students who finish early and have time on their hands. These include availability of high-interest activities such as special reading materials or educational games that students can complete on their own, or (for older students) procedures for moving to special laboratories to work on other projects. Effective teachers also establish the expectation that those who finish early assist others.

Late finishers present a different set of problems. In some instances, teachers may give lagging students more time. Of course, this action results in the early finishers having even more downtime. Teachers may alternately decide to get late finishers to put in extra time after school or on the weekend. However, this action is often problematic. If students are working in teams, it could be difficult for them to get together outside school. Furthermore, students who are falling behind often are those who do not work well alone and who need a teacher's assistance to complete important tasks and assignments.

Monitor and Manage Student Work

Unlike some other types of instruction in which all students complete the same assignment on the same date, problem-based instruction generates multiple assignments, multiple artifacts, and often varying completion dates. Consequently, monitoring and managing student work is crucial when using this teaching model. Three important management tasks are critical if student accountability is to be maintained and if teachers are to keep a degree of momentum in the overall instructional process: (1) work requirements for all students must be clearly delineated, (2) student work must be monitored and feedback provided on work in progress, and (3) records must be maintained.

Special management problems of PBI include adjusting to different finishing rates, monitoring student work, managing materials and equipment, and regulating movement outside the classroom.

Many teachers manage all three of these tasks through the use of *student project forms*. Maintained on each individual, the student project form (Figure 4.2) is a written record of the work the individual or small group has agreed to complete, agreed-on time lines for completion, and an ongoing summary of progress.

Manage Materials and Equipment

Almost all teaching situations require some use of materials and equipment, and managing these is often troublesome for teachers. A problem-based situation, however, places greater demands on this aspect of classroom management than other teaching models, because it requires the use of a rich array of materials and investigative tools. Effective teachers must develop procedures for organizing, storing, and distributing equipment and materials. Many teachers get students to help them with this process. Students can be expected to keep equipment and supplies organized in a science classroom and to distribute books and collect papers in other classrooms. Getting this aspect of management under firm control is very important, because without clear procedures and routines, teachers can be overwhelmed with problem-based lesson details.

Regulate Movement and Behavior outside the Classroom

When teachers encourage students to conduct investigations outside the classroom in such places as the library or the computer lab, they need to make sure that students understand schoolwide procedures for movement and use of these facilities. If hall passes are required, teachers must ensure

Student's Name: _____

Study Team's Name: _____

Project Name and Scope: _____

_____
_____
_____
_____

Particular Assignments and Deadlines
Project 1 _____
Feedback on 1 _____

Project 2 _____
Feedback on 2 _____

Project 3 _____
Feedback on 3 _____

Project 4 _____
Feedback on 4 _____

Final Artifact or Exhibit _____
_____

FIGURE 4.2
Student Project Form

that students use them appropriately. If movement in halls is regulated, students must understand the rules associated with this movement. Similarly, teachers must establish rules and routines to govern student behavior when they are conducting their investigations in the community. For example, students should be taught the etiquette of interviewing and the need to obtain permission before looking at certain records or taking certain kinds of pictures.

ASSESSMENT AND EVALUATION

Most of the general assessment and evaluation guidelines provided in earlier chapters also pertain to problem-based instruction. Assessment procedures must always be tailored to the instructional goals the model is intended to achieve, and it is always important for teachers to gather reliable and valid assessment information. As with cooperative learning in which the instructional intents are *not* the acquisition of declarative knowledge, assessment tasks for problem-based lessons cannot consist solely of paper-and-pencil tests. Most appropriate assessment and evaluation techniques for problem-based instruction assess the work products created by students as a result of their investigations.

Trends in Assessment of Student Performance

Over the past decade, there has been nationwide demand for more school and teacher accountability and for higher academic standards. There is a general belief that assessment practices keyed to *minimal* competencies and measured with standardized, objective-type tests have failed to promote and measure the higher-level thinking and problem-solving skills required in today's world. Many educators, citizens, and measurement experts believe that this situation can be corrected by introducing such new approaches to student assessment as performance assessment, authentic assessment, student portfolios, and grading for team effort. Essentially, these assessment procedures allow students to show what they can do when confronted with authentic problem situations that do not lend themselves to assessment by paper-and-pencil tests.

There has been a movement away from paper-and-pencil testing and toward performance assessments, which allow students to show what they can do when confronted with real problem situations.

Performance Assessment

Instead of having students respond to multiple-choice questions on paper-and-pencil tests, advocates of **performance assessment** would have students demonstrate that they can *perform* particular tasks, such as writing an essay, doing an experiment, interpreting the solution to a problem, playing a song, or painting a picture. This type of assessment lends itself naturally to problem-based instruction because of the artifacts and exhibits students are expected to create. Figures 4.3 (pp. 182–183) and 4.4 (p. 184) display examinations considered good examples of performance assessments.

Figure 4.3 shows the procedures developed by the state of Maryland to test students' abilities to perform particular tasks in reading and writing. Note how students are asked to perform particular tasks, how the performance assessment is spread over several days, and how efforts are made to examine the broader connections in the reading and writing process rather than to measure discrete reading or writing skills.

Figure 4.4 shows the scoring form used to grade a performance task developed by Richard Shavelson and his colleagues at the University of California, Santa Clara. The task presented to students was to "determine which of three paper towels held the most and least water" (Shavelson & Baxter, 1992, p. 21). Students could use any of the equipment in their science laboratory to complete this task. Notice that the scoring form strives to measure performance not only in terms of *outcomes*, but also in terms of *scientific processes*.

The reading and writing tasks developed in Maryland and the paper towel experiment in California are efforts to measure rather complex intellectual skills and processes. Obvious questions that might be asked are "Why aren't these approaches used more often?" and "Why did it take so long to invent them?" Most measurement experts agree (as do teachers who have tried to devise and use performance assessments) that performance tests take a great amount of time to construct and administer and

Maryland is using performance assessment as a lever to improve programs. Assessments were developed by the State Education Department and Maryland teachers with the technical assistance of CTB/McGraw-Hill. Following is an example from the reading-writing examination.

Maryland has taken the natural parallel between reading and writing to the point where they are integrated into one assessment. The entire process models how to teach reading and writing together, directly in opposition to the skills approach, which breaks down reading (and then writing) into tiny steps, tests each through workbook drills, and uses basal readers with controlled vocabulary. To show how it works, I will describe the sample grade 8 reading-writing/language use assessment.

Each student is given a reading book, which contains a map of North America on the first page, with Canada, Alaska, and Yukon Territory marked on it; a short story by Jack London entitled "To Build a Fire"; and an excerpt from *Hypothermia: Causes, Effects, Prevention*, by Robert S. Pozos and

David O'Born, published by New Century Publishers in 1982. Students also have response books into which they write answers.

The assessment begins with a prereading activity, which focuses students on the topic—the deadly cold of the Yukon Territory and its dangers—by asking them to think about their own experiences of being cold. They are asked to spend 10 minutes writing a journal entry describing their experience on the appropriate page of their books. Then they read London's "To Build a Fire" and respond to a series of questions probing their comprehension of the story. The first question can be answered with a drawing of the scene of the action if the student prefers to draw rather than write. A question later in the sequence asks the students to compare their own experience, described in the journal entry, with that of the man in the story who dies in the extreme cold. The final three questions probe the students' reading abilities by asking them to assess the difficulty of the story and explain why they rated it "very easy," "somewhat easy," "about average," "somewhat hard," or "very hard"

that in most instances they are much more expensive than short-answer tests. Think, for instance, how long and expensive it would be to create and to administer performance assessments to cover all the topics currently found on the SAT. Furthermore, the creation of good performance assessments requires considerable technical knowledge that is beyond that currently held by many teachers.

and describe their reading strategies, that is, what they do to make sense of the story when they come to a word or a reference they do not understand.

On the second day of the assessment, the students begin by writing a 5-minute letter to the man in London's story giving him some advice that might have saved his life. Before they read the excerpt *Hypothermia: Causes, Effects, Prevention*, there is class discussion about the topic, with the teacher writing on the board a cluster of the students' ideas as they respond to the words *(succumb, insidious)* that they will find in the excerpt. After they read the piece, they respond to a series of questions, again including the option to draw a picture or a diagram for at least one of them.

On the third day of the assessment, the students are expected to integrate the information from the two pieces into a written response to one of three situations: informing a group of friends of what they will need to do to stay safe on a winter weekend trip; writing a poem, story, or short play expressing their feelings about extreme states, not only cold but also heat,

hunger, or fatigue; or writing a speech to persuade people to avoid travel in the Yukon. As in the case of Arizona and California, teachers will cover these three kinds of writing because they know that one of them—but they do not know which one—will be used in the assessment.

In each case, the student is asked to go through a process of first brainstorming ideas and either listing them or making a web of words with lines connecting them to major ideas. (These graphic organizers are now a recognized part of teaching the writing process.) Students write a rough draft, pause to consider whether it meets the needs of the situation, and then revise the piece. Finally, they use a proofreading guidesheet supplied in the response book to prepare a final copy. . . . The material is graded according to two rubrics: one for the answers to the questions designed to measure reading comprehension and the other for the persuasive or informative writing. The prereading and prewriting activities and the class discussion are recorded but not scored.

Authentic Assessment

Whereas performance assessments ask students to demonstrate certain behaviors or skills in a testing situation, **authentic assessments** take these demonstrations a step further and ask students to demonstrate what they can do in authentic (real life) settings. Although performance and authentic assessments have many characteristics in common, they also differ as illustrated in Figure 4.5.

Performance assessments *have students demonstrate skills in a testing situation;* authentic assessments *ask them to perform in real life settings.*

Student _____   Observer _____   Score _____   Script _____
1. **Method**   A. Container   B. Drops   C. Tray (surface)
                   Pour water in/put towel in   Towel on tray/
                   Put towel in/pour water in   Pour water on
                   1 pitcher or 3 beakers/   Pour water on
                   glasses   tray/wipe up
2. **Saturation**   A. Yes   B. No   C. Controlled
3. **Determine Result**
   A. Weigh towel
   B. Squeeze towel/measure water (weight or volume)
   C. Measure water in/out
   D. Time to soak up water
   E. No measurement
   F. Count number of drops until saturated
   G. See how far drops spread out
   H. Other _____
4. **Care in Measuring**   Yes   No
5. **Correct Result**   Yes   No

Grade	Method	Saturate	Determine Result	Care in Measuring	Correct Answer
A	Yes	Yes	Yes	Yes	Yes
B	Yes	Yes	Yes	No	Yes/No
C	Yes	Yes/ Controlled	Error		Yes/No
D	Yes	No	Missing		Yes/No
F	---------------------------------- No Attempt ----------------------------------

FIGURE 4.4
Paper Towel Investigation— Hands-On Scoring Form
SOURCE: From R. J. Shavelson and G. P. Baxter (1992), What we've learned about assessing hands-on science. *Educational Leadership*, 49, 8, p. 21. Reprinted with permission.

Student Portfolios

Teachers use portfolios (collections of student work) to assess students; students use them to reflect on their own learning.

Procedures closely related to performance and authentic assessments are those connected with evaluating *student portfolios.* Since it has been used for a long time, most people in the visual arts field are aware of the portfolio process. It is common practice for painters, graphic designers, and cartoonists to select illustrative pieces of their work and organize them into a portfolio that can be used to demonstrate their abilities to potential clients or employers. Often actors, musicians, and fashion models have portfolios that include video- and audiotapes of their performances. You, yourselves, have been encouraged to develop a teaching portfolio throughout this book.

Some schools, such as those in Winnetka, Illinois, and Manhattan, Kansas, have students develop portfolios both to assess and to report student achievement. The portfolios in these schools include a sample of artifacts, journal entries, and reflections that represent what the student has done and can do in all subject areas. In both Winnetka and Manhattan, students prepare their portfolios to be shared with parents, and they are guided by such questions as:

Peformance assessment and authentic assessment are often used interchangeably, but do they mean the same thing? Although both labels might appropriately apply to some types of assessment, they are not synonymous. We must be clear about the differences if we are to support each other in developing improved assessments.

To distinguish between the two terms, let's look at a familiar form of assessment with which we have a wealth of experience. Following are two examples of a direct writing assessment in which students produce writing samples.

Case 1

Every May school district X conducts a direct writing assessment. For four days, all students at selected grade levels participate in a standardized series of activities to produce their writing samples. Using a carefully scripted manual, teachers guide students through the assessment with limited teacher directions and extended student writing time (up to 45 minutes) each day: Topic Introduction and Pre-writing (Day 1), Rough Drafting (Day 2), Revising and Editing (Day 3), and Final Copying and Proofreading (Day 4). The assessment clearly supports the Writing-as-a-Process instructional model.

Case 2

School district Y also conducts a direct writing assessment annually in May. Each student has a conference with his or her teacher to determine which paper from the student's portfolio to submit for assessment purposes. The papers in the portfolio have not been generated under standardized conditions but, rather, represent the ongoing work of the student for the year. All the papers were developed by the student, with as much or as little time allocated to each of the Writing-as-a-Process stages as he or she saw fit.

Assessing the Cases

Is Case 1 an example of performance assessment? Yes. The students are asked to perform specific behaviors that are to be assessed: to prove that they can write, the students produce a writing sample. Is Case 2 an example of a performance assessment? Yes also. The portfolio contains numerous examples of actual student performance, although much of the structure associated with testing has been removed.

Is Case 1 an example of an authentic assessment? No. While the students are asked to perform the specific behavior to be assessed, the context is contrived. In real life, individuals seldom write under the conditions imposed during a standardized direct writing assessment. Is Case 2 an example of an authentic assessment? Yes. Performance is assessed in a context more like that encountered in real life; for example, students independently determined how long to spend on the various stages of the writing process, creating as many or as few rough drafts as they saw necessary to complete their final copies.

FIGURE 4.5

Examples of Performance and Authentic Assessment
SOURCE: From C. A. Meyer (1992), What is the difference between authentic and performance assessment? *Educational Leadership*, 49, 8, pp. 39–40. Reprinted with permission.

FIGURE 4.6
The Learning Experiences Form

SOURCE: From E. A. Hebert (1992), Portfolios invite reflection—from students and staff, *Educational Leadership,* 49, 8, p. 60. Reprinted with permission.

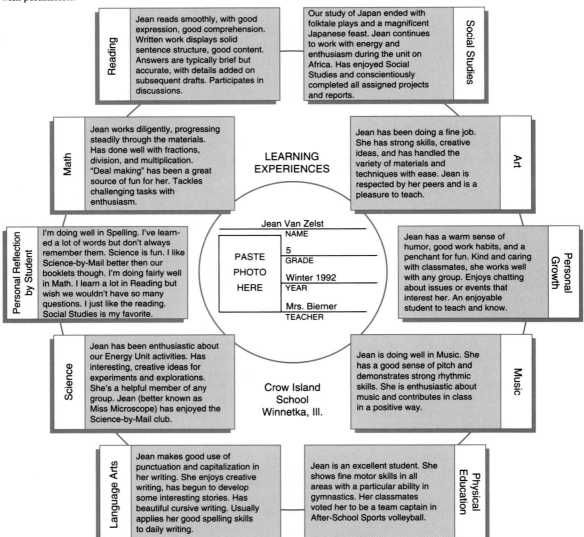

◆ How has my writing changed since last year?

◆ What do I know about numbers now that I didn't know in September?

◆ What is unique about my portfolio?

Portfolios are used by many teachers not only as an assessment tool but also as a tool to help students reflect on their own learning. In addition, the teachers in Winnetka have combined portfolios, student reflections, and their own judgments into a visual reporting device, which is illustrated in Figure 4.6.

Assessment of Learning Potential

Most tests, whether paper and pencil or performance oriented, are designed to measure knowledge and skills at specific points in time. They do not necessarily assess learning potential or readiness to learn. Vygotsky's idea about the zone of proximal development, described earlier, has prompted measurement experts and teachers to consider how a student's learning potential might be measured, particularly potential that could be enhanced with the guidance of a teacher or more advanced peer. Readiness (learning potential) tests exist for reading and other language development areas. Assessment devices that present students with problem-solving tasks which diagnose their ability to benefit from particular kinds of instruction also exist. Assessment tasks that measure learning potential in most areas, however, are still in their infancy stage with much work yet to be done.

Assessment of Group Effort

Chapter 3 on cooperative learning described assessment procedures used to assess and reward students for both individual and group work. These procedures can also be used for problem-based instruction. Assessing group effort reduces the harmful competition that often results from comparing students with their peers and makes school-based learning and assessment more like that found in real life situations.

Checklists and Rating Scales

Finding valid and reliable measurement techniques is one of the problems faced by teachers who want to use authentic assessment procedures. Some have turned to such fields as sports and the performing arts in which systems have been developed to measure complex performance tasks. Criterion-referenced checklists and rating scales are two devices that are often used in these fields. For example, individuals who judge diving or ice skating competitions use rating scales that compare individual performances to agreed-on standards. Rating scales are similarly used to evaluate musical or dance performances.

Criterion-referenced checklists and rating scales are two assessment devices often used in PBI classrooms.

Robert Rothman (1995) provided an example of a rating scale used by the teachers at Mark Twain Elementary School in Littleton, Colorado, to evaluate student work. Teachers there have developed a series of units that require students to address such real world questions as, "How are chimpanzees and people alike? How are wooden baseball bats made? How

1. Student clearly describes the question and gives reasons for its importance.	Student states question, but does not describe it or give reasons for its importance.	Student does not state question.
2. Evidence of preparation and organization strong.	Some evidence of preparation and organization present.	No evidence of preparation or organization.
3. Delivery engaging.	Delivery somewhat engaging.	Delivery flat.
4. Sentence structure is correct.	Sentence structure is somewhat correct.	Sentence structure has many errors.
5. Visual aid used to enhance presentation.	Visual aid referred to separately.	Visual aid is not mentioned.
6. Questions from audience answered clearly and with specific information.	Questions from audience somewhat answered.	Questions from audience not answered.

FIGURE 4.7
Sample Rating Scale for Oral Presentations
SOURCE: Adapted from R. Rothman (1995), *Measuring OP: Standards, Assessment, and School Reform.* San Francisco: Tossey-BASS. pp. 12–13 Reprinted with permission.

do parrots learn to talk? After completing their investigations, students write a report (artifact) about their topic using a computer; develop a visual representation (exhibit) of their topic; and deliver oral presentations to students, the principal, and a parent or community representative. The oral presentation is judged using the rating scale illustrated in Figure 4.7.

REFLECTION BOX   REFLECTING ON PROBLEM-BASED INSTRUCTION

The current interest in problem-based instruction is quite extensive. The model is based on solid theoretical principles, and a modest research base supports its use. In addition, there appears to be considerable teacher and student enthusiasm for the model. It provides an attractive alternative for teachers who wish to move beyond more teacher-centered approaches to challenge students with the active-learning aspect of the model.

However, problem-based instruction also has some obstacles to overcome if its use is to become widespread. The organizational structures currently found in most schools are not conducive to problem-based approaches. For instance, many schools lack sufficient library and technology resources to support the investigative aspect of the model. The standard 40- or 50-minute class period found in most secondary schools does not allow time for stu-

Rothman (1995) reported that similar rating scales are used to evaluate the written assignment and the visual exhibit.

Experimenting with New Approaches

Some teachers will find themselves in schools in which a great deal of experimentation is going on with alternative assessment procedures. Others will find more traditional paper-and-pencil approaches being used. Alone, without the assistance of colleagues, it is doubtful that inexperienced teachers can implement an alternative classroom assessment system. They can, however, experiment with alternative assessments within their own classroom. For instance, a science teacher could devise a few performance tests, such as the paper towel experiment described earlier, or the language arts or English teacher could make part of a student's grade depend on the performance of authentic writing tasks. Some use of portfolios can be introduced at almost every grade level and in every subject area. These steps would be movements in the right direction as the next generation of teachers work to find better and fairer ways to assess and make judgments about the students' work. Indeed, new teachers are fortunate, because they are starting their careers at a time when an extremely wide range of assessment and evaluation techniques is available.

dents to become deeply involved in out-of-school activities. Additionally, since the model does not lend itself to coverage of a great deal of information or foundational knowledge, some administrators and teachers do not encourage its use.

Drawbacks such as these cause some critics to predict that problem-based instruction will fare no better than Dewey's and Kilpatrick's *project method* or the *hands-on, process-oriented* curricula of the 1960s and 1970s.

What do you think? Is problem-based instruction here to stay? What use will you make of this model in your classroom? What might you do to work around current school structures and procedures? How would you answer critics who might accuse you of spending too much time on your projects and not covering enough materials? What about local businesspeople who complain that your "kids" are downtown interviewing people when they should be in school learning?

SUMMARY

- Unlike other models in which the emphasis is on presenting ideas and demonstrating skills, problem-based instruction consists of teachers presenting problem situations to students and getting them to investigate and find solutions on their own.

- Problem-based instruction has its intellectual roots in the Socratic method dating back to the early Greeks but has been expanded by ideas stemming from twentieth-century cognitive psychology.

- Over the past three decades, considerable attention has been devoted to a teaching approach known by various names—discovery learning, inquiry training, higher-level thinking—that focuses on helping students become independent, autonomous learners capable of figuring things out for themselves.

- The knowledge base on problem-based instruction is rich and complex. Several meta-analyses done in the last few years provide a rather clear picture of the main instructional effects of the model, which are to help students develop investigative skills, get experience with adult intellectual roles, and gain confidence in their own ability to think.

- The learning environment of problem-based instruction is characterized by openness, active student involvement, and an atmosphere of intellectual freedom.

- The general flow or syntax of a problem-based lesson consists of five major phases: orienting students to the problem, organizing students for study, assisting with independent and group investigation, developing and presenting artifacts and exhibits, and analyzing and evaluating work.

- Major preinstructional tasks associated with problem-based instruction consist of communicating goals clearly, designing interesting and appropriate problem situations, and logistical preparation.

- During the investigative phase of problem-based lessons, teachers serve as facilitators and guides of student investigations.

- Particular management tasks associated with problem-based instruction include: dealing with a multitask learning environment; adjusting to different finishing rates; finding ways to monitor student work; and managing an array of materials, supplies, and out-of-class logistics.

- Assessment and evaluation tasks appropriate for problem-based learning consist mainly of finding alternative assessment procedures to measure student work, such as by performances and exhibits. These procedures go by the names of performance assessment, authentic assessment, and portfolios.

LESSON PLAN FORMAT FOR PROJECT-BASED INSTRUCTION LESSON

PURPOSE: This is a suggested format for making a lesson plan tailored specifically to planning requirements of the problem-based teaching model. You can try it out as you plan for teaching or microteaching. Revise the format as you see the need.

DIRECTIONS: Follow the guidelines below as you plan a problem-based lesson.

Planning Tasks

Content That Is Focus of Lesson _____

_____

Lesson Objectives

    Content objective _____

    _____

    Investigation objectives _____

    _____

Problem Situation

    Statement of problem if teacher designed _____

    _____

    _____

    _____

    _____

    General domain if student designed _____

    _____

    _____

    _____

    _____

Composition of Study Teams
  Number and size of groups _____

  _____

  Criteria for membership _____

  _____

Materials and Logistics Requirements
  Materials needed _____

  Supplies and equipment needed _____

  People to contact _____

Conducting the Lesson
Procedures for orienting students to the problem _____

_____

_____

_____

Procedures for organizing students in study teams _____

_____

_____

_____

Notes/hints to remember as students work _____

_____

Important dates to remember _____   _____

                            _____   _____

Gannt Chart of dates and activities

_____

_____

_____

Procedures for presentation of artifact and exhibits _____

_____

_____

_____

_____

Pitfalls to Avoid

L E A R N I N G A I D 4.2

OBSERVING PROBLEM-BASED INSTRUCTION IN MICROTEACHING OR CLASSROOMS

DIRECTIONS: This form highlights key aspects of a problem-based lesson. It can be used to observe a peer in a microteaching laboratory or an experienced classroom teacher. It can also be used to assess a lesson you have taught and videotaped. As you observe the lesson, check the category you believe describes the level of performance of the teacher you are observing. Also answer the general questions about the lesson at the bottom of the form. Because most problem-based lessons take several days or weeks to complete, it may take several days to complete this form.

Teacher Behavior	Level of Performance			
	Excellent	Acceptable	Needs Improvement	Not Needed
Planning				
How appropriate was the lesson's content?	_____	_____	_____	_____
How clear were the content objectives?	_____	_____	_____	_____
How clear were the investigative objectives?	_____	_____	_____	_____
How well did the problem situation meet criteria?	_____	_____	_____	_____
How well were study teams organized?	_____	_____	_____	_____
How appropriate and sufficient were materials and supplies to support lesson?	_____	_____	_____	_____
How well prepared was the teacher overall?	_____	_____	_____	_____
Execution				
How well did the teacher				
Explain purposes and goals?	_____	_____	_____	_____
Orient students to problem situation?	_____	_____	_____	_____
Organize students in study teams?	_____	_____	_____	_____
Assist students in study teams?	_____	_____	_____	_____
How well did the teacher				
Explain expectations for presentations/artifacts/exhibits?	_____	_____	_____	_____
Organize presentations or exhibits?	_____	_____	_____	_____
Recognize individual effort?	_____	_____	_____	_____
Recognize team effort?	_____	_____	_____	_____

Overall Planning

What did you like best about the way the lesson was planned and organized?

_____

_____

What could be improved? _____

_____

Lesson Execution

What did you like best about the way the lesson was conducted? _____

_____

_____

What could be improved? _____

_____

If you were a student in microteaching, how did you feel about the teacher's interaction with you during the lesson? _____

_____

_____

INTERVIEWING TEACHERS ABOUT THEIR USE OF PROBLEM-BASED INSTRUCTION

PURPOSE: For many years, educators have promoted and fostered inquiry and discovery approaches to learning. Since Dewey's time, teachers have been admonished to spend less time teaching low-level basic information to students and more time developing critical thinking skills and helping students construct their own knowledge. Some observers do not believe much progress has been made over the years. This aid will give you an opportunity to investigate beliefs held by experienced teachers about inquiry-oriented, problem-based instruction.

DIRECTIONS: Use the questions below as a guide for interviewing teachers about their use or nonuse of problem-based instruction.

1. In what situations in your teaching do you use teaching methods that might be classified as inquiry-oriented teaching or problem-based instruction?

2. What do you see as the major strengths of this type of teaching?

3. What do you see as the major drawbacks of this type of teaching?

4. Some people believe that American schools spend too much time teaching basic information and not enough time promoting higher-level thinking and problem solving. What do you think?

5. If you want to spend more time on problem-based instruction in your classroom, are their barriers that prevent you from doing so? If so, what are they?

DESIGNING AND ILLUSTRATING PROBLEM SITUATIONS

PURPOSE: Thinking up unique and interesting topics and situations for problem-based lessons is among the most difficult aspects of this model. The purpose of this portfolio activity is to help you gain skill in designing problem situations and to develop products of your work that can become part of your teaching portfolio.

DIRECTIONS: Follow the steps here to design two problem situations and to display them in words and pictures in your portfolio.

Step 1: Choose two topical areas from one of your teaching fields for which you might used problem-based instruction. Choose one of these areas because it would lend itself to a few days of instruction. Choose the other because it would take several weeks to complete a problem-based lesson.

Step 2: Make problem situations out of both topics and draw a web (see Chapters 2 and 6) showing how the problem situation can be divided into subtopics. Put the subtopics in some logical order showing how they relate to one another. Use the criteria provided in this chapter to guide your problem selection.

Step 3: Make a plan showing how you would visually illustrate and introduce the two problem situations. For one of the situations, assume that you are defining the problem for students. For the other, assume that you are helping students define the problem for themselves within the broad confines of your school curriculum.

Step 4: Critique your work with a reflective essay. How appropriate were the problem situations you selected? What kinds of problems did you face in planning your introduction?

Step 5: Arrange the following in your portfolio: the two problem situations and your introduction of them, pictures illustrating the problems for students, your web showing relationships among the subtopics, and your critique.

BOOKS FOR THE PROFESSIONAL

Brooks, J. G., & Brooks, M. G. (1993). *In search of understanding: The case for constructivist classrooms.* Alexandria, Va.: Association for Supervision and Curriculum Development. The authors describe how to set up a classroom based on constructivist principles and how to use strategies similar to those labeled problem-based instruction in this book. This is a very readable book.

Costa, A. L. (1985). *Developing minds: A resource book for teaching thinking.* Alexandria, Va.: Association for Supervision and Curriculum Development. An excellent set of resources for teachers interested in making their classrooms more inquiry and thinking oriented.

Duckworth, E. (1987). *The having of wonderful ideas and other essays on teaching and learning.* New York: Teachers College Press. A delightful and insightful essay on teaching and learning and using problem-based methods.

Jervis, K., & Montag, C. (eds.). (1991). *Progressive education for the 1990s: Transforming practice.* New York: Teachers College Press. An excellent and timely collection of readings that consider progressive education and its traditional emphasis on teaching students how to inquire, to think, and to learn on their own.

Kaplan, M. (1992). *Thinking in education.* Cambridge, Mass.: Cambridge University Press. Provides an excellent and contemporary analysis of what it means to teach children how to think and what needs to be done at all levels of education if we are to convert our classrooms into "communities for inquiry."

Resnick, L. B. (1987). *Education and learning to think.* Washington, D.C.: National Academy Press. A review of cognitive research along with justification and means for helping students develop dispositions and skills for higher-level thinking.

Resnick, L. B., & Klopfer, L. E. (eds.). (1989). *Toward the thinking curriculum: Current cognitive research.* Alexandria, Va.: Association for Supervision and Curriculum Development. The yearbook of ASCD provides an excellent review of the research in the cognitive sciences that has implications for both curriculum development in the various subject areas and teaching students how to think and inquire.

CLASSROOM DISCUSSION

C hapters 2, 3, and 4 described three specific teaching models: direct instruction, cooperative learning, and problem-based instruction. In all of these approaches, some form of dialogue or discussion was required at some point during the lessons. For instance, recitation, one type of teacher-student discourse, comes toward the end of direct instruction lessons as teachers strive to check for understanding and to help students extend their thinking about particular information or behaviors. During cooperative learning lessons, discussion occurs mainly in small groups, whereas in problem-based lessons, constant dialogue is needed to accomplish the instructional goals of the model.

Discussion is really not a full-blown teaching model; rather, it is a teaching procedure that is a crucial part of almost all teaching models.

This chapter focuses on what is normally labeled **classroom discussion.** Discussion, you will find, is not a true teaching model like those presented in previous chapters. Instead, it is a particular teaching procedure or strategy that is a useful and much used part of the syntax of most other models. The preceding chapters of this text presented a particular way for thinking about instruction, that is, considering instructional goals, syntax, and the learning environment, and these same categories and labels are used to describe classroom discussion. The chapter begins with an overview of classroom discussion, presents its theoretical and empirical support, and examines the specific procedures involved in planning, conducting, and evaluating classroom discussions. The final section highlights the importance of teaching students how to become effective participants within the classroom discourse system and describes how teachers can change some of the unproductive communication patterns that characterize many classrooms today.

OVERVIEW OF CLASSROOM DISCUSSION

Because classroom discussion and discourse are so central to all aspects of teaching, it is difficult to examine them separately. Nonetheless, this section and the one that follows provide an overview of classroom discussion as if it were a distinct approach to teaching.

Classroom Discourse, Discussion, and Recitation

Effective use of classroom discussion strategies requires an understanding of several important topics pertaining to classroom discourse and discussion.

Discourse and discussion are communication in which people talk to one another, sharing ideas and opinions.

The dictionary definitions of *discourse* and *discussion* are almost identical: to engage in an orderly verbal interchange and to express thoughts on particular subjects. Teachers are more likely to use the term **discussion,** since it describes the *procedures* they use to encourage verbal interchange among students. Scholars and researchers are more likely to use the term **discourse,** since it reflects their interest in the *larger patterns* of exchange and communication found in classrooms. The term *discourse* is used to provide the overall perspective about classroom communication described in the section on theoretical support. The term *discussion* is used when specific teaching procedures are described.

Sometimes discussions are confused with *recitations*. As is described in more detail later, discussions are situations in which teachers and students or students and other students talk with one another and share ideas and opinions. Questions employed to stimulate discussion are usually at a higher cognitive level. **Recitations,** on the other hand, are those exchanges, such as in a direct instruction lesson, in which teachers ask students a series of lower-level or factual questions aimed at checking how well they understand a particular idea or concept.

Recitations are question-and-answer exchanges in which teachers check how well students recall factual information or understand a concept or idea.

Instructional Goals and Learner Outcomes

Discussions are used by teachers to achieve at least three important instructional objectives. First, discussion improves student thinking and helps them construct their own understanding of academic content. As described in previous chapters, telling students about something does not necessarily ensure their comprehension. Discussing a topic helps students strengthen and extend their existing knowledge of the topic and increase their ability to think about it.

Second, discussion promotes student involvement and engagement. Research, as well as the wisdom of experienced teachers, demonstrates that for true learning to take place students must take responsibility for their own learning and not depend solely on a teacher. Using discussion is one means of doing this. It gives students public opportunities to talk about and play with their own ideas and provides motivation to engage in discourse beyond the classroom.

Third, discussion is used by teachers to help students learn important communication skills and thinking processes. Because discussions are public, they provide a means for a teacher to find out what students are thinking and how they are processing the ideas and information being taught. Discussions thus provide social settings in which teachers can help students analyze their thinking processes and learn important communication skills such as stating ideas clearly, listening to others, responding to others in appropriate ways, and learning how to ask good questions.

Discussions are used to improve student thinking and communication skills and to promote student involvement in the lesson.

Syntax

Although several different approaches to discussion are presented here, the major phases generally remain the same. They are described briefly in Table 5.1. Although most discussions follow a similar pattern, variations do exist depending on the teacher's goals for a particular lesson and the nature of the students involved. Four variations are described in more detail later in the chapter.

TABLE 5.1 SYNTAX FOR HOLDING DISCUSSION

Phase	Teacher Behavior
Phase 1 Provide objectives and set	Teacher goes over the objectives for the discussion and gets students ready to participate.
Phase 2 Focus the discussion	Teacher provides a focus for discussion by describing ground rules, asking an initial question, presenting a puzzling situation, or describing a discussion issue.
Phase 3 Hold the discussion	Teacher monitors students' interactions, asks questions, listens to ideas, responds to ideas, enforces the ground rules, keeps records of the discussion, expresses own ideas.
Phase 4 End the discussion	Teacher helps bring the discussion to a close by summarizing or expressing the meaning the discussion has had for him or her.
Phase 5 Debrief the discussion	Teacher asks students to examine their discussion and thinking processes.

Learning Environment and Management System

Discussion-based teaching requires a great amount of student self-management.

The learning environment and management system surrounding discussion are incredibly important. The environment for conducting discussions is characterized by open processes and active student roles. It also demands careful attention to the use of physical space. The teacher may provide varying degrees of structure and focus for a particular discussion, depending on the nature of the class and the learning objectives. However, in many ways the students themselves control the specific minute-to-minute interactions. This approach to teaching requires a large degree of student self-management and control, a topic that is explored more fully later in this chapter.

THEORETICAL AND EMPIRICAL SUPPORT

Much of the theoretical support for the use of discussion stems from the fields in which scholars study language, communicative processes, and patterns of exchange. These studies extend to virtually every setting in which human beings come together. To consider the role of language, think for a moment about the many everyday situations in which success depends largely on the use of language and communication. Friendships, for instance, are initiated and maintained mainly through language—friends talk and share experiences with one another. Families maintain their unique histories by building patterns of discourse, sometimes even in the form of secret codes, that are natural to family members but are strange to outsiders, such as newly acquired in-laws. Youth culture develops special patterns of communication that provide member identity and group cohesion. The secret codes used by gangs are an example of communication used to maintain group identity. It is difficult to imagine a cocktail party, a dinner party, a church social, or any other social event existing for very long if people could not verbally express their ideas and listen to the ideas of others. The popularity of radio talk shows and computer networking adds additional evidence to how central interaction through the medium of language is to human beings.

Discourse through language is also central to what goes on in classrooms. Courtney Cazden, one of America's foremost scholars on the topic of classroom discourse, wrote that "spoken language is the medium by which much teaching takes place and in which students demonstrate to teachers much of what they have learned" (1986, p. 432). Spoken language provides the means for students to talk about what they already know and to form meaning from new knowledge as it is acquired. Spoken language affects the thought processes of students and provides them with their identity as learners and as members of the classroom group.

Discourse and Cognition

A strong relationship exists between language and logic, and both lead to the ability to analyze, to reason deductively and inductively, and to make sound inferences based on knowledge. Discourse is one way for students to practice their thinking processes and to enhance their thinking skills. Mary Budd Rowe (1986) summarized this important point nicely.

> To "grow," a complex thought system requires a great deal of shared experience and conversation. It is in talking about what we have done and observed, and in arguing about what we make of our experiences, that ideas multiply, become refined, and finally produce new questions and further explorations. (p. 43)

Discourse can be thought of as the externalization of thinking, that is, exposing one's invisible thoughts for others to see. Through public discourse, then, teachers are given a partial window for viewing the thinking skills of their students and a setting for providing correction and feedback when they observe faulty, incomplete reasoning. Thinking out loud also provides students opportunities to "hear" their own thinking and to learn how to monitor their own thinking processes. This is a very important point, and was mentioned in previous chapters. Learners don't acquire knowledge simply by recording new information on a blank slate; instead,

Discourse provides an opportunity for students to monitor their own thinking and for teachers to correct faulty reasoning.

they actively build knowledge structures over a period of time as they interpret new knowledge and integrate it into their prior knowledge.

Social Aspect of Discourse

In addition to promoting cognitive growth, classroom discussion can also be used to further a positive social environment in the classroom.

One aspect of classroom discourse, then, is its ability to promote cognitive growth. Another aspect is its ability to connect and unite the cognitive and the social aspects of learning. Indeed, the classroom discourse system is central to creating positive learning environments. It helps define participation patterns and, consequently, has a great deal of impact on classroom management. The talk of teachers and students provides much of the social glue that holds classroom life together.

The cognitive-social connection is most clear in the way social participation affects thinking and cognitive growth. Lauren Resnick and Leopold Klopfer (1989) observed, for instance, that the

> social setting provides occasions for modeling effective thinking strategies. Skilled thinkers (often the instructor, but sometimes more advanced fellow students) can demonstrate desirable ways of attacking problems, analyzing texts, or constructing argument. . . . But most important of all, the social setting may let students know that all the elements of critical thought—interpretation, questioning, trying possibilities, demanding rational justification—are socially valued. (pp. 8–9)

Discourse provides opportunities not only for engagement in thinking but, when properly handled, helps students establish a positive attitude toward thinking.

Teacher Talk

Working from a variety of perspectives and with diverse methods, researchers who study classroom discourse have found that most teachers talk a great deal and that a basic communication pattern exists in most classrooms. Also, they have found that this pattern is not necessarily the best one for promoting student thinking. This basic pattern of recitation, familiar to us all, is a teaching activity in which students in a whole-class setting are quizzed over their lessons by way of a question-answer format. Larry Cuban (1982) documented how the recitation pattern emerged early in the history of formal schooling and how it has persisted throughout the twentieth century at almost all levels of schooling and across all academic subjects. Teacher dominance of classroom communication was also thoroughly documented by Ned Flanders in the late 1960s and early 1970s with numerous studies on teacher-student interaction. Flanders (1970) concluded that in most classrooms, two-thirds of the talk is by teachers.

John Goodlad in his extensive study of schools made essentially the same observation in 1984.

The pattern is still very much with us today. Richard and Patricia Schmuck visited and collected information on rural schools in the United States. They studied 25 school districts in 21 states. They interviewed 212 teenagers about their school experience and observed lessons in over 30 high school classrooms. In 22 out of the 30 classrooms, they reported seeing mainly recitation lessons. The Schmucks (1989) reported teachers talking three-fourths of the time and commented this was more than the two-thirds teacher talk Flanders observed two decades ago. Only twice did the Schmucks observe students talking in pairs, and only four times did they observe small-group interaction and exchange.

Studies have repeatedly shown that teacher talk routinely constitutes about two-thirds to three-fourths of classroom discourse.

Teacher Questioning

Recitation teaching relies on teachers' talking and asking questions. The ways teachers ask questions and the types of questions they ask have been the focus of considerable inquiry and concern for quite some time. Mark Gall (1970), who has on several occasions reviewed the research on questioning, highlighted how frequently questions are asked in classrooms and, like Cuban, illustrated how a persistent pattern has existed over time.

Certainly teachers ask many questions during an average school day. A half-century ago, Stevens (1912) estimated that four-fifths of school time was occupied with question-and-answer recitations. Stevens found that a sample of high school teachers asked a mean number of 395 questions each day. High frequencies of questions used by teachers were also found in recent investigations: ten primary-grade teachers asked an average of 348 questions each day during a school day (Floyd, 1960); twelve elementary-school teachers asked an average of 180 questions each in a science lesson (Moyer, 1966); and fourteen fifth-grade teachers asked an average of sixty-four questions each in a 30-minute social studies lesson (Schreiber, 1967). (p. 11)

Because questions are asked so often in classrooms, an obvious concern is what effects they have on student learning. In particular, what is the effect of factual and higher-order questions on student learning and thinking? For many years, the conventional wisdom held that higher-order questions lead to greater cognitive growth than that resulting from more concrete, factual questions. However, reviews of research in the early 1970s reported that no clear evidence existed one way or the other (Rosenshine, 1971; Dunkin & Biddle, 1974). By 1976, Barak Rosenshine was prepared to challenge the conventional wisdom when he concluded that "narrow" (factual) questions actually seemed to be the most useful, particularly when teachers provided immediate feedback about the correct and incorrect answers. It is important to point out that Rosenshine reviewed studies done in early-grade classrooms that had a large proportion of children from lower social and economic backgrounds. A few years later, in a review by Redfield and Rousseau (1981), the conclusion about the use of factual questions was challenged, and the researchers reported that asking higher-level and thought-provoking questions had positive effects on student achievement and thinking.

During the past decade, researchers have continued to study the controversy over the effects of question types on student achievement and thinking. There appears to be an emerging consensus that the type of questions teachers ask should depend on the students with whom they are working and the type of educational objectives they are trying to achieve. Gall (1984), for example, interpreted this research in the following way.

◆ Emphasis on fact questions is more effective for promoting young disadvantaged children's achievement, which involves primarily mastery of basic skills
◆ Emphasis on higher cognitive questions is more effective for students of average and high ability, especially as they enter high school, where more independent thinking is required

In addition to the types of questions teachers ask, researchers have also been interested in the questions' level of difficulty and in teachers' overall pattern of questioning. *Level of difficulty* refers to students' ability to answer questions correctly regardless of cognitive level. Research on this topic has also produced mixed results. However, after a thorough review of the research, Jere Brophy and Tom Good (1986) concluded that three guidelines should be considered by teachers when deciding how difficult to make their questions:

◆ A large proportion (perhaps as high as three-fourths) of a teacher's questions should be at a level that will elicit correct answers.
◆ The other one-fourth of the questions should be at a level of difficulty that will elicit some response from students, even if the response is incomplete.
◆ No question should be so difficult that students will not be able to respond at all.

Some researchers, such as Cazden (1986) and Cazden and Mehan (1989), have not been so concerned with the types of questions teachers ask, but instead have focused on the overall pattern of questioning. They discovered important "unspoken classroom rules," which have been missed by other researchers. For example, Cazden and Mehan (1989) write that in most classrooms: "(1) It is the teacher who asks the questions; (2) The teacher knows the answers; and (3) Repeated questions imply wrong answers" (p. 50). They argue that these implicit rules must be confronted directly if teachers want discourse in their classrooms to promote higher-level thinking. This issue is discussed more fully later in the chapter.

Wait-Time

An additional important line of research in relation to classroom discussion and discourse focuses on the pace of interchange and a variable known as *wait-time*. **Wait-time** is the pause between a teacher's question and the student's response and between the response and the teacher's subsequent reaction or follow-up question. This variable was first observed in the 1960s, a time when considerable effort was under way to improve curricula in almost all academic subjects. These new curricula, particularly in the sciences and the social sciences, were developed to help students learn how to inquire and discover relationships among social and/or natural phenomena. The recommended method for virtually all curricula was inquiry or discovery-oriented discussions. However, researchers found that these types of discussions were not occurring. The research by Mary Budd Rowe on this important topic is highlighted in the research box in this chapter for two reasons: Her investigations highlighted an important problem with classroom discourse and offered a cure. They also illustrated how research in education sometimes moves from observation of teacher behavior in regular classrooms to experimentation and the testing of new practices.

Wait-time is the pause between teacher question and student response and between student response and teacher reaction.

Increasing wait-time produces more and better student responses.

CONDUCTING A DISCUSSION LESSON

As with the teaching models described in the preceding chapters, effective discussion requires that teachers perform a set of planning, interactive, management, and assessment tasks. Planning and interactive tasks are described in this section followed by a discussion of management and assessment tasks.

Planning Tasks

Two common misconceptions held by many teachers are that planning for a discussion requires less effort than planning for other kinds of teaching and that discussions cannot really be planned at all because they rely on spontaneous and unpredictable interactions among students. Both these ideas are wrong. Planning for a discussion necessitates every bit as much effort, perhaps more, as planning for other types of lessons, and even though spontaneity and flexibility are important in discussions, it is a teacher's prior planning that makes these features possible.

Proper planning for a discussion lesson increases the opportunities for spontaneity and flexibility within the lesson.

Consider Purpose

Deciding that discussion is appropriate for a given lesson is the first step in planning a discussion. Preparing the lesson and making decisions about

RESEARCH BOX   MOVING FROM OBSERVATION TO EXPERIMENTATION

In Chapter 2, the concept of finding relationships between teacher behavior and student learning by observing teachers in regular classrooms was introduced. Although product-process research is an important approach to research, it was pointed out that this research, which focuses mainly on existing practices, does not lead to effective innovations. Chapter 3, on the other hand, described how some educational research has resulted from conducting experiments and comparing the effects of innovative teaching practices, such as cooperative learning, with traditional practices. Sometimes a researcher may employ both observation in natural settings and experimentation with new practices. One good example of research that moved from observation of teachers in regular classrooms to experimentation with a new procedure is studies on a variable referred to as wait-time.

Observation of Teacher Discourse Patterns

The wait-time variable was first observed in the 1960s, a time when considerable effort was under way to improve curricula in almost all academic subjects. These new curricula were developed to help students learn how to inquire and to discover relationships among social and/or natural phenomena. The recommended teaching method for these curricula was inquiry or discovery-oriented discussions.

Initially, curriculum developers and researchers who observed regular teachers working with these new curricula were disappointed because the amount and quality of discourse fell far below their expectations. Some believed that this was true because the teachers lacked sufficient scientific knowledge. Mary Budd Rowe (1974a, 1974b) and her colleagues, however, found evidence that challenged this idea. They observed 36 elementary teachers who had extensive training in the science content of the new programs, and these teachers did not have substantially different discourse patterns from those who had little or no training. They also compared the discourse patterns of 54 prominent scientists, who had helped develop a particular science curriculum, to the patterns of regular classroom teachers. They found that the "patterns of questions and responses were remarkably alike" (Rowe, 1974b, p. 82).

This led Rowe and her colleagues to consider other reasons for the low quality of discourse. The pattern that emerged from these early observations

what type of discussion to hold and specific strategies to employ are next. As described earlier, although discussions can stand alone as a teaching strategy, they are more frequently used in connection with other teaching models. Although the particular uses of discussion are practically infinite, teachers generally want their discussion to accomplish one of the three objectives described in the previous section: to check for student understanding of reading assignments or presentations through recitations, to teach thinking skills, or to share experiences.

showed that discourse in classrooms was characterized not only by recitation but also by speed. They found that when teachers asked questions, they would wait less than 1 second for a response before moving on to another question or another student. This phenomenon was labeled *wait-time 1*. They also found that when students provided a response, teachers similarly waited less than 1 second before reacting or asking the next question. This phenomenon was labeled *wait-time 2*.

These observations concerning the rapid pace of classroom discourse motivated Rowe and others to develop a concept of classroom life that would explain the discourse patterns and help to account for changes if different wait-time patterns could be established. Rowe's view characterized the classroom as a game in which two players, the teacher and the students, carried on discussions. The researchers found teachers' roles were to structure the discussion, to give directions, to ask questions, and to respond to student answers. The single role for students was to respond, one at a time, to the teacher. Obviously, as in any game, it is not much fun if all players cannot play and some have to sit on the bench most of the time, but this is what seemed to be happening when the pace moved at such a rapid rate.

Wait-Time Experiment

The observational studies and theories led Rowe to ask if longer pauses by the teacher might not improve classroom discourse and thereby promote higher-level thought processes. Following this line of inquiry, Rowe conducted a controlled experiment to see if teachers could be taught to slow down the pace of their discussions by using wait-times of at least 3 seconds and if a slower pace would impact on important outcome variables. Ninety-six teachers from two locations were recruited and trained to employ wait-times of at least 3 seconds. From a pool of lessons prepared by the researchers using various curricula and aimed at various grade levels, teachers were asked to teach six lessons to students who were assigned to four-member learning groups. Each lesson was recorded on audiotape.

Rowe found that teacher behavior changed as a result of being trained to use longer wait-times. A sharp drop—from 38 questions every 15 minutes to 8 questions every 15 minutes—occurred after wait-time training Also, the number of informational questions asked by teachers declined from 82 to 34, whereas the number of probing and thought-provoking questions increased significantly.

(cont.)

Consider Students

Knowing about students' prior knowledge is just as important in planning a discussion as it is in planning other kinds of lessons. Experienced teachers know that they must also take into consideration their students' discourse and communication skills. They consider, for instance, how particular students in the class will respond differently to various kinds of questions or foci; they predict how some will want to talk all the time

Teachers should plan discussions with their students in mind.

RESEARCH BOX (continued)   MOVING FROM
OBSERVATION TO EXPERIMENTATION

The researchers had hypothesized that if teachers could slow down their pace, this behavior would affect the way their students responded. Following is what they found out.

◆ The length of student responses increased from 8 words per response under the fast pace to 27 words under the slower pace. This signifies that considerably longer statements were made by students after teachers were trained to use wait-time.

◆ The number of unsolicited but appropriate responses increased from a mean of 5 to a mean of 17.

◆ Failures to respond ("I don't know" or silence) decreased. In classrooms prior to training, the no-response was sometimes as high as 30 percent. This changed dramatically to less than 5 percent once teachers started to wait at least 3 seconds for students to think.

◆ Students provided more evidence to support the inferences they were making when wait-time was lengthened.

◆ Students asked more questions, and the number of structuring and soliciting moves increased with the slower pace.

What is striking about this study and others is that (1) teachers, left to their natural inclinations, pace instruction much too fast for serious dialogue and (2) a rather simple intervention—waiting—can bring striking changes in discourse patterns. Learning to wait results in fewer and different types of questions by teachers, and, more important, different student responses. Given more time, students will less often respond with "I don't know," and they will increase the length of their responses. The quality of responses will also change. Students in classrooms in which teachers use wait-time engage in inquiry-oriented and speculative thinking.

Another important outcome of this study is the model it and others have provided for educational researchers. It demonstrated how through observation of natural teacher behavior researchers could identify behavior (fast-pace instruction) thought to prohibit good instruction and then invent a new strategy (wait-time) that could subsequently be tested to find out whether or not it affected student behavior and learning.

whereas others will be reluctant to say anything. When planning discussions, it is important to devise ways to encourage participation by as many students as possible, not just the bright ones, and to be prepared with questions and ideas that will spark the interest of a diverse student group. More is said about this aspect of discussion later.

Choose an Approach

As mentioned previously there are several different kinds of discussions, and the approach chosen should reflect a teacher's purposes and the nature of the students involved.

Recitation Exchange.   Although recitation, most often associated with direct instruction, is often overused, it nonetheless has its place. One important use is when teachers ask students to listen to or read about information on a particular topic. A reading assignment in history may vary in length from a paragraph to a whole book. A teacher's talk on ecosystems may be as long as a full-hour lecture or as short as 5 or 10 minutes. Either can cover a variety of topics. Teachers generally ask students to read or listen with a definite purpose in mind. Sometimes it is to glean important information about a topic, whereas at other times it is to become familiar with a particular author, a specific type of literature, or a point of view or particular interpretation. Brief question-and-answer sessions (recitation discussions) about assigned reading materials or a lecture can provide teachers with a means of checking for student understanding as well as provide motivation for students to complete their reading assignments or to listen carefully when the teacher is talking.

Brief question-and-answer or recitation sessions covering assigned material are useful in checking student understanding and in motivating student work.

Problem-Based Discussion.   As described earlier, discussions are sometime used to engage students in higher-order thinking and, thereby, to motivate their own intellectual investigation. Normally, such discussion is part of some type of problem-based teaching. Although a number of specific approaches have been developed, they all have a common syntax in which the teacher opens the lesson by presenting students with what Suchman (1962) labeled a *discrepant event* or what Palincsar and Brown (1989) called *mystery spots*. Both refer to puzzling situations that are not immediately explainable, such as water appearing to run uphill, metal changing shape when heated, and social data that confront conventional wisdom. Because these situations are puzzling to students and create cognitive dissonance, they provide a natural motivation to think. When using this approach, teachers encourage students to ask questions, to generate empirical data, and to formulate theories and hypotheses to explain the puzzling situation. In this type of discussion, teachers help students become conscious of their own reasoning processes and teach them to monitor and evaluate their own learning strategies.

Problem-based lessons centered around a discrepant event encourage discussion and help students become aware of their own reasoning processes.

Sharing-Based Discussion.   Often teachers hold discussions for the purpose of helping students develop shared meaning from common experiences or to confront one another with differences of opinions. Younger children may be asked to talk about what they learned from their visit to the zoo or the apple farm. Older students may be asked to talk about what they learned from a science experiment they all performed or from a

*Sharing-based
discussions help
students form and
express independent
thoughts and opinions.*

novel they read. Important current events such as a breakthrough in an arms treaty, new abortion legislation, or a natural disaster are often discussed in the classroom so that different points of view may be explored. Unlike recitation discussions, during which teachers ask students *to recall* specific information, or problem-based discussions, in which teachers get students *to reason,* shared discussions help students *to form and to express thought and opinions independently.* Through dialogue about shared experiences and discussion about what these experiences mean, ideas are refined or expanded and questions are raised for future study.

Make a Plan

A lesson plan for a discussion consists of a set of objectives and a content outline. The plan should include not only the targeted content but also a well-conceived focus statement, the description of a puzzling event, and/or a list of questions. If the discussion is to follow a lecture, it is likely that the teacher already has the content firmly in mind and has explored the important conceptual relationships. When the discussion follows assigned readings, experienced teachers know that they must have read the materials themselves and, in most instances, must have taken extensive notes not only about specific facts but, more important, about the main ideas, points of view, and key relationships highlighted in the reading.

Sometimes teachers find using the **conceptual web** technique a useful planning device. A web provides a visual image of the characteristics and relationships around a central idea. To make a conceptual web you identify the key ideas associated with a particular topic and arrange them in

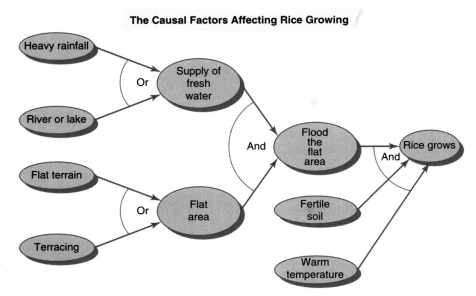

FIGURE 5.1
Conceptual Web
SOURCE: From A. Collins (1977), Processes in acquiring knowledge. In R. C. Anderson, R. J. Spiro, and W. E. Montague (eds.). *Schooling and the acquisition of knowledge.* Hillsdale, N.J.: Lawrence Erlbaum Assoc. Publishers, Fig. 1, p. 341. Reprinted with permission.

The Causal Factors Affecting Rice Growing

some logical pattern. Sometimes conceptual webs are hierarchical diagrams; sometimes they focus on causal relationships. Figure 5.1 provides an example of a conceptual web that focuses on a set of causal relationships.

Teachers will find that careful attention to preparation will assist immensely as they strive to keep details straight for students and as they help facilitate student understanding and higher-order thinking. For some types of discussions, asking students questions becomes a key feature. In preparing their questioning strategy, teachers need to consider both the cognitive level of questions and their level of difficulty.

During the past three decades, many systems have been developed for classifying the cognitive level of teacher questions. Most of the classification systems have similarities; all consider questions in terms of the cognitive processing they require students to perform. Bloom's **taxonomy of educational objectives** is one means used by teachers to design ques-

TABLE 5.2 SIX QUESTION TYPES ACCORDING TO BLOOM'S TAXONOMY

Level		Examples of Questions	Cognitive Processes
Level 1	Knowledge	Which region of the United States is Ohio in? What does H_2O stand for?	Recalling factual information
Level 2	Comprehension	What is the difference between longitude and latitude? What is the book *The Old Man and the Sea* about?	Using information
Level 3	Application	If John has 12 feet of lumber, how many 2-foot boards can he make?	Applying principles
Level 4	Analysis	Why do you think the red liquid moves? Why do some trees lose their leaves in winter?	Explaining relationships or making inferences
Level 5	Synthesis	If the North had not won the Civil War, what would life be like in the United States today? What if John Brown had succeeded at Harpers Ferry? What might happen if the Earth experienced a continuing warming trend?	Making predictions
Level 6	Evaluation	Which novel do you think is the best piece of literature? What do you think about the recycling program?	Making judgments or stating opinions

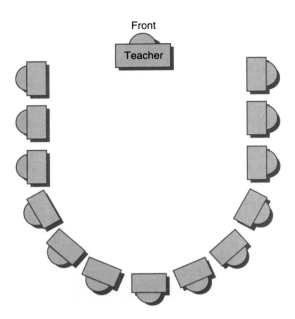

FIGURE 5.2
U-Shaped Seating Arrangement

A good discussion includes both lower- and higher-level questions.

tions for classroom discussion. Table 5.2 shows six categories of classroom questions and examples of each.

As described earlier, the research about the effects of using various types of questions is still unclear. However, beginning teachers should keep in mind one important truth, that is, that different questions require different types of thinking and that a good lesson should include both lower- and higher-level questions. One way to achieve this is to start by asking simple recall questions to see if students have grasped the basic ideas under consideration, follow with comprehension and analysis questions ("why" questions), and then conclude with more thought-provoking synthesis and evaluation questions.

In preparing the lesson plan and questioning strategies, remember to think through the issues associated with question difficulty, discussed earlier. Experience helps teachers to know their students and to devise questions of appropriate difficulty. Decisions about question type and difficulty can be better made during the quiet of advanced planning than during the discussion itself.

Use Physical Space Appropriately

Another planning task involves making arrangements for appropriate use of physical space. Chapters 2 and 3 discussed how different seating patterns affect communication patterns within the classroom. The best seating arrangements for discussion are the U-shape and the circle formations illustrated in Figures 5.2 and 5.3. Both seating patterns allow students to see each other, an important condition for verbal interaction. Both can be

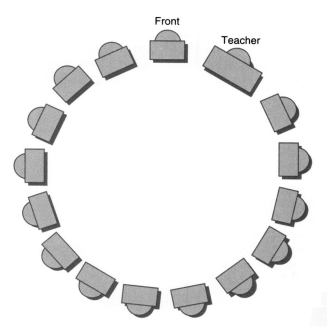

FIGURE 5.3
Circle Seating Arrangement

accommodated in most classrooms. Each, however, has some advantages and disadvantages that should be considered.

The **U-shape seating pattern,** with the teacher situated in front at the open end of the U, gives a bit more authority to the teacher, an important feature when working with groups of students who lack discussion skills or where behavior management is a problem. The U-shape also allows freedom of movement for teachers. They have ready access to the chalkboard or flip charts, which may be important during the course of a discussion, and they can move into the U to make closer contact with particular students when that is needed. The disadvantage of the U is that it establishes some emotional distance between the teacher, as discussion leader, and students. It also puts considerable physical distance between students who are sitting at the head of the U and those sitting at the end.

The **circle seating pattern,** on the other hand, minimizes both emotional and physical distance among participants and maximizes opportunities for students to talk freely with one another. The disadvantage of the circle is that it inhibits the teacher from moving freely to the chalkboard or among students. There is simply something about the circle that requires the teacher to be seated along with the students.

Many elementary and secondary schools today have furniture and other features that make movement from one seating arrangement to another possible. In some instances, however, teachers will be confronted with situations that will severely limit this possibility. For example, some science laboratories and shop classes have fixed tables that make moving furniture impossible. Some drama and English classes may be held in the school's theater with fixed seating. These conditions require special prob-

The best seating arrangements for a discussion are either a U-shape or a circle.

lem solving on the part of teachers. Some experienced science teachers have students stand in a U-shape during discussion sessions; drama teachers have their students sit on the floor of the stage. The specifics of the classroom space and the teacher's own personal preferences certainly are strong considerations when making planning decisions about use of the space prior to a discussion.

Interactive Tasks

As discussion leader, a teacher should focus the discussion, keep it on track, encourage participation, and keep a visible record of it.

For whole-class discussions to be successful demands some rather sophisticated communication and interaction skills on the part of both teachers and students. It also requires norms that support open exchange and mutual respect. As discussion leader, a teacher should clearly focus the discussion, keep it on track by refocusing student digressions, encourage participation by listening carefully to all ideas and points of view, and help keep a record of the discussion.

Establish Set and Focus the Discussion

Establishing set in a discussion lesson includes stating the focus question or issue clearly and relating it to students' prior knowledge.

Many classroom discussions are characterized by talk and more talk, much of which has little to do with either the main aims of the lesson or with encouraging student thinking. An effective discussion, just like an effective demonstration is clearly focused and to the point. At the beginning, teachers must explain the purposes of the discussion and get students set to participate. They should also pose a specific question, raise an appropriate issue, or present a puzzling situation associated with the topic. These activities have to be in a form students can understand and respond to. Stating the focus question or issue clearly is one key to getting a good discussion started. Another way to establish set and spark student interest is to relate the beginning discussion question or focus to students' prior knowledge or experiences.

Conduct the Discussion

As a whole-class discussion proceeds, many circumstances can get it off track. In some cases students will purposely try to get the teacher off the topic, as, for instance, when they want to talk about last Friday's ball game instead of the causes of World War I. Talking about Friday's game is fine if that is the objective of the lesson, but it is not appropriate if the aim is to encourage student reasoning.

A second example of wandering is when a student expresses an idea or raises a question that has little or nothing to do with the topic. This happens often, particularly with students who have trouble concentrating in school. It is also likely to happen with younger students who have not been taught good listening and discussion skills.

In both instances, effective teachers acknowledge what students are doing—"We are now talking about last Friday night's game." or, "You say your father had a good time in New York last weekend."—and then refocus the class's attention on the topic with a comment such as, "Talking about the game seems to be of great interest to all of you. I will let you do that during the last 5 minutes of the class period, but now I want us to get back to the question I asked you." or, "I know you are very interested in what your father did in New York, and I would love it if you would spend some time during lunch telling me more. Right now we want to talk about. . . ."

Effective discussion leaders acknowledge students' off-track remarks and then refocus their attention to the topic at hand.

Keeping Records. Most experienced teachers know that verbal exchange during a discussion proceeds more orderly if they keep some type of written record of the discussion as it unfolds. Writing students' main ideas or points of view on the chalkboard or on flip charts provides this written record. Or it may consist of constructing conceptual webs that illustrate the various ideas and relationships being discussed.

A dilemma faced by beginning teachers in keeping a discussion record is how much detail to include and whether or not all ideas should be written down. These decisions, obviously, depend on the nature of the students involved and the purposes of the discussion. When a teacher is working with a group that lacks confidence in discourse skills, it is probably a good idea to write down as much as possible. Seeing many ideas on the chalkboard or flip chart provides a public display of the many good thoughts that exist within the group and can encourage participation. With a more experienced and confident group, the teacher may want to list only key words, thus affording a more open exchange of ideas and opinions.

Discussions proceed in a more orderly fashion if some type of visible written record is kept as the discussion unfolds.

If the teacher has asked students specifically for their theories or ideas about a topic, it is important to list all ideas and treat these equally, regardless of their quality. On the other hand, if questions focus on direct recall of right answers, then only right answers should be recorded. How to respond to incorrect responses will be discussed in a moment.

Listening to Students' Ideas. A favorite discussion technique used by many teachers at the high school and college levels is "playing the devil's advocate." Teachers using this technique purposely take the opposite point of view from that being expressed by individual students or groups of students. Even though this approach can create lively exchange between a teacher and a few of the more verbal students, it does not work well with younger students or with many older students who lack good verbal and communication skills. Debate and argument arouse emotions, and despite their motivational potential may divert the students' attention from the topic. They also cause many less articulate or shy students to shrink from participation. If the teacher's goal is to help students understand a lesson and extend their thinking, then the teacher should listen carefully to each student's ideas. In this case, the teacher should remain nonjudgmental and inquiry oriented, rather than challenge and argue with students.

Free and open discussion is enhanced when teachers listen carefully and nonjudgmentally to students' ideas.

In most circumstances, teachers should practice waiting at least 3 seconds for a student's response.

Using Wait-Time. Earlier we discussed how many teachers do not give students sufficient time to think and to respond. There are probably several reasons for this. One is that there is a strong cultural norm in our society against silence. Silence makes many people uncomfortable and, consequently, they jump in to keep the conversation moving. Another is that waiting for student response can be perceived by teachers as threatening to the pace and momentum of a lesson. Additionally, silence or waiting can give uninvolved students opportunities to start talking or otherwise misbehaving. Although many contextual conditions influence wait-time, the general recommendations are for beginning teachers to practice waiting at least 3 seconds for a student's response, to ask the question again or in a slightly different way if there is no response, and never to move on to a second question without some closure on the first. The amount of wait-time should probably be less for direct recall questions and more for questions aimed at higher-level thinking and more complex content. After a student response, teachers should also wait a sufficient time before moving on.

Responding to Student Answers. When students respond correctly to teachers' questions, effective teachers acknowledge the correct answer with brief affirmations such as "That's right." "Okay." "Yes." They do not spend time providing overly gushy praise. Most teachers learn these behaviors quite quickly. However, responding to incorrect responses or to incomplete responses is a more complicated situation. The guidelines provided by Madeline Hunter (1982) and described in Chapter 2 are repeated here.

1. *Dignify* a student's incorrect response or performance by giving a question for which the response would have been correct: For example, "George Washington would have been the right answer if I asked you who was the first president of the United States."
2. Provide the student with an *assist,* or prompt: For example, "Remember the president in 1828 was also a hero in the War of 1812."
3. Hold the student *accountable:* For example, "You didn't know President Jackson today, but I bet you will tomorrow when I ask you again." (p. 86)

Responding to Student Ideas and Opinions. Although the art of questioning is important for effective discussions, other verbal behaviors by teachers are equally important, especially those for responding to students' ideas and opinions. These are responses aimed at getting students to extend their thinking and to be more conscious of their thinking processes. Statements and/or questions such as the following provide illustrations on how to do this.

◆ Reflect on student ideas
    "I heard you say . . ."
    "What I think you're telling me is . . ."
    "That's an interesting idea. I have never thought of it in quite that way . . ."

◆ Get students to consider alternatives

"That's an interesting idea. I wonder, though, if you have ever considered this as an alternative . . ."

"You have provided one point of view about the issue. How does it compare with the point of view expressed by . . . ?"

"Evelyn has just expressed an interesting point of view. I wonder if someone else would like to say why they agree or disagree with her idea?"

"Do you think the author would agree with your idea? Why? Why not?"

◆ Seek clarification

"I think you have a good idea. But, I'm a bit confused. Can you expand your thought a bit to help me understand it more fully?"

◆ Label thinking processes and ask for supportive evidence

"It sounds to me like you have been performing a mental *experiment* with these data."

"You have made a very strong *inference* from the information given you."

"Can you think of an *experiment* that would put that hypothesis to a good test?"

"What if I told you (give new information)? What would that do to your *hypothesis*?"

"That's an interesting position, what *values* led you to it?"

"If everyone held the *judgment* you just expressed, what would the result be?"

Student thinking can be extended by teacher reactions that review student ideas, ask for alternative ideas, and/or seek clarification or supporting evidence.

Expressing Opinions. Many beginning teachers are uncertain about whether or not they should express their own ideas and opinions during a discussion. Although teachers do not want to dominate discussions or make it appear that they are the only ones with good ideas, expressing ideas appropriately can be beneficial. It provides opportunities for teachers to model their own reasoning processes and to show students the way they tackle problems. It also communicates to students that the teacher sees himself or herself as part of a learning community interested in sharing ideas and discovering knowledge.

End the Discussion

As with other types of lessons, discussions need to be brought to proper closure. Effective teachers do this in a variety of ways. In some instances, they may choose to summarize in a few sentences what has been said and try to tie various ideas together or to relate them to the larger topic being studied. In other instances, teachers may want to close the discussion with a short presentation highlighting new or previously studied information. Some teachers ask students to summarize the discussion by posing a final question such as, "What is the main thing you got from our discussion today?" or, "What do you think was the most provocative point made during our discussion?"

One popular way of closing a discussion is for either the teacher or students to summarize the key ideas and relate them to the topic at hand.

Debrief the Discussion

From time to time discussions should be debriefed. Here the focus is not on the content of the discussion but on the way the discussion proceeded. To conduct a successful debriefing teachers must teach students the differences between the discussion itself and the debriefing and then pose questions such as: How do you think our discussion went today? Did we give everyone a chance to participate? Did we listen to one another's ideas? Were there times when we seemed to get bogged down? Why? What can we all do next time to make our discussion more stimulating or provocative?

LEARNING ENVIRONMENT AND MANAGEMENT TASKS

Many of the management tasks described in previous chapters also apply to discussion lessons. For example, pacing the lesson appropriately and dealing quickly and decisively with misbehavior are both essential teacher management behaviors when conducting a discussion. However, the most important management tasks are those aimed at improving discussion and discourse patterns in the classroom: teaching students specific discussion skills and establishing classroom norms that support productive discourse patterns. Several skills and norms are critical. In this section, skills and strategies to broaden participation, to promote interpersonal regard, and to heighten classroom thinking are described. Underlying the presentation is the premise that if discussion and discourse are to improve substantially, rather dramatic changes in the classroom discourse patterns must occur.

Slowing the Pace and Broadening Participation

To broaden participation in discussions, the pace must be slowed down and the norms for questioning and turn taking modified.

An often heard statement of inexperienced teachers is, "I tried to hold a discussion, but no one said anything." It is not uncommon for discussions, even those led by experienced teachers, to follow a pattern in which the teacher's questions are all answered by 4 or 5 of the 30 students present. Remember the action zone described in Chapter 2 and the rapid discourse pattern described by Rowe earlier in this chapter? To broaden participation and to get real discussions going requires substantial changes to this limited pattern of discourse. The pace must be slowed down and the norms about questioning and turn taking modified. Below are strategies that work and are used by experienced teachers.

Think-Pair-Share

The *think-pair-share* strategy was described in Chapter 3 as a cooperative learning structure that increased student participation. It is also an effective way to slow down the pace of a lesson and extend student thinking. This is true because it has built-in procedures for giving students more time to think and to respond and can affect the pattern of participation. For a description of the three-step think-pair-share strategy, return to Chapter 3.

Buzz Groups

The use of *buzz groups* is another effective means of increasing student participation. When using buzz groups, a teacher asks students to form into groups of three to six to discuss ideas they have about a particular topic or lesson. Each group assigns a member to list all the ideas generated by the group. After a few minutes, the teacher asks the recorders to summarize for the whole class the major ideas and opinions expressed in their group. Buzz groups, like think-pair-share, allow for more student participation with the learning materials and make it difficult for one or a few class members to dominate discussions. Using buzz groups can change the dynamics and basic patterns of classroom discourse and are easy for most teachers to use.

Beach Ball

A third technique, particularly effective with younger students, for broadening participation and promoting one person's talking a time, is *beach ball*. The teacher gives the ball to one student to start the discussion with the understanding that only the person with the ball is permitted to talk. Other students raise their hands for the ball when they want a turn.

Increasing Interpersonal Regard and Understanding

An open and honest communication process is perhaps the single most important variable for promoting positive classroom discourse and discussion. Fortunately, the way discourse occurs in classrooms can be greatly influenced by a teacher's leadership, particularly if he or she teaches skills that promote worthwhile communication as well as a positive regard for it among students.

Since communication is essentially a process of sending and receiving messages, effective communication requires the sender of a message to express clearly what he or she intends to communicate and the receiver to interpret that message accurately. In reality, however, the message a per-

Communication gaps develop whenever a sender's intended message is misinterpreted because it was poorly expressed or was foreign to the listener's prior experience.

son intends to send often is not the one the other person receives. The meaning intended in the sender's mind may not be accurately expressed or may be expressed in a manner that does not fit the receiver's prior experiences. Whenever either of these conditions occurs, a *communication gap* develops.

In the 1970s, John Wallen, then an organizational psychologist in a large electronics firm and a consultant in the Pacific Northwest, described four skills people can use to make the process of sending and receiving messages more effective and thereby reduce the gap in communication. Two of these skills assist the sender; two assist the receiver.

1. Paraphrase

To improve communication, teachers can paraphrase responses, describe behavior and feelings, and check impressions.

Paraphrasing is a skill for checking whether or not you understand the ideas being communicated to you. Any means of revealing your understanding of a message constitutes a paraphrase. Paraphrasing is more than word swapping or merely saying back what another person says. It answers the question, "What exactly does the sender's statement mean to me?" and requests the sender to verify the correctness of the receiver's interpretation. The sender's statement may convey specific information, an example, or a more general idea, as shown in the following examples.

Example 1

Sender: I'd sure like to own this book.

   You: (*Being more specific*) Does it have useful information in it?

Sender: I don't know about that, but the binding is beautiful.

Example 2

Sender: This book is too hard to use.

   You: (*Giving an example*) Do you mean, for example, that it fails to cite research?

Sender: Yes, that's one example. It also lacks an adequate index.

Example 3

Sender: Do you have a book on teaching?

   You: (*Being more general*) Do you just want information on that topic? I have several articles about it.

Sender: No, I want to find out about cooperative learning.

2. Describe Behavior

In using a behavior description, one person reports specific observable behaviors of another person without evaluating them or making inferences about the other's motives. If you tell me that I am rude (a trait) or that I do not care about your opinion (my motivations) when I am not trying to be rude and do care about your opinion, I may not understand what you are trying to communicate. However, if you point out that I have interrupted you several times in the last 10 minutes, I would receive a clearer picture of what actions of mine were affecting you. Sometimes it is helpful to preface a behavior description with "I noticed that. . . ." or, "I hear you say. . . ." to remind yourself that you are trying to describe specific actions. Consider the following examples.

"Jim, you've talked more than others on this topic."

instead of

"Jim, you always have to be the center of attention."

Or

"Bob, I really felt good when you complimented me on my presentation before the class."

instead of

"Bob, you sure go out of your way to say nice things to people."

3. Describe Feelings

Although people often take pains to make sure that others understand their ideas, only rarely do they describe how they are feeling. Instead, they act on their feelings, sending messages that others draw inferences from. If you think that others are failing to take your feelings into account, it is helpful to put those feelings into words. Instead of blushing and saying nothing, try "I feel embarrassed." or, "I feel pleased." Instead of, "Shut up!" try, "I hurt too much to hear any more." or "I'm angry with you."

4. Check Impressions

Checking impressions is a skill that complements describing your own feelings and involves checking your sense of what is going on inside the other person. You transform the other's expression of feelings (the blush, the silence, the tone of voice) into a tentative description of feelings and check it out for accuracy. An impression check describes what you think the other's feelings may be, and does not express disapproval or approval. It merely conveys, "This is how I understand your feelings. Am I accurate?" Examples include the following.

"I get the impression you are angry with me. Are you?"

"Am I right that you feel disappointed that nobody commented on your suggestions?"

Often an impression check can be coupled easily with a behavior description, as in these examples.

"Ellen, you've said nothing so far and seem upset with the class. Are you?

"Jim, you've made that proposal a couple of times. Are you feeling put down because we haven't accepted it?"

Direct instruction is the best model to use to teach specific communication skills.

Teachers can learn and model these skills in their classrooms. They can also teach them directly to students just as they teach many other skills. The training model described in Chapter 2 provides an appropriate strategy for teaching communication skills initially. A typical lesson is outlined in Figure 5.4.

Tools for Highlighting Discourse and Thinking Skills

Frank Lyman and James McTighe have written extensively about the use of teaching tools, particularly visual ones that help teachers and students learn discourse and thinking skills (Lyman, 1986; McTighe & Lyman, 1988).

Visual Cues for Think-Pair-Share

The think-pair-share discussion strategy described previously (see Chapter 3) is not easy for students to use at first. Old habits, such as responding to

---

Step 1 Introduce and explain the four communication skills, and define a topic for students to talk about.

Step 2 Have students get into groups of three for practice purposes. Each person in each trio is assigned a role—either sender, receiver, or observer. The sender begins a conversation and tries to describe his or her feelings or the receiver's behavior while discussing the topic. The receiver listens and either paraphrases or checks his or her impressions of the sender's feelings. The observer notes instances of communication skill use and instances where there are gaps in communication.

Step 3 Roles are exchanged so different people become senders, receivers, and observers.

Step 4 Finally, the teacher holds a class discussion about which skills are easy and which are difficult to learn and about how these skills can be applied in areas of classroom life as well as outside the classroom. During the discussion, the teacher should model use of the skills and encourage students to use them.

FIGURE 5.4
Typical Lesson Plan for Teaching Communication Skills

teacher questions before thinking, or blurting out answers without wait-ing, are difficult to change. Lyman and teachers working with him have developed various ways of teaching students how to employ think-pair-share, particularly how and when to switch from one mode to another. A favorite strategy is to make and use cueing devices such as those illus-trated in Figure 5.5.

Thinking Matrix

McTighe and Lyman (1988) also studied how to get students and their teachers to ask more questions that promote higher-level thinking and to analyze the nature of responses made to various types of questions. They created a device they call the "thinking matrix." Lyman (1986) recom-mends that teachers create symbols which illustrate the various thinking processes described in Bloom's taxonomy and then construct symbol cards that can be placed on the wall or held in the teacher's hand. Dur-ing a discussion teachers point to these symbols as they ask various types of questions. They also encourage students to categorize the questions they ask and the responses they give using the symbol cards. Figure 5.6 shows the symbol system developed by Lyman and teachers who work with him.

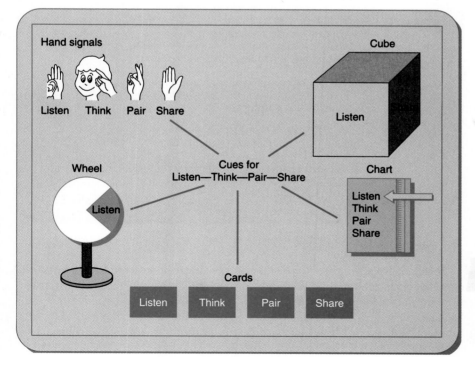

FIGURE 5.5

Cues for Using Think-Pair-Share

SOURCE: From F. Lyman, (1985), *Think-pair-share.* (Mimeographed.) College Park, Maryland: University of Maryland. Reprinted with permission.

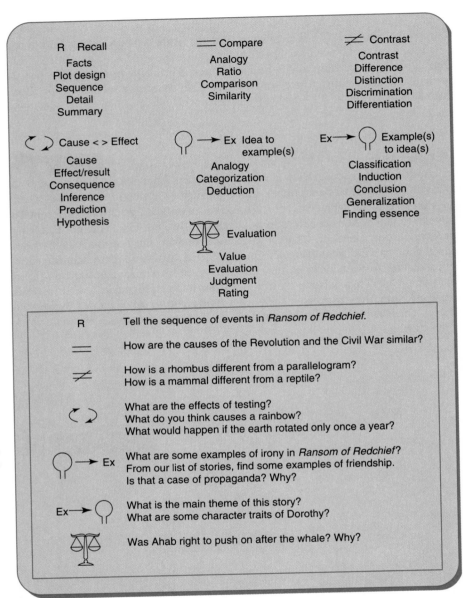

FIGURE 5.6
*Teaching Thinking
Skills with Question-
Response Cues*
Source: From F. Lyman,
(1986), *Procedures for using
the question/response cues.*
(Mimeographed.) College
Park, Maryland: University
of Maryland and the
Howard County Public
Schools. Reprinted with
permission.

Teaching specific discourse skills is no different from teaching content-specific skills or social skills. As described in Chapter 2, the direct instruction model, which requires teachers to demonstrate and model the skill being taught and to provide time for students to practice the skill and receive feedback on how they are doing, is the best approach to use.

ASSESSMENT AND EVALUATION

As with the other teaching approaches, there are assessment and evaluation tasks for teachers to perform following a discussion. One is considering how a particular discussion should be followed up in subsequent lessons; the other is grading.

Following Up Discussions

Experienced teachers make both formal and mental notes for themselves following discussions. Sometimes these notes pertain to the content of the discussion and help determine subsequent lessons. For example, perhaps a discussion identifies some serious gaps in students' knowledge about a topic. Learning this might prompt a teacher to plan a presentation on a particular topic that came up in the discussion or to find suitable reading materials to assign students. A discussion can also identify aspects of a topic in which students are particularly interested. Teachers use the information they gain during discussions to plan lessons that will take advantage of this natural interest. The conduct of the discussion itself will give the teacher information about the strengths and weaknesses of students' thinking processes as well as the group's ability to engage in purposeful dialogue. Future lessons can then be planned to strengthen areas targeted for improvement.

Grading Classroom Discussions

Grading classroom discussion can pose a perplexing problem for many teachers. On the one hand, if participation is not graded, students may view this part of their work as less important than work for which a grade is given. Remember the "work for grade exchange" concept described in Chapter 1? On the other hand, it is practically impossible to quantify participation in any satisfactory way. The questions teachers are confronted with when they try to grade discussions are: Do I reward quantity or quality? What constitutes a quality contribution? What about the student who talks all the time but says nothing? What about the student who is naturally shy but has good ideas?

There are two ways experienced teachers have confronted this grading dilemma. One is to give bonus points to students who consistently appear to be prepared for discussions and who make significant contributions. If this method is used, it needs to be discussed thoroughly with the class and opportunities provided that allow each student equal access to the bonus points available.

Two ways to grade a discussion are to award bonus points for student participation and to have students do a reflective writing assignment based on the discussion.

A second way to grade discussions is to use the discussion as a springboard for a reflective writing assignment. The grade in this instance is given not for participation but for the student's ability to reflect on the discussion and put in words what the discussion meant to him or her. Properly conceived and managed, when students know they are responsible for a postdiscussion reflective essay, it can heighten student attention during the discussion and extend student thinking about the discussion after it is over. The obvious disadvantage of using this type of assignment is the time required to read and assign grades to the essays.

Using Essay Exams

Many teachers and test experts agree that essay tests do the best job of tapping students' higher-level thought processes and their creativity. Obviously, this is a decided advantage an essay test has over an objective test, particularly when teachers are trying to assess what students have learned in discussions. Another advantage of the essay test is that it normally takes less time to construct than an objective test does. A note of caution is in order, however, about preparation time. Good, clear essay questions also require time to construct. They just don't happen. Teachers need to keep in mind the time it takes to construct sample answers and to read and grade essay questions.

Probably the most serious criticisms of essay tests are that they can cover fewer topics than objective tests and they are difficult to grade objectively. The first criticism can be partially resolved by using a combination of objective and essay items in a test. Use objective items to measure student understanding of basic knowledge and use essay items when it is important to measure higher-level objectives. Several guidelines that help to reduce grading bias have been developed by experienced teachers and evaluation specialists including those listed here.

1. Write the essay question so it is clear and explains to students what should be covered in the answer.

For example, if a teacher wants students to apply information, the questions should say that. If the teacher wants students to compare two different ideas or principles, the question should state that clearly. Take the following example, for instance: "Discuss the Civil War." This item is too broad and does not tell students what information the teacher is looking for. Consequently, answers will vary greatly and will be difficult for the teacher to score. On the other hand, an essay item such as: "Describe and compare economic conditions in the North and the South during the 1840s and 1850s, and explain how these conditions influenced decisions by both sides to engage in civil war." This question describes more clearly the relevant topics to be covered in the essay and the type of thinking about the topic the teacher wants.

2. Write a sample answer to the question ahead of time and assign points to various parts of the answer.

Writing a sample answer can become a criterion on which to judge each of the essays. Assigning points to various aspects of the answer (for instance, 5 points for organization, 5 points for coverage, and perhaps 5 points overall) helps deal with the problem of uneven quality that may exist across a given answer. Students should be made aware of the point distribution, if this technique is used by the teacher.

3. Use techniques to reduce expectancy effects.

Expectancy effects is a phenomenon that causes teachers to expect some students to do well and others to do poorly, regardless of their actual performance. Having students write their names on the back of their essays is one technique used to prevent this type of bias. However, this strategy has limited value, because most teachers soon find they readily recognize a particular student's handwriting. If an essay test has two or three questions, reading all the responses to a single question and then shuffling the papers before reading responses to the next question is another procedure teachers use to reduce expectancy effects. If teachers are working in teams, checking each other's grading is also helpful.

4. Consider using holistic scoring.

Some evaluation specialists argue that the best procedure for scoring essay questions and other types of student writing (reports, essays, and so on) is one they have labeled *holistic scoring*. The logic behind this procedure is that the total essay written by a student is more than the sum of its parts and should be judged accordingly. Teachers who use this approach normally skim through all the essays and select samples that could be judged as very poor, average, and outstanding. These samples then become the models or criteria on which to judge the other papers. Some teachers use this same process but add a second procedure of stacking the papers in appropriate piles as they read, for instance an A pile, a B pile, and so on. They then reread selected papers from the various piles to check their initial judgments and to check for comparability of papers within a given pile.

Obviously, constructing essay items and making judgments about students' work this way can be difficult and time consuming. The use of essay questions, however, remains one of the best means for measuring the more complex and higher-level abilities of students, particularly those connected with classroom discussion. Subjective grading will probably always be an unattractive feature of essay testing, but employing the safeguards described here greatly reduces this factor.

> ## REFLECTION BOX   REFLECTING ON CLASSROOM DISCOURSE PATTERNS
>
> There is almost universal agreement among scholars and researchers that for real learning to occur a different discourse pattern than the one currently found in most classrooms must be established. When asked about how they are going to teach, most beginning teachers will attest to the importance of providing opportunities for students to discuss important topics and to exchange ideas with each other and with the teacher.
>
> Yet year after year, classroom observers say this is not happening. Teachers continue to dominate the talk that goes on in classrooms, by presenting information and giving directions for students to follow. When they ask students questions, most of them are the kind that require direct recall rather than higher-level thinking, and if students don't answer immediately, another question is asked or another student called on. All this takes place at a very rapid pace. We know from research that teacher dominance of classroom discourse patterns and the rapid pace of this discourse is harmful. We also know that slowing down the pace of discourse and using different discourse patterns such as think-pair-share will produce more and better student thinking.
>
> If this is true, why is it so difficult to change the discourse patterns in classrooms? What do you think? Are there some underlying causes for this phenomenon? Do students really want to participate in discussions? Perhaps it is easier to sit and listen. Do teachers really want to have discussions? Perhaps it is easier just to talk.
>
> What about you and your teaching? Do you value discussion and open dialogue with students? Why? Why not? If you plan to be a teacher who uses a lot of discussion, why will you be successful when so many other teachers have not?

SUMMARY

- ◆ Discourse and discussion are key ingredients for enhancing student thinking and uniting the cognitive and social aspects of learning.
- ◆ When experienced teachers refer to classroom discourse, they often call it *discussion.*
- ◆ Discourse can be thought of as externalization of thinking and has both cognitive and social importance.
- ◆ Studies for a good many years have described how discourse patterns in most classrooms do not afford effective dialogue among students or promote much discovery or higher-level thinking.
- ◆ A substantial knowledge base exists that informs teachers on how to create positive discourse systems and to hold productive discussions. Studies also provide

guidelines about the types of questions to ask and how to provide appropriate pacing for students to think and to respond.

◆ Most classroom discourse proceeds at too rapid a pace. Teachers can obtain better classroom discourse by slowing down the pace and giving themselves and their students opportunities to think before they respond.

◆ Classroom discussions are characterized by students as well as teachers talking about academic materials and by students willingly displaying their thinking processes publicly.

◆ The primary instructional effects of a discussion lesson are to improve student thinking, to promote involvement and engagement around academic materials, and to learn important communication and thinking skills.

◆ There are many variations to discussions. Three of the major approaches include recitation discussions, discovery or inquiry discussions, and discussions to clarify values and to share personal experiences.

◆ Regardless of the approach, the general flow or syntax for a discussion lesson consists of five major phases: providing objectives and set, focusing the discussion, holding the discussion, ending the discussion, and debriefing the discussion.

◆ The structure of the learning environment for discussion lessons is characterized by open processes and active student roles.

◆ Important planning tasks for teachers to consider include determining the purposes of the discussion, being aware of students' prior knowledge and discourse skills, making plans for how to approach the discussion, and determining the type of questions to ask.

◆ Placing students in circle or U-shape seating arrangements facilitates classroom discussions.

◆ Primary tasks for teachers as they conduct a discussion consist of focusing the discussion, keeping the discussion on track, keeping a record of the discussion, making sure students' ideas are listened to, and providing appropriate wait-time.

◆ Students' ideas should be responded to with dignity, and teachers should help students extend their ideas by seeking clarification, getting students to consider alternative ideas, and labeling thinking processes students are displaying.

◆ In general, discussion and classroom discourse patterns can be improved if teachers slow the pace, use methods to broaden participation, and teach students to try to understand one another and have high interpersonal regard for one another's ideas.

◆ Teaching students four specific interpersonal communication skills—paraphrasing, behavior description, feeling description, and impression checking—can enhance the quality of classroom discourse and the interpersonal regard students hold for each other.

◆ Specific visual tools, such as the think-pair-share cueing device and the thinking matrix, can help students learn discourse and thinking skills.

◆ For students to become effective in the discourse system and during specific discussions requires teaching students discourse skills just as directly as academic content and other academic skills are taught.

◆ Assessment and evaluation tasks appropriate for discussion consist of finding ways to follow up on discussions and ways to grade students for their contributions.

◆ Teachers use two ways to grade discussions: giving bonus points to students who consistently appear to be prepared and who make contributions, and grading reflective writing assignments based on the content of discussions.

◆ If essay tests are to be used to assess student understanding of the content of discussions, procedures to reduce grading bias should be used.

LESSON PLAN FORMAT FOR DISCUSSION

PURPOSE: This is a suggested format for making a lesson plan tailored specifically to planning requirements of a discussion. You can try it out as you plan for teaching or microteaching. Revise the format as you see the need.

DIRECTIONS: Follow the guidelines below as you plan a discussion lesson.

Planning Tasks

Content That Is Focus of Discussion _____

_____

Lesson Objectives

    Content objectives _____

    _____

    Discourse objectives _____

    _____

Discussion Approach

    Recitation type _____

    Problem-based type _____

    Sharing ideas type _____

Web of Major Ideas

Plan for Use of Physical Space

Key Questions to Use_____

_____

_____

_____

Conducting the Lesson

Procedures for introducing and explaining discussion _____

_____

_____

_____

Notes/hints to remember as discussion proceeds _____

_____

_____

_____

Procedure for ending discussion _____

_____

_____

_____

Questions to guide debriefing of discussion _____

_____

_____

_____

Pitfalls to Avoid

During Introduction of Discussion	As Discussion Proceeds	Closing and Debriefing Discussion

OBSERVING DISCUSSION IN MICROTEACHING OR CLASSROOMS

DIRECTIONS: This form highlights key aspects of a classroom discussion lesson. It can be used to observe a peer in a microteaching laboratory or an experienced classroom teacher. It can also be used to assess a lesson you have taught and videotaped. As you observe the lesson, check the category you believe describes the level of performance of the teacher you are observing. Also answer the general questions about the lesson at the bottom of the form.

Teacher Behavior	Excellent	Acceptable	Needs Improvement	Not Needed
Planning				
How appropriate was the discussion's focus?	____	____	____	____
How clear were the content objectives?	____	____	____	____
How clear were the discourse objectives?	____	____	____	____
How appropriate was the type of discussion?	____	____	____	____
How appropriate was the way the teacher used the physical space?	____	____	____	____
How well prepared was the teacher overall?	____	____	____	____
Execution				
How well did the teacher				
Explain purposes and goals?	____	____	____	____
Orient students to the discussion?	____	____	____	____
Keep the discussion focused?	____	____	____	____
Use methods to record the discussion?	____	____	____	____
Encourage broad participation	____	____	____	____
Use wait-time?	____	____	____	____
How well did the teacher				
Bring the discussion to a close?	____	____	____	____
Debrief the discussion?	____	____	____	____

Level of Performance

Overall Planning

What did you like best about the way the lesson was planned and organized?

_____

_____

What could be improved? _____

_____

_____

Lesson Execution

What did you like best about the way the lesson was conducted? _____

_____

_____

What could be improved? _____

_____

_____

If you were a student in microteaching, how did you feel about the teacher's interaction with you during the lesson? _____

_____

_____

OBSERVING STUDENT PARTICIPATION IN DISCUSSION

PURPOSE: Broad student participation is an important goal in classroom discussions. This aid can be used to gather information about patterns of student participation in class discussions.

DIRECTIONS: Obtain a copy of the class seating chart, or if observing a small group, note everyone's name and location on your paper. You can use a format like the one pictured below. Whenever a student contributes to the discussion, make a "tick" on your chart by that student's name.

Front

☐ _____   ☐ _____   ☐ _____   ☐ _____
☐ _____   ☐ _____   ☐ _____   ☐ _____
☐ _____   ☐ _____   ☐ _____   ☐ _____
☐ _____   ☐ _____   ☐ _____   ☐ _____
☐ _____   ☐ _____   ☐ _____   ☐ _____

Analysis and Reflection: Who talks the most? The least? Is there an action zone, that is, an area of the room that the teacher seems to favor during whole-class discus-sions? Are there any sex differences in participation? Racial differ-ences? Any other pat-terns observed? How might the quieter students be encouraged to participate?

DEMONSTRATING YOUR EXECUTIVE CONTROL OF QUESTIONING

PURPOSE: To help you gain skill in questioning and to develop understanding of the effects of various questions. The result can become a work product for your portfolio.

DIRECTIONS: Following the steps below, develop a list of questions that might be asked in a discussion, try them out with an audience, and visually document this work for your portfolio.

Step 1: Choose a topic in your teaching field and develop a list of questions that might be asked in a discussion. Have one question from each of the six levels of Bloom's taxonomy. Use Table 5.2 on page 213 as a guide in developing the different types of questions.

Step 2: Find a small group of three or four students, friends, family who would be willing to have you question them in a discussion-type format, and have this activity videotaped.

Step 3: Ask the group each of your prepared questions and record their responses.

Step 4: Review your video recording and analyze the responses elicited by the various levels of questions

Step 5: Write a critique of your questioning. Did it go as you planned? How did response differ according to the level of question asked?

Step 6: Arrange the following in your portfolio: your questions, your video, and your critique.

BOOKS FOR THE PROFESSIONAL

Morine-Dershimer, G. (1985). *Talking, listening, and learning in elementary class-rooms.* New York: Longman. This book describes students' perceptions of classroom discourse as well as effects of various types of discourse and interaction patterns.

Resnick, L. B. (1987). *Education and learning to think.* Washington, D.C.: National Academy Press. This book provides a review of cognitive research along with justification and means for helping students develop dispositions and skills for higher-level thinking.

Resnick, L. B., and Klopfer, L. E. (eds.). (1989). *Toward the thinking curriculum: Current cognitive research.* Alexandria, Va.: Association for Supervision and Curriculum Development. The yearbook of ASCD provides an excellent review of the research in the cognitive sciences that has implications for curriculum development in the various subject areas and for teaching students how to think.

CHAPTER 6

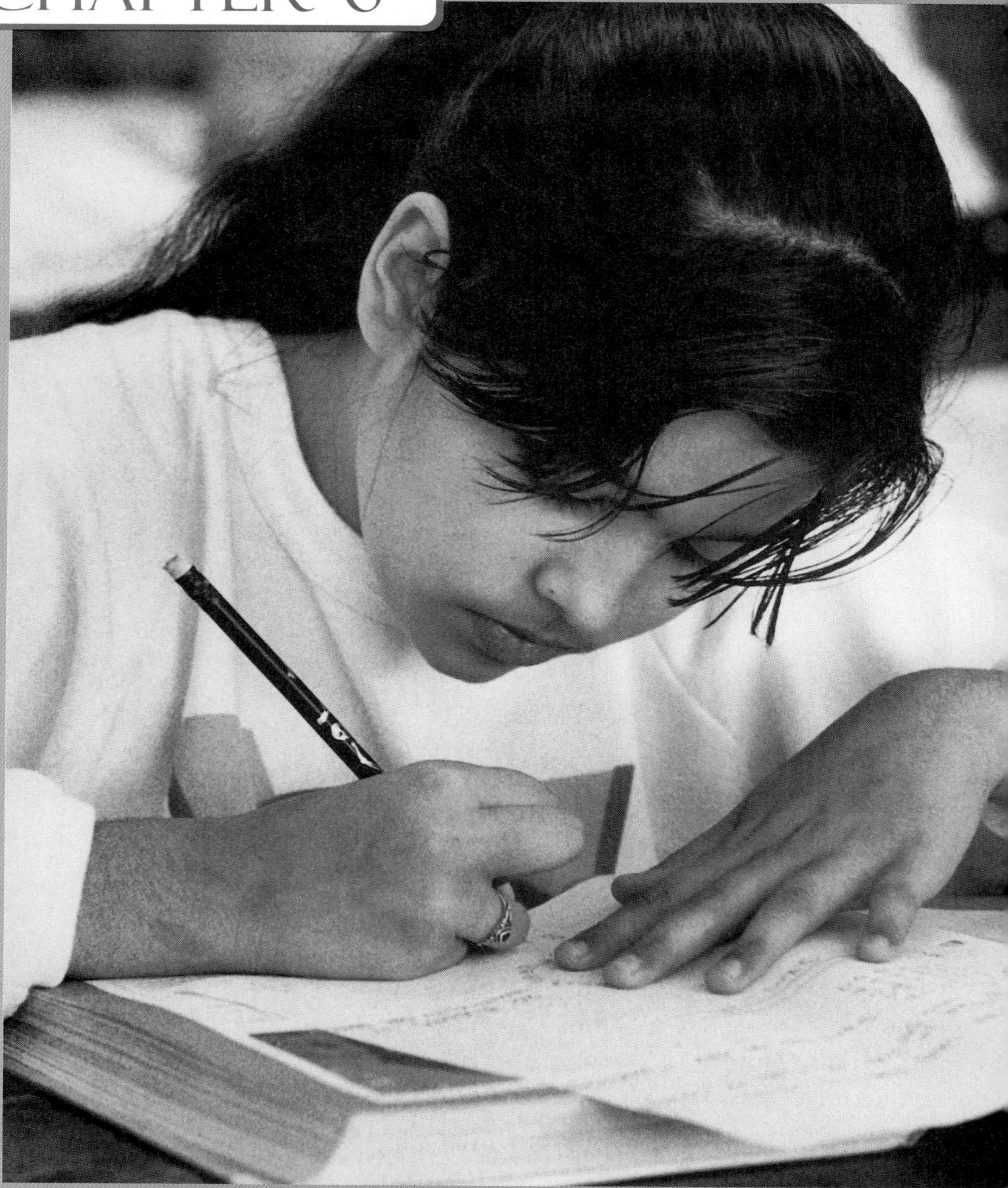

LEARNING AND STUDY STRATEGIES

T his chapter turns from a description of particular teaching strategies to a focus on student learning and study strategies. Thus, we shift our attention from looking primarily at what teachers do and think to what students do and think. The chapter begins with an overview of learning and study strategies and their importance and then examines the theoretical support behind learning and study strategies.* Next, an array of learning and study strategies are examined, some dating back to ancient times and others the result of recent developments. The final sections describe how teachers teach learning strategies to students and how they set up classrooms and manage learning environments in ways that promote "learning how to learn."

OVERVIEW OF LEARNING STRATEGIES

In Chapter 1, you visited Ms. Cuevas's classroom and saw the many different learning activities going on there, including students working in small groups, students working independently, and students misbehaving. You did not, however, get to observe particular lessons being taught; neither were you privy to how Ms. Cuevas works with her students to help them become independent, self-regulated learners. Let's revisit Ms. Cuevas's classroom now for these purposes. As we enter, we find her teaching reading and talking to a small group of students.

"Today we're going to learn a new way to check whether we understand what we're reading. There are several steps in this process, and the first is *summarizing*. After every paragraph that we read, we need to make a statement that summarizes the main ideas in it. Then we'll ask a *question* about the material in that paragraph. Our passage today is about *snakes*. I'll read the first paragraph out loud and then try to summarize it for you.

"The snake's skeleton and parts of its body are very flexible—almost like a rubber hose with bones. A snake's backbone can have almost 300 vertebrae, about 10 times as many as a human backbone. These vertebrae are connected by cartilage that allows easy movement. Because of this bendable, twistable spinal construction, a snake can turn its body in almost any direction at almost any moment.

"Hmmm. Let's see—what would be a sentence that summarizes this paragraph? How about: 'Snakes have lots of bones'? Hmmm, that's okay, but it doesn't tell why having so many bones is important. How about: 'Snakes have lots of bones in their backbone, and that allows them to move and bend'?

*Sometimes distinctions are made between the terms *learning strategies* and *study skills,* the latter of which is reserved to refer to a subset of learning strategies used by students to retain information from text or verbal presentation. The ability to take notes, for instance, could be defined as a study skill. This chapter uses the term *learning strategy* to encompass all types of learning strategies and study skills.

"Yes, that's better. Now I need a good *question*. *How, why,* and *when* words are often helpful. How about this one: 'Why do snakes have so many bones in their backbones?' That's a good question, because it has to do with the main idea in the paragraph.

"Now, let's see. Are there any ideas in the paragraph that aren't clear? *(pause)* What is *cartilage? (pause)* Oh, yes. That is the flexible material between bones, like the cartilage in our knees between the bones in our upper leg and our lower leg.

"What [can you *predict*] that the next paragraph will be about? *(pause)* I wonder if it will explain how snakes' flexible spines help them to survive and hunt? *(pause)* Now let's try another paragraph, and I want one of you to try these four steps." (after Brown & Palincsar, 1985)

Ms. Cuevas is using an approach called **reciprocal teaching,** an instructional procedure developed to teach students learning strategies that improve reading comprehension. Students are taught four strategies: summarization, question asking, clarification, and prediction. In the beginning, the strategies are demonstrated to students as the teacher is doing here, and gradually, through dialogue between students and teacher and among students themselves, students learn to perform them on their own. The aims of this type of instruction are to help students become better and more self-regulated learners and to enhance their motivation and abilities to learn on their own.

Importance and Purposes of Strategy Instruction

You may ask, "Why include a chapter on learning and study strategies in a book on teaching?" One answer to this question was provided sometime ago by Claire Weinstein and Richard Meyer (1986) when they wrote, "good teaching includes teaching students how to learn, how to remember, how to think, and how to motivate themselves" (p. 315).

Many educators agree with Weinstein and Meyer that teaching students how to learn is a very important—perhaps the ultimate—educational goal. They also recognize that educators have not always done a very good job of accomplishing this goal. Norman (1980) described our shortcomings in this area, and he argued for spending more time teaching students just these things.

It is strange that we expect students to learn yet seldom teach them about learning. We expect students to solve problems yet seldom teach them about problem solving. And, similarly, we sometimes require students to remember a considerable body of material yet seldom teach them the art of memory. It is time we made up for this lack, time we developed the applied disciplines of learning and problem solving and memory. We need to develop the general principles of how to learn, how to remember, how to solve problems, and then to develop applied courses, and then to establish the place of these methods in an academic curriculum." (Weinstein & Meyer, 1986, p. 315)

Norman's argument is insightful and provides strong argument for the importance of strategy instruction. Strategy instruction rests on the premise that the students' success depends, to a large extent, on their proficiency to learn on their own and to monitor their own learning. This makes it imperative that learning and study strategies be explicitly taught to students, starting in the early grades and continuing throughout secondary and higher education. Students must learn about the various strategies that are available and when to use them appropriately. In the past, such instruction was rarely provided. Durkin (1978, 1979), for example, found that elementary teachers were good assignment givers but provided little instruction about how to study or learn. A study by Moely and colleagues (1986) reinforced this finding, as did Sirotnik's (1983) study of middle and high school teachers.

More recently this situation has improved. Researchers and teachers have begun to develop specific learning strategies and to use them with students. Many of these strategies focused initially on reading but subsequently have been applied successfully to most fields, including mathematics, physics, and writing.

Defining Learning Strategies

The term learning strategies *refers to the behaviors and thought processes students use as they carry out learning tasks.*

Learning strategies refers to the behaviors and thought processes used by students that influence what is learned, including memory and metacognitive processes. In Michael Pressley's (1991) words, they are "the cognitive operators over and above the processes directly involved in carrying out a [learning] task. They are the strategies students use to attack particular learning problem." (p. 7). For example, students are often assigned specific learning tasks, such as completing a work sheet in reading or locating source material for a history report. To complete these learning tasks requires engaging in particular thought processes and behaviors, such as skimming main headings, summarizing, and taking notes, as well as monitoring one's own thinking. So, in order to perform the assigned learning tasks, students must accomplish several learning strategies.

Another name for learning strategies is **cognitive strategies,** because they achieve cognitive rather than behavioral learning goals. Examples of traditional cognitive goals students are asked to achieve in school include understanding a passage in a book, solving a mathematics or science problem, remembering a list of dates or spelling words, and memorizing a poem. We return to this topic in more detail later in the chapter and describe specific learning strategies and their use.

Self-Regulated Learners

The main purpose of strategy instruction is to teach learners to learn on their own. Several terms are used to describe this type of learner including *independent learner, strategic learner,* and *self-regulated learner.* This chapter uses primarily the term **self-regulated learner,** which refers to those learners who can do four important things:

1. Accurately diagnose a particular learning situation
2. Select a learning strategy to attack the learning problem posed
3. Monitor the effectiveness of the strategy
4. Be sufficiently motivated to engage in the learning situation until it is accomplished

An example of a self-regulated learner is one who knows it is important to summarize or to ask questions while reading a passage in a book or listening to a teacher's presentation and one who is motivated to perform such an operation and to monitor its success. This learner also knows when it was not important to employ a particular strategy, such as when the teacher is telling a joke or recalling an interesting experience.

A self-regulated learner can choose an appropriate learning strategy and use it successfully to complete a learning task.

THEORETICAL SUPPORT FOR STRATEGY INSTRUCTION

Before we describe specific learning and study strategies, we will discuss the theory behind strategy instruction. This theory is important because it helps explain when particular learning and study strategies should be used by teachers and why they work the way they do. The support for learning strategies stems primarily from two theoretical sources, Vygotsky's work as described in Chapter 4 and contemporary cognitive psychology. To summarize Vygotsky, he emphasized three main ideas: that the intellect develops as individuals confront new and puzzling ideas and link these ideas to what they already know; that interactions with others enhance intellectual development; and that a teacher's primary role is to serve as a helper and mediator of student learning. The contribution of cognitive psychology stems from those theories that explain how the mind works and how individuals acquire and process information. The perspectives offered by Vygotsky and more recent cognitive psychologists are important in understanding the use of learning strategies for three reasons. One, they highlight the important role that prior knowledge plays in the learning process. Two, they help us understand what knowledge is and the difference among various types of knowledge, and three, they help explain how knowledge is acquired by humans and processed in the mind's memory system.

Importance of Prior Knowledge

For many years, indeed dating back to the early Greeks, philosophers and teachers have theorized that what individuals already know influences to a great extent what they can learn. One learns, it seems, by associating new ideas with old ideas. Contemporary cognitive psychologists have refined these ancient truths and have shown more precisely how relating new information to information already stored in memory enhances learning.

Cognitive psychologists refer to the information and experiences stored in long-term memory as *prior knowledge*. **Prior knowledge** is the sum of an individual's knowledge and experiences gained during the course of their lives, and what he or she brings to a new learning experience. Research has been conducted during the past two decades on the influence prior knowledge has on learning to read and write and learning to use new information of all kinds. A common finding that has emerged from this research is that a learner's prior knowledge controls new learning possibilities. That is, specific new knowledge—facts, concepts, and skills—cannot be learned until a foundation of related knowledge has been established.

Prior knowledge refers to the sum of one's knowledge and experience to date.

Peter Mosenthal and his colleagues (1985) illustrated the significance of prior knowledge in a particularly interesting study relating it to children's production of narrative text. The researchers selected a representative group of fourth-grade teachers and picked two whose teaching styles were characterized by asking students questions related to their prior knowledge and two who did little questioning of this type. Each teacher was then asked to conduct a writing lesson in his or her class. The lesson consisted of presenting students with a series of 13 pictures representing a baseball episode and asking them to write a story about the picture sequences. The results from this study showed that students who were questioned about their prior experience and knowledge of baseball produced stories that were more complex and creative than those produced by students in the nonquestioning classrooms.

This and many other studies point out how important it is in teaching to help students build bridges between the new and the known. Figure 6.1 illustrates this idea.

Advance organizers help to connect new learning materials to prior knowledge.

The use of **advance organizers** is a pedagogical tool recommended by Ausubel (1960) to anchor new learning materials to prior knowledge. Advance organizers, according to Ausubel, highlight the major ideas in a new learning situation and relate them to the learner's existing knowledge. He described them as the anchors or intellectual scaffolding that help learners activate relevant prior knowledge. Although Ausubel suggested that advance organizers should be slightly more abstract than the

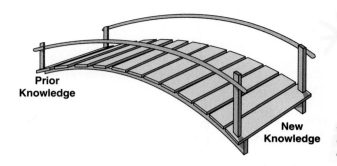

FIGURE 6.1
Making Bridges between the New and the Known

content to be taught, more recent research suggests that concrete examples from a forthcoming lesson work better than more abstract advance organizers (Mayer, 1984). It is also recommended that advance organizers should contain materials familiar to the students.

Advance organizers come in a variety of forms. They can be verbal explanations, passages of text, pictures, or diagrams. Following is an example of a verbal advance organizer. A history teacher is about to present information about the Vietnam War. After reviewing the previous day's lesson, telling students the goals of today's lesson, and asking students to recall what they already know about Vietnam, the teacher presents this advance organizer.

> "I want to give you an idea that will help you understand why Americans became involved in the Vietnam War. The idea is that *"most wars reflect conflict between peoples over one of the following: ideology, territory, or access to trade."* As I describe the United States's involvement in Southeast Asia between 1945 and 1965, I want you to look for examples of how conflict over ideology, territory, or access to trade may have influenced later decisions to fight in Vietnam."

Advance organizers can also be used to introduce students to passages of text. Figure 6.2 shows a series of diagrams used by a teacher prior to having students read a passage about radar, a topic many people have a difficult time understanding. Students were instructed to study the illustrations in Figure 6.2 for a minute or two before reading the assigned passage. A diagram such as this can also be used to introduce a presentation by the teacher.

Kinds of Knowledge

Contemporary cognitive psychology not only emphasizes the importance of prior knowledge in learning, it also divides knowledge into three categories: declarative, procedural, and conditional (see, for instance, Ryle, 1949; Gagné, 1977; Gagné, E., 1985; & Paris, Lipson, & Wixson, 1983). **Declarative knowledge** is knowledge a learner has about something or

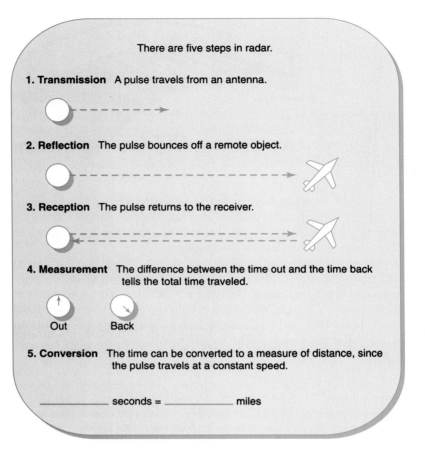

There are five steps in radar.

1. Transmission A pulse travels from an antenna.

2. Reflection The pulse bounces off a remote object.

3. Reception The pulse returns to the receiver.

4. Measurement The difference between the time out and the time back tells the total time traveled.

Out   Back

5. Conversion The time can be converted to a measure of distance, since the pulse travels at a constant speed.

_____ seconds = _____ miles

FIGURE 6.2
An Advance Organizer for a Lesson on Radar
SOURCE: Adapted from R. E. Mayer (1984) "Aids to prose comprehension." *Educational Psychologist, 19,* 30–42, Reprinted with permission.

Facts, generalizations, and opinions are examples of declarative knowledge.

knowledge that something is the case. Knowing a poem, a group of facts, a list of dates, or rules for a game are examples of declarative knowledge. More complex examples of declarative knowledge include concepts and generalizations about the physical or social world, such as that water is required for plants to live; the earth revolves around the sun; and the legislative branch of the government has two chambers, the House and the Senate. Personal preferences and opinions (for example, democracy is better than totalitarianism) are also forms of declarative knowledge.

Knowing how to do something, how to take action, is called procedural knowledge.

Procedural knowledge, on the other hand, is knowledge a learner has about how to do something. Being able to divide fractions, recite a poem, and play a game are examples of procedural knowledge. Notice that knowing the rules of a game is categorized as declarative knowledge, whereas knowing how to play the game is procedural. Teachers want students to have both kinds of knowledge. They want students to acquire large bodies of declarative knowledge that they can then use to understand problems and make decisions. They also want them to have the procedural knowledge required for taking action. For example, both declarative knowledge and procedural knowledge of American government are needed to understand political processes and to be able to vote intelligently on election day or to write a letter to a member of Congress.

A third category of knowledge is referred to as **conditional knowledge,** which is knowing when and why to use particular declarative or procedural knowledge. Knowing when to apply a certain algorithm to solve a mathematics problem is an example of conditional knowledge as is knowing when to use the various learning strategies described in this chapter. For example, with a history assignment, when should a learner read carefully and underline key ideas? When should he or she skim the materials and pay attention to its overall structure? Or in football, when should a quarterback choose to run instead of pass on a run-pass option? Learners and football players with good conditional knowledge know which action will be the most effective for them in particular situations. Many learners in school do poorly because they do not have sufficient conditional knowledge to use the declarative and procedural knowledge they possess.

Conditional knowledge refers to knowing when or why to use specific declarative or procedural knowledge.

Understanding the distinctions among these three types of knowledge is important for teachers, because students acquire declarative, procedural, and conditional knowledge in different ways that require different teaching approaches. Direct instruction, for instance, is best to teach procedural knowledge or declarative knowledge that can be ordered in a straightforward, linear fashion. Problem-based instruction, on the other hand, helps students to construct complex and authentic declarative knowledge and to practice using conditional knowledge.

Table 6.1 summarizes the three kinds of knowledge and provides definitions and examples of each.

TABLE 6.1 THREE KINDS OF KNOWLEDGE		
Kinds of Knowledge	**Definition**	**Example**
Declarative	Knowing about something or that something is the case	Rules of a game; definition of a triangle
Procedural	Knowing how to do something	Play basketball; use word processing
Conditional	Knowing when to use particular declarative or procedural knowledge	When to dribble; when to subtract; when to highlight

The Memory System

The importance of prior knowledge and the way knowledge is represented in the mind are two ingredients for understanding how individuals learn and how they employ particular learning strategies. How the mind's memory system works is another. Some cognitive psychologist have developed what they call the **information processing** perspective of learning. These theorists rely heavily on the computer as the metaphor or analog for how the mind and its memory system work. From this perspective, information enters the mind through the senses (analogous to entering data on a computer keyboard) and is stored temporarily in a work space called *short-term memory* (the desktop storage space of a computer). From short-term memory it is then transferred to *long-term memory* (a computer's hard disk) and stored (saved) until retrieved for later use. Figure 6.3 shows how a computer serves as a metaphor for how the information processing system works. This is followed by a more detailed explanation of how the memory system works.

Short-Term and Long-Term Memory

As shown in Figure 6.3, new ideas and information begin as sensory input into our visual, auditory, and olfactory registers. Much of the sensory stimulation bombarding us at any given time fails to be registered (attended to) and, consequently, never makes it into consciousness. Once the sensory input has been perceived and registered, however, it moves into **short-term memory,** the place in the mind where conscious mental work is done and the place where it is either acted on in some way or forgotten.

Short-term memory, or working memory, initially receives new ideas and information.

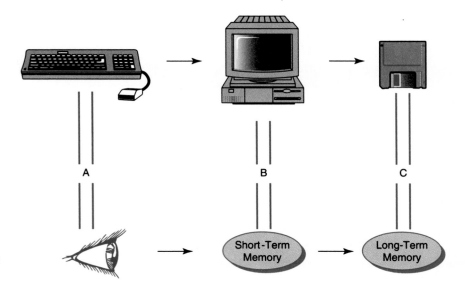

FIGURE 6.3
Computers and Human Information Processing

For instance, if you are solving the problem 26 × 32 mentally, you hold the intermediate products 52 and 78 in short-term memory and add them together there. Short-term memory also corresponds to what we think of as our consciousness at a particular moment.

The storage space in short-term memory is very limited. However, it governs what learners attend to, how new information initially enters the memory system, and how it is subsequently transferred to **long-term memory,** the place where knowledge is stored permanently for later retrieval and use.

Figure 6.4 illustrates an analogy between short-term memory, long-term memory, and a kitchen's countertop. A cook gathers pot, pans, and the ingredients for an apple pie on the countertop where food preparation is done. But the countertop space is rather limited and requires the use of other space (cabinets) to store a vast array of cooking tools and ingredients. In the mind, this storage space is called long-term memory and is analogous to cabinet space in a kitchen.

As described later, getting students to activate prior knowledge and to focus their attention on particular learning materials are critical conditions for bringing new information to short-term memory. However, information in short-term memory will soon be forgotten unless acted on by

To be retained, new information must be transferred to long-term memory.

FIGURE 6.4
Short-Term and Long-Term Memory

the learner. The more effort expended during this active processing phase while in short-term memory, the better the chances are that the new information will be permanently transferred to long-term memory. This process of transferring new information from short-term memory to long-term memory is called **encoding.** Once in long-term memory, information is thought to be stored for a lifetime. However, storing information in long-term memory is meaningless unless ways can be found to activate and retrieve it. That, of course, is a major goal of teaching and of the several learning strategies presented in this chapter.

The permanent transfer of new information from short-term to long-term memory is called encoding.

Knowledge Networks and Schemata

The average person (child or adult) holds a tremendous amount of information and knowledge in long-term memory. Information processing theorists refer to the way knowledge is organized and stored in our memory systems as **knowledge representation.** According to them, knowledge in long-term memory is represented in a variety of ways. Cognitive psychologists believe that humans process knowledge in terms of basic units, called propositions and productions. **Propositions** are units of declarative knowledge, whereas **productions** are the basic units of procedural knowledge. Together they form **knowledge networks** that mentally link related concepts and bits of knowledge.

Knowledge is organized and stored in the mind through propositions, productions, and schemata.

Propositions and productions are used to represent rather small units of declarative or procedural knowledge. The term **schemata** (the plural form of *schema*) refers to more complex knowledge structures, such as the vast array of concepts stored in long-term memory. A learner develops schemata through experience, and these, in turn, form the learner's prior knowledge. Some theorists have compared a person's schemata to a large filing system (Anderson & Pearson, 1984; Cooper, 1993). Various pieces of knowledge and information are stored in particular files (the schema). As new information or knowledge enters consciousness, the mind creates new files (new schema) or adds the information to existing files. Over a period of time, the whole filing system develops and expands. Mental systems, analogous to computer programs, are developed to make connections among the various files and to retrieve information from the filing system as needed. Figure 6.5 illustrates how a learner's filing system or schema influences understanding about a particular written passage.

In summary, knowledge enters short-term memory of the mind as sensory input. It is then encoded (transferred) and organized in long-term memory in the form of propositions, productions, and schemata. These knowledge networks are linked together in various relationships. Although psychologists are not always in agreement about the exact nature of the networks, there is a high degree of consensus that knowledge networks actively filter new information and thereby determine how well it will be received and retained by students.

FIGURE 6.5
*Reader Interacting
with Text to Activate
Schema and Learn
New Information*

TYPES OF LEARNING STRATEGIES

Traditionally, students are asked to perform numerous learning tasks in school, such as practicing the multiplication tables, rehearsing a speech, writing in a journal, and collecting library information. Although successfully completing these tasks is the most visible learning goal, a more important one is mastering the learning process itself: accurately diagnosing the learning situation, choosing an appropriate learning strategy, and monitoring the effectiveness of the strategy. This section describes how teachers can convert cognitive and information processing theory into specific learning strategies for students. Detailed descriptions of four major types of learning strategies are given, including rehearsal strategies, elaboration strategies, organization strategies, and metacognitive strategies.

Rehearsal Strategies

As you read in the previous section, for learning to occur, learners must act on the new information and connect it to prior information. Strategies used for this encoding process are called **rehearsal strategies,** of which there are two kinds: *rote rehearsal* and *complex rehearsal.*

Rehearsal strategies help transfer learning from short- to long-term memory but do not help make meaning out of new information.

We are all familiar with the most basic of all rehearsal strategies, simply repeating out loud or subvocalizing information we want to remember. This is **rote rehearsal,** and is used to remember phone numbers and the directions to a particular location for a short period of time, say, when we don't have pencil and paper to write them down. We also use rote rehearsal to remember lists of items to buy at the store or chores that need to be done. Simply repeating information over and over helps keep simple information in short-term memory, but unless we elaborate on the information—link the phone numbers to something meaningful, for instance—there is little likelihood that it will transfer to long-term memory. Furthermore, simply repeating and vocalizing does not provide much assistance when more complex information is involved. A learner cannot remember all the words or ideas in a book simply by reading the book out loud.

Retaining more complex materials requires **complex rehearsal** strategies that go beyond merely repeating information. Underlining key ideas and making marginal notes are two complex rehearsal strategies that can be taught to students to help them remember more complex learning materials.

Underlining

Underlining key ideas or text passages is a technique most students have learned by the time they reach college. Underlining helps students learn more from text for several reasons. First, it physically locates key ideas, thereby making review and memorization quicker and more efficient. Second, the process of selecting what to underline assists in connecting new information to existing knowledge. Unfortunately, students do not always use the underlining procedure very effectively. A common error is to underline almost everything. Obviously, this does not help highlight important information or allow for quick review before a test. Sometimes students also underline information that is irrelevant. This is particularly true of younger students who have difficulty determining what information is most and least important.

Marginal Notes

Making marginal notes and other annotations helps supplement underlining and is another example of a complex rehearsal strategy. Figure 6.6 provides examples of marginal notes and other types of notations. Notice that the student has circled words she didn't know, underlined important definitions, numbered and made a list of events, identified a confusing sentence, and written memory notes and comments. Rehearsal, particularly complex rehearsal strategies, helps students attend to specific new information and assists with encoding. It does not help students make new information more meaningful, however. This requires other, more complex learning strategies.

Type of Note or Annotation	Example
Mark definitions	The amount of time the teacher spends on academic tasks is called *allocated time.*
Circle unknown words	At least eleven of its ⟨denizens⟩ are on the federal list of endangered species
Place asterisks next to important idea	** The system for making choices must be ethical
Mark possible test item	*Test item* How? negotiate a favorable lease
Number list (key ideas, causes, reasons)	Weather patterns are influenced by 1 low pressure; 2 high pressure.
Note confusing passages	?? Rehearsal, particularly complex, strategies help students . . . *do what??*
Mark summary statements	New teachers are fortunate because they are starting their careers at an optimum time.
Note similarities	Kilpatrick argued that learning should be purposeful—*similar to Dewey?*

FIGURE 6.6
Examples of Marginal Notes and Annotations
SOURCE: After K. T. McWhorter, (1992), *Study and Thinking Skills in College.* New York: HarperCollins.

Elaboration Strategies

Elaboration strategies make up the second category of learning strategies. As the name implies, elaboration is the process of adding detail so new information will become more meaningful, thereby making encoding easier and more definitive. Elaboration strategies help transfer new information from short-term to long-term memory by creating associations and connections between new information and what is already known. For example, relating a telephone number to a significant date such as one's birthday makes the number more meaningful and increases the likelihood that it will be retained in long-term memory. People use this strategy when creating "PIN" numbers for their bank cards or code numbers for voice mail accounts. These strategies use the mind's existing schemata to make sense out of new information. Note taking, the use of analogies, and the PQ4R method are three frequently used elaboration strategies.

Note taking and using analogies are frequently used elaboration strategies that build connections between new and old knowledge.

Note Taking

A great deal of information is given to students through teacher presentations and demonstrations. Note taking assists students in learning this information by compactly storing it for later review and rehearsal. Done correctly, note taking also helps organize information so that it can be processed and connected to existing knowledge more effectively. However, as with underlining, many students are ineffective note takers. Some students attempt to write down everything teachers say, whereas others have difficulty identifying relevant and important ideas. Effective note takers, on the other hand, capture the main ideas of a presentation in their own words in outline form so that they spend time making sense by synthesizing and summarizing important points and ideas. Kiewra (1989) has suggested the use of **matrix note taking** as a way of elaborating and making comparisons within complex information. An example of this is shown in Figure 6.7.

Analogies

Using analogies is another way of providing for elaboration. **Analogies** are comparisons made to show the similarities between like features of things or ideas that otherwise are different, such as a heart and a pump. Here are two more examples.

> Our mind is like a computer that takes in and stores information. Our sensory registers are like the computer's keyboard where information enters. Information is stored in the mind's long-term memory just as it is stored on the computer's hard disk.

> Schools are like factories. Students are the raw resources that are processed into a final product, an educated person.

Topic   Loons and Cormorants

Loons, with their heavy, solid bones, enjoy a wet habitat. Loons range between 30"–36" and can be identified by their loud yodeling call. They have a black and white checkerboard pattern.

Cormorants are heavy-bodied diving birds that paddle across the water's surface. Cormorants are usually silent, and their size ranges between 30"–36". These birds are black with bare patches of orange skin.

Matrix Notes from Passage on Loons and Cormorants

	Loon	Cormorant
Similarities		
structure	heavy, solid bones	heavy bodied
habitat	water	water
size	30"–36"	30"–36"
Differences		
voice	loud, yodeling	silent
color	black/white	black/orange

FIGURE 6.7
Example of Matrix Notes

When used as a learning strategy, note how analogies link new ideas—the way the mind or schools work—to already familiar ideas—the computer or factories.

PQ4R

Another elaboration strategy that has long been very popular with teachers is the **PQ4R method** used to help students remember what they read. It is likely that you were taught this method during your elementary or middle school career. P stands for preview, Q for question, and the 4Rs consist of read, reflect, recite, and review (Robinson, 1961; Thomas & Robinson, 1972). A student using PQ4R would be instructed to approach a reading assignment using the following steps.

Step 1   *Preview* the reading assignment. Look at major headings and topics, read the overview and summary, and predict what the reading will be about.

Step 2   Consider the major topics and headings and ask *questions* for which the text might provide answers.

Step 3   *Read* the material. Pay attention to main ideas and seek answers to the questions posed.

Step 4   *Reflect* while reading. Create visual images from the text. Try to connect the new information in the text with what you already know.

Step 5   After reading, *recite* by answering the questions you asked out loud and without the book. Recall lists or other important facts included in the text either out loud or subvocally.

Step 6   *Review* by going back over the material, reread when necessary, and again answer the questions that were posed.

There has been substantial research on PQR4-type learning strategies, and the method has been shown to be effective in helping students recall information from text (see, for example, Meyer, Brandt, & Bluth, 1980; Doctorow, Wittrock, & Marks, 1978). Previewing and asking questions before reading activates prior knowledge and starts the process of making connections between new information and what is already known. Looking at headings and major topics helps readers become aware of the organization of the new materials, thus facilitating its transfer from short-term to long-term memory. Recitation of basic information, particularly when accompanied by some form of elaboration, likewise enhances encoding.

Organization Strategies

A third category of learning strategies involves what are referred to as organization strategies. As with elaboration strategies, these aim at helping learners increase the meaningfulness of new materials, mainly by imposing new organizational structures on the materials. **Organization strategies** may consist of regrouping or clustering ideas or terms or of dividing them into smaller subsets. They also consist of identifying key ideas or facts from a larger array of information. Outlining, mapping, and mnemonics are common organization strategies.

Outlining

Organization strategies, such as outlining, mnemonics, and conceptual mapping, help students identify key ideas and topics.

In outlining, students learn to relate a variety of topics or ideas to some main idea. In traditional outlines the only kind of relation is subordination of one topic to another. The first page of each chapter in this text shows an outline of the chapter and is there to give readers a preview of the key ideas and topics in the chapter and their relationship to each other. As with other learning strategies, students are rarely good outliners at first, but they can learn to write good outlines if they are given appropriate instruction and sufficient practice.

Mapping

Mapping, sometimes referred to as conceptual mapping, is an alternative to outlining and, in some instances, is more effective than outlining in learning complex materials. Mapping is accomplished by making a visual representation or a diagram of how important ideas on a particular topic are connected to one another. George Posner and Alan Rudnitsky (1986) wrote that "conceptual maps are like road maps, but they are concerned with relationships among ideas, rather than places" (p. 25).

To make a conceptual map, students are taught to identify the key ideas associated with any topic and to arrange these ideas in some logical pattern. Sometimes conceptual maps are hierarchical diagrams, sometimes they focus on causal relations. Figure 6.8 shows how main topics and subtopics are illustrated in a conceptual map of stars. The following steps are those usually followed to create a concept map.

Step 1   Identify the main idea or overarching principle
Step 2   Identify secondary ideas or concepts supporting the main idea
Step 3   Put the main idea in the center or at the top of the map
Step 4   Cluster secondary ideas around the main ideas visually showing their relationship to the main idea and to each other

Most students find conceptual maps fun to make, and their visual nature helps them to understand relationships among various ideas and to learn new materials more effectively than with word outlines.

Mnemonics

Mnemonics form a special category and technically can be classified as either elaboration or organization strategies. Essentially, **mnemonics**

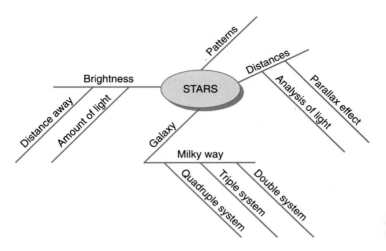

FIGURE 6.8
Example of a
Conceptual Map

refers to techniques or strategies to assist memory by helping form associations that don't naturally exist. A mnemonic helps to organize information that reaches working memory in familiar patterns so that it more easily fits the schema pattern in long-term memory. Pattern recognition is an important part of connecting new information into long-term memory. Although you may never have labeled them as such, you have likely employed several different types of mnemonics in your life, both in and outside school. Several examples of this device are provided here.

Mnemonics *refers to learning strategies that assist memory by forming associations that will be familiar to the learner's schema pattern.*

Chunking. Because an individual's working memory has such limited capacity, it is difficult for most people to learn a long list of numbers such as those used to identify a credit card or an automobile registration. If, however, numbers can be placed in chunks, they are more easily remembered. For instance, most people can remember a 10-digit telephone number because it has been divided into three chunks: the area code (203), the neighborhood code (231), and the individual's four-digit number (2137). Thus most people can remember 203-231-2137, whereas they have difficulty with 2032312137. Automobile license plate numbers are assigned using the same chunking principle, often three letters and three- or four-number combinations, such as LIA-6335. Vanity plates in which the letters and numbers are personally meaningful (e.g., one's initials and birth date) make the chunking product even more memorable.

Acronyms. Another mnemonic is the use of **acronyms** representing the first letter of each item in a list of items. Every Good Boy Does Fine (EGBDF) is a mnemonic used by beginning music students to remember the letters of the scale. HOMES is a familiar word to help us remember the names of the Great Lakes (Huron, Ontario, Michigan, Erie, Superior). Likewise, the first letters of the words Dad, Mom, Sister, Brother are used to help remember the steps in long division: divide, multiply, subtract, and bring down. Acronyms assist memory by making associations between new information and familiar information.

Link-Word. Perhaps the most well known mnemonic used in school is the key-word or **link-word method.** Created initially by Richard Atkinson (1975) as a mnemonic to learn foreign language vocabulary, the link-word method teaches students how to create a mental image that links a familiar English word to an unfamiliar foreign language word. The example shown in Figure 6.9 consists of getting students to link the Spanish word *carta,* which means postal letter, to an image of a letter being transported in a shopping *cart.* Because the familiar image has the same sound as the foreign language word being learned (cart and carta), both the meaning and the pronunciation of the new word are captured.

Metacognitive Strategies

A fourth type of learning strategy has been labeled **metacognitive strategies.** *Metacognition* refers to learners' thinking about their own thinking and their abilities to use particular learning strategies appropriately. John Flavel (1985) provided a more complete definition when he wrote that metacognition is

> one's knowledge concerning one's own cognitive processes and products or anything related to them, e.g., the learning-relevant properties of information or data. . . . Metacognition refers, among other things, to the active monitoring and consequent regulation and orchestration of these processes in relation to the cognitive objective on which they bear, usually in the service of some concrete goal or objective. (p. 232)

Carta means letter

↓

(cart)

FIGURE 6.9
Example of the Link-Word Method

Most authorities agree that metacognition has two components: knowledge about cognition, and self-regulating mechanisms such as cognitive control and monitoring (Baker & Brown, 1984; Brown, 1982; Gagné, E., 1985; 1993). *Knowledge about cognition* consists of the information and understanding that a learner has about his or her own thinking processes as well as knowledge about various learning strategies to use in particular learning situations. An example is when a visually oriented student knows that making a conceptual map is a good way for him or her to understand and remember a large amount of new information. Knowledge about cognition is a form of declarative knowledge and, as such, can be taught to students like any other form of declarative knowledge.

Another learning strategy, metacognition, involves students' thinking about their own thinking and the ability to properly use learning strategies.

The research box for this chapter consists of an extremely provocative study done in Sweden by Ingrid Pramling. It demonstrates how simple it is for teachers to help students be more aware of their metacognitive processes.

The second component of metacognition, **cognitive monitoring,** is a learner's ability to select, use, and monitor learning strategies that are appropriate both for their own learning style and for the situation at hand. A visual learner's use of concept mapping is one example. Another example of this form of metacognition would be a learner's ability to select and to use an appropriate elaboration strategy (say, the link-word method) to accomplish a specific learning task (say, mastering a new foreign language word) and then to check the effectiveness of this method. This component of metacognition is a form of procedural and conditional knowledge that can also be taught to students.

Table 6.2 lists the four types of cognitive strategies and provides examples of each.

TABLE 6.2 FOUR CATEGORIES OF COGNITIVE STRATEGIES

Strategy	Definition	Example
Rehearsal	Committing materials to memory by repeating them	Repeating a new phone number
Elaboration	Adding detail to new information and creating associations	Using mnemonic techniques and adding detail, such as relating a new phone number to one's social security number
Organization	Reorganizing or picking out main ideas from large bodies of information	Outlining or highlighting
Metacognition	Thinking about thinking and monitoring cognitive processing	Deciding that the best strategy for comprehending a body of new text is to create an outline of main ideas

RESEARCH BOX   STUDYING LEARNING HOW TO LEARN

Studying how teachers can help students learn about their own learning presents interesting challenges to educational researchers. Unlike the procedures used in process-product research in which the researcher is most interested in observable teacher and student behaviors—such as teacher clarity or student time-on-task—procedures used to understand cognitive and metacognitive processes require ways of getting inside students' minds to find out what they are thinking and understanding. Such research is time consuming and results in the researcher's using small samples and employing interviewing techniques for gathering data. A Swedish study conducted by Ingrid Pramling (1988) is an interesting illustration of this type of research.

Pramling was concerned mainly with one aspect of metacognition, children's awareness of their own thinking. She knew that most young children view learning as "doing" something: completing a drawing, saying good-bye in a foreign language, counting to ten, sorting colors. Conceptions about how one learns or awareness of understanding is seldom grasped by young learners. Pramling, however, wondered whether or not it was possible to help young children develop a different concept of what it means to learn.

In a quasi-experimental-descriptive study, Pramling interviewed and observed 56 preschool children (5- and 7-year-olds) in three teachers' classrooms. Over a period of three weeks, teachers taught the children a unit called "the shop." Each teacher taught the same content, but their methods differed. Teachers A and B provided a conceptual structure for the children by studying the shop from two perspectives: the shopkeeper's perspective, or how the shop works, and the customer's point of view of shopping. Teacher C did not use this conceptual structure. Furthermore, teacher C taught the shop unit by engaging students in a variety of activities involving special materials and play, a traditional preschool method. Teacher B used the conceptual structure and spent a lot of time explaining the unit's content to students, labeling main ideas and questioning students about them. Teacher A, on the other hand, taught the content *metacognitively*. Throughout the lesson, she focused the children's attention not only on the conceptual structure, but also on the learning aspect of the lessons. Through what was labeled *metacognitive dialogues*, teacher A got children to ponder and reflect on the following types of questions: "How come we went to the shop yesterday?" "Did you find out anything that you didn't know before?" "How did you go about finding it out?" How would you go about teaching other people all you have learned about the shop?"

All the children were interviewed three times and asked questions about their conceptions of learning one week before the unit, after the unit was completed, and six months later. Pramling reports that the interviews were semistructured, similar to a Piagetian interview. Here are examples of the types of questions that were asked.

"Tell me about something you have learned in preschool!" followed by, "Anything else?"

"Now that you have been working on shops, tell me something you have learned!" followed by, "Anything else?"

"Now that you have been in preschool a whole year, tell me something you have learned!" followed by, "Anything else?"

Children were also asked:

"If you were the one who had to decide what the children will have to learn next in preschool, what would you suggest?" Or, "Imagine you are as old as your teacher, and have to teach children . . . what you have learned when working with the shop. How would you go about that?"

Before the unit was taught, Pramling reported that the children in all three classrooms responded to questions the same ways. Most children (over 90 percent) conceived learning as something to do. However, as a result of the metacognitive dialogues, something dramatic happened in classroom A. After the unit, 75 percent of the children explained learning as "learning to know and to understand." This compared to only 15 and 25 percent respectively of children in classrooms B and C. In these classrooms, the large majority of children still expressed learning as something "to do." When students responded to the question about teaching others, almost half teacher A's children described things that were associated with learning as "knowing" such as "being able to tell time" or "how the first ape men grew up," whereas over 90 percent of the students in the other classrooms described "learning to do" types of things, such as "to draw," "to color," "to walk on stilts." Finally, Pramling found that the differences between children in classroom A and the other two groups were even greater 6 months later, at the end of the school year. Only one child in group A conceptualized learning as merely something "to do" at the end of the year, but well over 90 percent of the children in the other groups still described learning in this way.

This study demonstrates that young children typically conceive of learning as doing something and rarely view it as understanding or knowing something. However, Pramling found that if a teacher carried on conversations with the children and asked them certain kinds of questions, their conceptions of learning could be changed. Children can be helped to become aware of what learning means and to become reflective about their own learning. This kind of teaching does not take much extra effort. It only requires creating an environment in which learning how to learn is valued and practiced.

This study also illustrates how some cognitive researchers do their work of trying to find out what students are thinking by finding ways to explore inside students' minds.

After Pramling, I. (1988). Developing young children's thinking about their own learning. *British Journal of Educational Psychology, 58*, 266–278.

TEACHING LEARNING STRATEGIES

Unless students possess cognitive and metacognitive skills, efforts to teach academic lessons or to promote independent learning will be frustrated. Indeed, the students' success in school rests, to a large extent, on their proficiency to learn on their own and to monitor their own learning. This makes it imperative that the learning strategies described in the previous section be introduced to students starting in the early grades and continued throughout secondary and higher education.

Selecting Learning Strategies to Teach

At the minimum, students should be taught the study, learning, and memory strategies described in this chapter. Younger students can be taught specific strategies such as outlining, mnemonic techniques, and PQ4R. Older students can then be taught how the memory system works and more advanced study and learning strategies, such as note taking, using marginal notes, and chunking. Students at every age should be introduced to such organization strategies as mapping and outlining. From the beginning grades, students should also be taught how to reflect on their metacognitive processes.

Using learning strategies effectively requires declarative, procedural, and conditional knowledge. Declarative knowledge about particular strategies should include how the strategy is defined, why it works the way it does, and how it is similar to or different from other strategies. For example, students need to know what matrix notes are and why this type of note taking is sometimes more effective in learning textual information than simple underlining is. They also need to know why underlining every word in a passage is not effective. Students require procedural knowledge as well, so they can use various learning strategies effectively. Knowing what a conceptual map is may be important declarative knowledge, but it is useless unless a student can actually make one and use it. Finally, conditional knowledge is required so students know when and why to use particular strategies. With the matrix notes example, for instance, students need to know when it is important to make matrix notes and when underlining will suffice.

Choosing an Instructional Approach

Learning strategies are taught using direct instruction and reciprocal teaching.

The process of teaching students learning strategies has been quite thoroughly studied (Collins & Brown, 1982; Duffy & Roehler, 1987; Palincsar & Brown, 1989; Pressley et al., 1989, 1991). Two major instructional approaches, direct instruction and reciprocal teaching, have been developed based on this research.

Direct Instruction

For the most part, learning strategies consist of rather straightforward declarative and procedural knowledge. Teaching learning strategies, therefore, is not much different from teaching content-specific knowledge or skills such as map reading or how to use a microscope. Chapter 2 described a model of instruction for the acquisition of skills and well-structured declarative knowledge. Labeled the *direct instruction model,* it requires teachers to provide background information, to demonstrate the skill being taught, and then to provide time for students to practice the skill and receive feedback on how they are doing. In general, this is the model that teachers should use when introducing learning strategies to their students. The steps of a typical direct instruction lesson are summarized below.

Step 1 Provide objectives for the lesson and establish set. Get students' attention and explain to them that the goal of the lesson is to acquire a learning strategy that will help them learn better. Point out connections between effective use of learning strategies and performance on tests.

Step 2 Explain and demonstrate a particular learning strategy. Teach the strategy to students using verbal presentation and demonstration. Explain why the strategy works, and tie new information about the strategy into what students already know about it. In demonstrating the mental processes, think out loud with students and describe what is going on in your own mind as you use the strategy.

Step 3 Provide opportunities for guided practice. Do this immediately, perhaps with another student, but under your supervision.

Step 4 Check for understanding and provide feedback. Stop the practice and check to see what kinds of problems students are having with the strategy. Have students think out loud about what is going on in their mind as they use the strategy. Give them feedback on how they are doing. Carry on a discussion about the strategy.

Step 5 Provide for independent practice and transfer. Give students an opportunity to use the strategy independently, and then evaluate their success on practice assignments.

Sometimes it takes several days to teach a particular learning strategy. Ellen Gagné and her colleagues (1985) used the direct instruction approach to help seventh-grade students to understand and to use elaboration strategies. They spent 50 minutes a day for 10 days to accomplish their instructional objectives. Table 6.3 shows how they sequenced topics and activities over the 10-day period of instructional time.

Reciprocal Teaching

An alternative to direct instruction for teaching learning strategies, particularly in the area of reading comprehension, is to use procedures associated with reciprocal teaching. You were introduced to this teaching procedure in the vignette at the beginning of this chapter. **Reciprocal teaching** requires teachers to become modelers and helpers rather than presenters in the learning process. According to Ann Brown (1982) and Annemarie Palincsar (1984) teachers teach students important cognitive skills by creating learning experiences in which they model particular behaviors and then help students develop these skills themselves by providing them with encouragement, support, and a scaffolding system.

Using reciprocal teaching, students are taught four specific, self-regulated comprehension strategies: summarizing, asking questions, clarifying, and predicting. To learn these strategies, teachers and students read assigned passages in small groups, and the teacher models the four skills—summarizing the passage, asking a question or two, clarifying hard or difficult points, and predicting what the next segment of the passage will say. As the lesson proceeds, students take turns assuming the teacher's role and serving as discussion leader for the group. The teacher provides support, feedback, and encouragement as students learn the strategies and help teach them to others. How teachers model and pro-

TABLE 6.3　SEQUENCE OF LESSON TOPICS AND ACTIVITIES FOR ELABORATION STRATEGY TRAINING USING DIRECT INSTRUCTION

Day	Topic	Activity
Day 1	What is an elaboration?	Explanation and guided practice
Day 2	Why use elaborations?	Explanation and guided practice
Days 3–4	Good elaborations generate much information.	Explanation and guided practice
Days 5–6	Good elaborations organize information.	Explanation and guided practice
Day 8	When to elaborate and how to recall.	Guided and independent practice
Days 9–10	Practice in deciding whether to elaborate and to recall.	Independent practice

vide assistance and prompts during the dialogue in a reciprocal teaching lesson is illustrated in the following examples of how to teach the "questioning" strategy.

> T: What is a good question about pit vipers that starts with the word "why"?
>
> S: *(No response)*
>
> T: How about, "Why are the snakes called pit vipers?"

or,

> T: That's good. Keep going.
>
> S: How do spinner's mate . . .? How am I going to say that?
>
> T: Take your time with it. You want to ask a question about the spinner's mate and what he does, beginning with the word "how."
>
> S: How do they spend most of his time sitting?
>
> T: You're very close. The question would be "How does spinner's mate spend most of his time?" Now you ask it.
>
> S: How does spinner's mate spend most of his time?

or,

> S: Snakes' backbones can have as many as 300 vertebrae, almost_____ times as many as humans.
>
> T: Not a bad beginning, but I would consider that a question about a detail. See if the next time you can find a main idea question and begin your question with a question word—how, why, when . . . (adapted from Palincsar & Brown, 1984)

Here is an example of teaching the summarizing strategy.

> T: That was a fine job, Ken, but I think there might be something to add to our summary. There is more information that I think we need to include. This paragraph is mostly about what?
>
> S: The third method of artificial evaporation. (adapted from Palincsar & Brown, 1984)

As this kind of dialogue continues, it is expected that students in the group will take on more and more teaching responsibility by providing prompts and hints to each other. Although the teacher remains with the group, he or she acts mainly as a mediator, modeler, and coach, providing what Vygotsky called *scaffolding*. The teacher is promoting self-regulated learning by gradually shifting the responsibility for teaching to the students and remaining ever present to help them monitor their own thinking and strategy use.

LEARNING ENVIRONMENT AND MANAGEMENT TASKS

As with any teaching activity, the effective use of learning strategies necessitates creating and managing a learning environment that will facilitate the goals of strategy instruction, namely producing self-regulated learners. This requires creating a physical environment that is rich in sensory stimuli and a social environment in which the importance of learning how to learn is communicated clearly and forcefully to students. Teachers need to teach important learning strategies explicitly to their students and to help students become effective in their use. Finally, students must be held accountable for mastery and use of learning strategies just as they are for learning other important knowledge and skills.

Creating Rich Learning Environments

A rich learning environment that communicates the importance of learning helps to attune students to become self-regulated learners.

A rich learning environment promotes independent and self-regulated learning. Stimulating bulletin boards and displays spark curiosity and serve as motivators for independent inquiry. The physical environment should also communicate clearly to students the importance teachers attach to self-regulated learning. Effective teachers accomplish this end by displaying the results of students' work and by encouraging students to display their own work when they think they have done a good job. Creating learning centers for younger students and providing many opportunities for older students to make choices also shows that the teacher values independent, self-regulated learning. Having a rich array of materials and supplies accessible for student use is beneficial as well.

Emphasizing the Importance of Self-Regulated Learning

The physical environment highlights the importance teachers attach to self-regulated learning. So too do the teacher's words and deeds. Effective teachers constantly remind students that most lessons have two big goals: acquisition of the content or skill being taught and mastery of the cognitive and metacognitive strategies needed to complete the learning task. Teachers should communicate to students the value they place on self-regulated learning and encourage all students to become independent learners. Whenever possible, teachers should permit students to run their own classrooms, to engage in peer tutoring, and to perform other activities that require independent action.

Using Attention-Getting Devices

A persistent problem facing all teachers in many settings is how to get their students' attention. Common sense tells us that attention is important, because unless students are paying attention, little learning can occur. Attention is also important from a theoretical, learning-strategies perspective. As described previously in the chapter, information enters the learner's short-term memory through one of the senses. However, short-term memory is very limited, and many stimuli compete for an individual's attention. Therefore, it is important to get learners to pay attention to certain stimuli and to ignore others. Effective teachers use a variety of strategies to attract and maintain their students' attention.

Establishing set for a lesson, as described in Chapter 2, is one way teachers attract their students' attention. Set activities help students get their minds off other things they have been doing—changing classes in secondary schools, changing subjects in elementary schools, lunch, and recess—and begin the process of attending to the forthcoming lesson. Teachers also use other attention-getting devices as a means to help students get ready to learn. They may begin a lesson by asking questions or relating an anecdote to spark interest and to activate and retrieve relevant information from long-term memory.

Additionally, teachers think of ways to arouse students' curiosity and to stimulate all their senses, including touch, taste, and smell. Effective teachers know that having young children touch a rabbit at the beginning of a lesson on mammals or coming dressed as Abraham Lincoln before a Civil War unit are actions likely to gain most students' attention. Visual displays, demonstrations, and interesting stories are further examples of techniques that can be used to gain students' attention to get them ready to learn.

Managing Seatwork, Homework, and Assignments

Teaching students the learning strategies covered in this chapter is one way of empowering them to learn on their own. Keep in mind, though, that as with all forms of learning, the acquisition of learning strategies takes practice, in this case independent practice in the form of seatwork and homework. The amount of time students are asked to work independently is sizable. One study (Fisher et al., 1978) found that students in a sample of California classrooms worked independently as much as 70 percent of the time. Other studies summarized by Carol Weinstein and Andrew Mignano (1993) found that students spend over half of their time working independently. Furthermore, most schools have policies that require teachers to assign homework to students on a regular basis. Younger students are expected to complete approximately 15 to 30 minutes of homework each evening. Thirty to 60 minutes per class is a typical homework assignment for older students.

Since so much of a student's time is spent in independent learning activities, it is extremely important that assignments, seatwork, and homework promote the goals of self-regulated learning. Also, students should perceive their assignments as more than just tasks to get done. The following sections discuss how teachers can structure and manage these important forms of school learning.

Seatwork

When giving a seatwork assignment, a teacher must give clear instructions about what students are to do, how they are to do it, and the purpose for the assignment.

Seatwork in which students study independently in the classroom, serves various purposes for teachers. It is an instructional tool that affords students practice and application opportunities in school. It also serves a management purpose, because it is a means to keep students engaged and busy. Regardless of purpose, it is very important that seatwork be structured so students will remain engaged, experience a high degree of success, and become effective independent learners.

Fortunately, a great deal of research has been conducted on the topic of seatwork that offers a number of guidelines and recommendations. The findings of a number of studies are summarized in the guidelines that follow (Anderson, L., 1985; Emmer et al., 1994; Kounin, 1970; Rosenshine & Stevens, 1986; Weinstein & Mignano, 1993).

1. Seatwork is best suited for practice of previously taught materials or as preparation for a forthcoming lesson. It is not an effective way to learn new, untaught material.

2. For seatwork to be effective, it is important to have sufficient materials available. It is also important that these materials be appropriate for students' ability level.

3. Students need to be convinced that a seatwork assignment has real value, that it is more than just academic busywork the objective of which is to get the right answers. Teachers must clearly emphasize the reasons for making particular assignments and the importance of self-regulated learning.

4. Students need clear instructions on what they are to do and how they are to do it. The cognitive strategies associated with completing the learning task should also be made clear.

5. It is important for teachers to monitor student progress on seatwork assignments and to make sure they complete assignments correctly.

Seatwork requires students to pace themselves through assignments. They do not have the benefit of their teacher directing them and keeping them on task. Consequently, it is very easy for students to daydream, to talk to their neighbors, to pass notes, or to completely ignore the assignment.

Effective management of seatwork, just as the management of any other classroom task, necessitates clearly stated rules and routines. For example, a teacher needs to be specific about when talking is allowed and when it is not. If the teacher is using seatwork to keep students busy so he or she can work with a particular group, then it is generally best to prohibit talking among the students who are working independently. On the other hand, if students are completing an assignment in cooperative learning groups, talking is expected. Talking during seatwork is something some experienced teachers phase in over time. They may begin the year with a no-talking rule and then gradually allow talking to evolve in controlled circumstances. For some assignments, teachers will want students to work together and help one another. For others, working alone silently will be required. The important point in   king and working together is to be clear about wh   llowed and when they are not.

Homework

Most schools today ask t   mework is considered necessary because many   lieve it is an effective means to extend learning time and thereby increase academic achievement. However, the results of research on the value of homework remain somewhat mixed. When Harris Cooper (1989) reviewed the research on the effects of homework, he found the following, among other things.

◆ The effect of homework on achievement was strongest for high school students, a little less strong but still positive for junior high students, and absent for upper-elementary students.

◆ Homework related to the learning of simple tasks is more effective than that related to complex tasks. This may mean that many of the more complex learning strategies cannot be learned through homework.

◆ Homework that focused on practice of previously taught content or preparation for forthcoming lessons was more effective than homework related to new materials.

This research suggests that whereas homework may be useful for some students at some grade levels, it should not be considered a solution to the time pressures that teachers may feel during the school day. Also, homework should not be given carelessly or frivolously. If the teacher does not value it, the students will not. Here are four general guidelines for homework assignments.

Homework should be a continuation of practice or preparation for the next day, not a continuation of instruction.

1. **Teachers should give homework students can perform successfully.** Homework should not involve the continuation of instruction but rather the continuation of practice of acquired materials or preparation for the next day's lesson.

2. **Teachers should emphasize that homework is an opportunity to practice and to monitor important cognitive strategies** in addition to other goals the homework may have. Students can practice, for instance, the use of mnemonics, underlining, and note taking.

3. **Parents should be informed of the level of involvement expected of them.** Are they expected to help their children with answers to difficult questions or simply to provide a quiet atmosphere in which students can complete their homework assignments on their own? Are parents supposed to check over assignments? Do they know the approximate frequency and duration of homework assignments?

4. **Teachers must provide feedback on the homework.** Many teachers simply check to determine whether it was performed. What this says to the students is that it doesn't matter how it is done, as long as it is done. Students soon figure out that the task is to get something, anything, on paper. One method of providing feedback is to involve other students in the correcting process.

General Assignment Guidelines

Regardless of whether an assignment is to be completed as seatwork or as homework, the following four principles will help students on their way toward becoming effective independent learners.

1. Make Assignments Meaningful, Clear, and Challenging. One of the most difficult challenges facing teachers when they use seatwork or homework is keeping students engaged. When working alone, it is very easy for students to lose interest and to become off task, particularly if assignments are routine. Most educators generally agree that independent seatwork and homework assignments which sustain student engagement share particular characteristics.

The management problems associated with independent study can often be prevented if a teacher makes the assignments meaningful and challenging, has clear rules and routines, and holds students accountable for their work.

To begin with, work assigned to be completed independently should be meaningful and have clarity of purpose. Students need to know exactly what they are to do, why they are doing it, and what is required to get it done. That students stay on task during seatwork and complete homework when they perceive assignments to be meaningful and not busywork seems an obvious conclusion. Yet Linda Anderson's research (1985) showed that teachers rarely attend to the purposes of seatwork or to the learning strategies involved. Instead, they stress procedural directions. For instance, teachers may spend considerable time explaining to students where to put their name on the paper or how to arrange the answers. While directions on "what to do" are important, they do not substitute for explanations of "why" something is to be done and the learning processes involved. Before giving an assignment, teachers should consider these features carefully and then spend sufficient time explaining them to students.

2. Vary the Nature of Assignments. As with life in general, variety adds spice to seatwork and homework assignments. Students are more likely to stay engaged and to complete their work if assignments are varied and interesting rather than routine and monotonous. Effective teachers change the length and the modality of assignments as well as the nature of learning tasks and cognitive strategies involved. Silent reading, reports, special projects, and multimedia materials offer various ways to complete independent work. The list of possibilities is endless and provides few excuses for teachers to make the same type of assignment day after day.

3. Pay Attention to Level of Difficulty. Achieving the appropriate level of difficulty of assignments is an important ingredient for sustaining the engagement needed for task completion. If students are expected to work on their own, the assignment should be at a difficulty level that affords a high success rate. Jere Brophy and Tom Good (1986), for instance, report that the success rate should be nearly 100 percent. It can be slightly lower if help is available to students when they need it. At the same time, students will not remain engaged with assignments that are too easy. They perceive such assignments as unchallenging busywork. In general, a good assignment needs to be difficult enough so that most students consider it challenging, yet easy enough that most can figure out what to do and complete the assignment on their own.

4. Monitor Student Progress. Finally, it is important that teachers monitor seatwork and homework assignments. Monitoring should include checking to see if students understand their assignments and the cognitive processes involved. It should also include checking student work and returning assignments with feedback. When some students are given seatwork so the teacher can work with other students, a general recommendation is for the teacher to spend 5 or 10 minutes circulating among the seatwork students to make sure they understand the assignment before joining the others. If work with a small group is planned for an extended period of time, it is a good idea for the teacher to leave the small group periodically and circulate among the students working independently. Although correcting assignments is very time consuming, it is critical that seatwork and homework assignments be returned to students with feedback. Guidelines for feedback presented in Chapter 2 can be followed for all types of assignments.

ASSESSMENT AND EVALUATION

Assessing students' use and understanding of learning strategies can be accomplished using paper-and-pencil and performance tests.

The same guidelines and procedures described in previous chapters apply to assessing and evaluating student proficiency with particular cognitive and metacognitive strategies.

Assessing a skill component or the procedural knowledge associated with learning strategies requires using the type of performance tests described in Chapters 2 and 4. As you recall, performance tests go beyond evaluating students' abilities to recall information about a topic. They necessitate that students demonstrate how well they can actually perform a particular skill. For example, students might be asked to show that they can construct an outline or identify key ideas from a passage. Because learning strategies are cognitive rather than behavioral, constructing performance tests can be difficult. "Thinking aloud" is one form of test used to get students to display their thinking processes so that cognitive performance can be checked.

Sometimes cognitive skills can be assessed using paper-and-pencil tests. Figure 6.10 shows how students' abilities to discriminate between examples and nonexamples of elaboration can be tested.

It is important not only that students possess a repertoire of cognitive strategies but that they actually use particular strategies appropriately. Thus, the assessment of conditional knowledge is as important as that of

FIGURE 6.10

Test Item to Assess Ability to Discriminate between Elaborations and Nonelaborations
SOURCE: E. D. Gagné (1985) *The Cognitive Psychology of School Learning.* Boston: Little Brown. Reprinted by permission.

Here are two examples that show elaboration and two that don't. Read each example. In the blank at the left of each example, write E if you think the example is an elaboration. Write NE in the blank if you think the example is not an elaboration.

E = Elaboration
NE = Not an Elaboration

1. _NE_ A student reads, "Columbus discovered America in 1492." and decides she wants to remember it. She repeats in her head, "Columbus discovered America in 1492."

2. _E_ John reads, "Columbus was a Spaniard. He sailed to America in 1492." He wants to remember this information, so he thinks, "Columbus most likely sailed west to America because the shortest way to get to America from Spain is to go west."

3. _NE_ Jack reads, "Columbus discovered America in 1492. Columbus was a Spaniard." He thinks, "I wonder what's for lunch?"

4. _E_ A student hears his science teacher say, "Molecules are farther apart in gases than in liquids, so gases are lighter." The student thinks, "That is like loosely woven cloth is lighter than tightly woven cloth of the same material."

declarative and procedural knowledge. Often conditional knowledge can be assessed using paper-and-pencil test items such as the one developed by Ellen Gagné and her colleagues (1985) shown in Figure 6.11.

For each of the following goals, decide whether you should think of elaborations or not. Write E if you should think of elaborations and NE if you should not think of elaborations.

_NE_ Goal 1: Remember your answer to a math problem the teacher is asking about long enough to raise your hand and say it.

_E_ Goal 2: Remember the rule for dividing fractions so you can divide fractions when you're 30 years old!

_NE_ Goal 3: Read a space odyssey book for fun. Don't care to remember it.

_E_ Goal 4: Understand the main ideas about how a computer works. Don't know whether you want to remember them or not.

_E_ Goal 5: Remember some information about early humans so you can use that information in a high school history class.

FIGURE 6.11

Test Item to Assess Conditional Knowledge of When One Does and Does Not Want to Use Elaboration to Remember Something
SOURCE: E. D. Gagné (1985) *The Cognitive Psychology of School Learning.* Boston: Little Brown. Reprinted by permission.

REFLECTION BOX   REFLECTION ON LEARNING STRATEGIES

Chapter 6 explored various strategies aimed at helping students study and learn on their own. It offered procedures for teaching learning strategies to students and for motivating them to become independent, self-regulated learners. However, teaching and using learning strategies are not widely practiced at this time and these concepts are not without their critics, as the following discussion indicates.

On the one hand, it is reasonable to argue that if we expect students to remember large quantities of information, to solve problems, and to take responsibility for their own learning, then they must be provided with the tools and strategies for accomplishing these goals. On the other hand, time used to teach learning strategies is time taken away from teaching other things, and time is a very scarce commodity in education. For instance, declarative and procedural knowledge of basic subjects represent an important part of any person's education. Adults in our society are expected to be literate in language and mathematics. They are expected to have command of substantial knowledge about their physical and natural worlds as well as to possess critical citizenship skills. They are presumed to be more widely educated and to be able to lead a more rewarding life if they have keen appreciations of the visual and performing arts. A question that must be

SUMMARY

- Good teaching includes teaching students how to learn on their own, that is, how to remember, how to think, how to motivate themselves, how to be self-regulated learners.

- Learning and cognitive strategies are meant to help students learn on their own. Learning strategies are the mental processes and tactics used by students to facilitate learning, including memory and metacognitive strategies.

- Learning and cognitive strategies refer to the same thing, namely the mental plans and tactics students use to accomplish learning.

- The major purpose of strategy instruction is to produce self-regulated learners defined as individuals who can: (1) accurately diagnose a particular learning situation, (2) select a learning strategy to attack the learning problem posed, (3) monitor the effectiveness of the strategy, and (4) be sufficiently motivated to engage in the learning situation until it is accomplished.

- The theoretical support for study and learning strategies stems mainly from cognitive theories of learning and information processing. These theories emphasize the importance of prior knowledge in learning and divide such knowledge into three categories: declarative, procedural, and conditional.

asked is whether or not possession of advanced cognitive and metacognitive strategies automatically leads to the acquisition of subject matter knowledge.

Similarly, some critics believe that the use of learning strategies and cognitive approaches may not work well for lower-ability and/or unmotivated students and that other approaches are preferable. For instance, many of the strategies described in this chapter assume that students have some degree of background knowledge. How will teachers approach students who do not have sufficient prior knowledge?

Common sense suggests the adoption of some type of middle ground in which *some* of a teacher's instructional energy goes into direct and nondirected instruction of learning strategies. At the same time the teacher must keep in mind the high value our society holds for subject matter knowledge and skills and the need to tailor instruction for particular students. Common sense also suggests that unless a student knows how to learn, any kind of teaching is lost.

What do you think about this issue? If you had your own classroom today, how would you deal with teaching students learning and study strategies? If you spent considerable time teaching learning strategies, how would you defend your actions?

◆ Declarative knowledge is knowledge about something (say, facts, concepts, and generalizations about public speaking), whereas procedural knowledge is knowledge about how to do something (say, actually making a speech). Conditional knowledge is knowing when and why to use particular declarative and procedural knowledge.

◆ Information processing perspectives rely on the computer as the metaphor for how the mind works and to illustrate how information is encoded, stored, and retrieved for later use.

◆ The memory system consists of two main parts: short-term memory, where conscious mental work occurs, and long-term memory, where knowledge is organized and stored.

◆ Knowledge is organized and stored in long-term memory in the form of propositions, productions, and knowledge networks. These act as filters for new information and thus determine how well new information can be learned.

◆ Propositions are units of declarative knowledge; productions are the basic units of procedural knowledge. *Schema* refers to the overall network of knowledge structures that constitutes one's long-term memory.

◆ Because the environment consists of many stimuli and because short-term memory is limited, getting students to attend to particular knowledge is important if lessons are to be successful. A variety of attention-getting devices exist for this purpose.

◆ Advance organizers are one pedagogical device used to activate schemata in long-term memory that are related to new information to be learned.

◆ Learning strategies can be divided into four categories: rehearsal strategies, elaboration strategies, organization strategies, and metacognitive strategies.

◆ Rote rehearsal strategies consist of verbally repeating information (phone numbers) over and over so that it can be kept in short-term memory long enough to act on it. Complex rehearsal strategies consist of adding something meaningful to the verbal rehearsal, such as relating it to one's birth date. By adding something meaningful to the information being rehearsed, complex rehearsal is more likely to encode information into long-term memory. Examples of the latter include underlining and marginal note taking.

◆ Elaboration strategies assist with the process of developing meaning out of new information by adding detail and finding connections. Common elaboration strategies include analogies, matrix note taking, and PQ4R.

◆ Organization strategies increase the meaningfulness of new learning materials by imposing new organizational structures on simple and complex ideas. Common organization strategies consist of mnemonics, outlining, and mapping.

◆ Metacognitive strategies refer to learners' thinking about their own thinking and their abilities to monitor cognitive processes. Metacognitive strategies include both knowledge about cognition and the ability to monitor, control, and evaluate one's own cognitive functioning.

◆ If students are to be successful in school, it is imperative that learning strategies be taught explicitly. The two primary ways of doing this are with direct instruction and reciprocal teaching.

◆ A large portion (as much as 50 percent) of a student's time in school is spent studying independently, and most schools have policies requiring teachers to assign homework on a regular basis. Independent study performed in the classroom is called seatwork whereas study performed in study halls or at home is called homework.

◆ Guidelines exist to help teachers make independent seatwork and homework effective. In general, seatwork is more effective if it allows practice of previously presented material as compared to learning new materials.

◆ The effects of using homework are mixed. Homework has been found to be more effective with older students and less so with younger students. As with seatwork, homework is most effective when it is used as an extension of practice rather than as a form of instruction. Students should be given only homework that they can perform successfully, and homework should be promptly corrected and returned to students with feedback.

◆ Important principles to follow for all types of assignments include making assignments clear and meaningful, varying assignments, paying careful attention to the difficulty level of an assignment, and monitoring student work.

◆ Assessment of study and learning strategies should consist of checking for student possession of declarative, procedural, and conditional knowledge. Declarative knowledge and conditional knowledge can often be assessed using paper-and-pencil tests, whereas procedural knowledge is best assessed using performance tests of some kind.

L E A R N I N G A I D 6 . 1

OBSERVING THE TEACHING OF LEARNING STRATEGIES

PURPOSE: Research suggests that many teachers rarely spend much time teaching students how to learn. This aid allows you to conduct your own investigation of how much teachers teach learning strategies.

DIRECTIONS: Shadow one teacher for at least half a day (two teachers would be better). Make a tick (√) whenever you observe one of the activities listed below. Also, in the space provided, estimate the amount of time the teacher spends on that activity, and jot down any other observations you make about the activity.

Learning Strategy	Observed	Time	Comment
Teaching students how to use the following or using the following in instruction			
Underlining	_____	____	_____
Marginal notes	_____	____	_____
Note taking	_____	____	_____
Chunking	_____	____	_____
Acronyms	_____	____	_____
Link-word method	_____	____	_____
PQ4R	_____	____	_____
Outlining	_____	____	_____
Mapping	_____	____	_____
Metacognitive	_____	____	_____

L   E   A   R   N   I   N   G   A   I   D   6 . 2

CONCEPTUAL MAPPING EXERCISE

PURPOSE: Conceptual mapping can be useful in your own teaching as well as a tool to help your students understand complex materials. This aid was developed to help you understand mapping by constructing one of your own on a topic of your choice.

DIRECTIONS: Choose a topic such as the Civil War or a concept such as protoplasm, and construct a conceptual map for the topic or concept. You may wish to use the following steps:

Step 1: Write the topic or concept word(s) in a circle in the center of the space at the bottom of this page.

Step 2: Think of all the subtopics and attributes and their relationship to the main topic and to each other. Write these words in circles or boxes.

Step 3: Draw strands branching out from the core connecting the major subtopics and critical attributes.

Step 4: Draw lines tying the various strands together to show relationships among them.

Below is my map for the topic or concept _____

DEVELOPING A LEARNING STRATEGIES LESSON

PURPOSE: This exercise gives you an opportunity to plan, teach, and critique a learning strategies lesson and add the products of your work to your portfolio.

DIRECTIONS: Use the following sequence to plan, teach, and critique your learning strategies lesson.

1. Using the lesson plan format recommended for a direct instruction lesson in Chapter 2, *plan* a 3-day 45-minutes-per-day lesson on one of the learning strategies described in Chapter 6. Refer back to the examples provided in the chapter for ideas. Make sure you devise a means of measuring student proficiency of the strategy.

2. *Teach* your lesson to a group of students. This could be a whole class, a small group, or just one or two students. If possible, get one of your classmates to videotape your lesson from beginning to end.

3. At the end of the lesson, ask the student(s) what they thought about the lesson. Do they think the learning strategy you taught them will be useful in future study and learning? Why? Why not?

4. Using the videotape and the student comments, write a one- or two-page critique of your lesson. How well did it work for you? What were the lesson's strengths? Weaknesses? How would you revise the lesson the next time you use it?

5. Place the following in your portfolio under the topic "Use of Learning Strategies."

   ◆ A brief discussion of your views of the importance of learning strategies
   ◆ Your lesson plan
   ◆ Visuals of you (video or still) teaching the lesson
   ◆ Examples of student work showing their proficiency
   ◆ Your critique

BOOKS FOR THE PROFESSIONAL

Gagné, E. D., Yekovich, C. W., & Yekovich, R. R. (1993). *The cognitive psychology of school learning* (2d ed.). New York: HarperCollins. This book discusses recent development in cognitive psychology as applied to school learning. It contains excellent discussion on cognition and learning and on student learning strategies.

Mastropiere, M. A., & Scruggs, T. E. (1991). *Teaching students ways to remember: Strategies for learning mnemonically.* Cambridge, Mass.: Brookline. This book contains a very good discussion of mnemonics and how teachers can teach and use them with students.

McWhorter, K. T. (1992). *Study and thinking skills in college.* New York: HarperCollins. Although designed for college students, many of the skills described are applicable for younger students.

Pressley, M. et al. (1991). *Cognitive instruction that really improves children's academic performance.* Cambridge, Mass.: Brookline. This book is filled with excellent examples of learning strategies and how to teach them to students.

GLOSSARY

academic learning time The amount of time a student spends engaged in a particular subject or learning task at which he or she is successful.

acronym A mnemonic that uses the first letter of familiar words to remember lists of names or other information.

action zone The section of the classroom (normally the front rows and center columns) where students tend to be called on most often and where most verbal interaction occurs.

active teaching Another term for *direct instruction.*

activity structure Patterns of behavior that characterize what teachers do as they teach and what students do as they engage in learning tasks; can be viewed as the basic unit of planning.

advance organizer A statement made by teachers before a presentation or before having students read textual materials that provides a structure for new information to be linked to prior knowledge.

analogy An elaboration learning strategy that makes comparisons and shows the similarities between like features of things or ideas that otherwise are different.

anchored instruction Another term for *problem-based instruction.*

anticipatory set A technique used by teachers at the beginning of a lesson to prepare students to learn and to establish a link between their prior knowledge and the new information to be presented. Same as *set induction* and *establishing set.*

art of teaching Aspects of teaching in which complex decisions are based on a teacher's experience and tacit knowledge instead of on research and scientific evidence.

artifacts The products produced by students in problem-based instruction, such as reports, videos, computer programs.

assessment The process of collecting a full range of information about students and classrooms for the purpose of making instructional decisions.

attended time The amount of time students actually attend school.

attribute A quality or characteristic of a person or thing.

authentic assessment Assessment procedures that have students demonstrate their abilities to perform particular tasks in real life situations.

authentic human relationship A relationship that is genuine or real and likely to build trust between individuals.

authentic investigation An investigation done by students that seeks real solutions to real problems.

authentic learning Another term for *problem-based instruction.*

autonomous learners Students who are motivated to take responsibility for their own learning and who have the skills and strategies to learn independently.

available time The amount of time actually available for academic activity.

behavior modeling theory A theory to describe how people learn as a result of observing and memorizing the behavior of others.

behavioral objective A model for writing an instructional objective that emphasizes precision and careful delineation of expected student behaviors, the testing situation, and performance criteria.

best practice Teaching practice that has been shown by research to be the most effective for sustaining student engagement and/or for enhancing achievement.

checking for understanding A technique used by teachers to see if students have grasped new information or skills that have been presented.

circle seating pattern A seating arrangement used in discussion that places teacher and students in a circle; maximizes free interchange among participants.

classroom discussion Another term for *discussion.*

284

classroom management The ways teachers organize and structure their classrooms for the purpose of maximizing student cooperation and engagement and minimizing disruptive behavior.

classroom properties Distinctive features of classrooms that shape behavior of participants, such as multidimensionality, simultaneity, immediacy, unpredictability, publicness, and history.

cognitive-constructivist perspective A view of learning which posits that learning occurs when learners are actively involved in the process of acquiring and constructing their own knowledge.

cognitive monitoring Learners' abilities to select, use, and monitor appropriate learning strategies.

cognitive processes The thinking processes engaged in by teachers and students.

cognitive psychology A view of human behavior that focuses on learning as an active mental process of acquiring and retaining knowledge.

cognitive strategy A learning and thinking strategy associated with receiving, storing, and retrieving information; used by students to be more proficient and self-regulated in their learning.

competitive goal structure A learning environment in which students perceive they can obtain their goal if, and only if, the other students with whom they work fail to obtain their goals.

complex rehearsal strategy A learning strategy, such as note taking and using analogies used to encode complex information.

conceptual mapping (webbing) A technique of visually organizing and diagramming a set of ideas or concepts in a logical pattern so relationships can be readily observed.

conditional knowledge Knowledge about when it is most appropriate to use particular declarative or procedural knowledge.

constructivism A perspective of teaching and learning in which a learner constructs meaning from experience and interaction with others, and the teacher's role is to provide meaningful experiences for students.

cooperative goal structure A learning environment in which students perceive they can obtain their goal if, and only if, the other students with whom they work can obtain their goals.

cooperative learning An approach to teaching in which students work in mixed-ability groups and are partially rewarded by group effort and success, not on individual accomplishment alone.

cooperative reward structure A learning environment in which students are interdependent for a reward they will share if they are successful as a group.

corrective feedback Information given to students about how well they are doing.

dangle A classroom occurrence in which a teacher starts an activity and then leaves it unfinished because of either an interruption or beginning a new activity.

declarative knowledge Knowledge about something or that something is the case; knowledge of facts, concepts, and principles.

desist behavior A teaching behavior aimed at stopping disruptive student behavior.

desist incident A disruptive classroom incident serious enough that if not dealt with will lead to widening management problems.

diagnostic testing A test used by teachers to determine students' prior knowledge and level of skill development; information used to assist in planning.

dignifying errors A technique used by teachers when responding to student answers which are wrong.

direct instruction An approach to teaching basic skills and straightforward declarative knowledge in which lessons are highly teacher directed and learning environments are tightly structured.

discourse A term used to describe the larger pattern of verbal exchange and communication that occurs in classrooms.

discovery learning An approach to teaching that encourages students to learn concepts and principles through their own explorations and to solve problems on their own.

discrepant event A puzzling situation that sparks curiosity and motivates inquiry into cause-and-effect relationships; used by teachers to engage students.

discussion A teaching method that relies on verbal exchange of ideas among the students and the teacher.

distributed practice Practice assigned to students to be done for brief periods spread over several sessions or periods of time.

distributing participation The process of equalizing verbal exchange and participation.

downtime Times in classrooms when lessons are completed early or when students are waiting for upcoming events, such as moving to another class or going home.

ecological system A view of classrooms in which inhabitants (teachers, students, and others) interact within a highly interdependent environment.

elaboration strategy A learning strategy that assists encoding by adding detail to new information so it becomes meaningful.

encoding The process of transferring new information from short-term to long-term memory.

engaged time The amount of time students actually spend on a particular subject or learning activity; also called *time-on-task*.

engagement The time students spend actively learning academic materials.

establishing set Another term for *anticipatory set* or *set induction*.

evaluation The process of making a judgment, assigning value, or deciding on the worth of a particular program, approach, or student's work.

exhibit A situation and venue in which students present artifacts *(products)* of their work from a problem-based lesson.

expectancy effect A situation in which teachers expect certain students to do well and others to do poorly, regardless of students' actual performance.

experienced-based education Another term for *problem-based instruction*.

explicit instruction Another term for *direct instruction*.

extending student thinking A process used by teachers following a presentation to help students strengthen their understanding of new material and expand their cognitive structures.

feedback Information given to students about their performance; same as *knowledge of results*.

flip-flop A situation in which a teacher starts an activity, stops it and starts another one, and finally returns to the original activity.

formative evaluation Evaluation that occurs before or during instruction; used to assist with planning or making adaptations.

fragmentation A situation in which a teacher breaks a learning activity into overly small units.

goal structures The way goals specify the degree of interdependence sought among students; the three different types are individualistic, competitive, and cooperative.

graphic organizers Visual images presented to students to provide structures for new information about to be presented; similar to an *advance organizer.*

group investigation An approach to cooperative learning in which students help define topics for study and work together to complete their investigations; similar to *problem-based instruction.*

guided practice Practice assigned to students to be completed under the guidance or watchful eye of the teacher.

high talker tap out An activity to teach students how to take turns and share participation.

higher-order thinking Thinking that goes beyond simple recall of facts and considers cause-and-effect relationships and nuanced judgments about complex situations.

independent learner Another term for *self-regulated learner.*

independent practice An assignment given to students to accomplish on their own without the teacher's guidance to practice newly presented material.

independent task A learning task that students complete alone.

individualistic goal structure A goal structure in which achievement of a goal by one student is unrelated to the achievement of the goal by other students.

inductive reasoning The process of determining general rules or principles based on information from specific examples or data.

inductive teaching An approach to teaching in which the emphasis is on helping students to inquire on their own and to develop such skills as asking questions and drawing conclusions from data.

information processing The process used by the mind to take in, store, and retrieve information for use.

inquiry process A thinking process or methods associated with inquiry in sciences or social sciences.

inquiry training Another term for *inductive teaching*.

instructional functions of teaching Those aspects of teachers' work in which they are providing face-to-face instruction to students.

instructional goals The learning goals or intents a particular teaching model has been designed to achieve.

instructional intents Same as *instructional goals*.

instructional objective A statement which describes the teacher's instructional intents or what they expect students to learn as a result of instruction.

intellectual processes Abstract thinking processes such as induction, deduction, and reasoning.

interaction patterns The overall design and nature of verbal interaction in classroom settings.

interactive functions of teaching Same as instructional functions; those aspects of teachers' work where they are providing face-to-face instruction to students in classrooms.

interactive planning Teacher planning and decision making that occurs "in-flight" or during a particular lesson.

interdependent task A learning task which students complete by working with others.

jigsaw An approach to cooperative learning where students work in mixed-ability groups and each student is responsible for a portion of the material.

knowledge acquisition The process in which students acquire and assimilate new information and knowledge.

knowledge base Information that informs teaching practices that has accumulated over time from research and from the wisdom of experienced teachers.

knowledge networks How information and related concepts are organized and linked together in the memory system.

knowledge of results Feedback given to students about their performance.

knowledge representation The way information is organized and stored in the memory system.

leadership functions of teaching The leadership aspects of teachers' work, such as planning, providing motivation, coordinating and controlling learning environments, and assessing student progress.

learning activities The learning and social tasks students are required to carry out including those associated with the ways they are organized for instruction.

learning environment The overall climate and structures of the classroom that influence how students respond to and remain engaged in learning tasks; the context in which teaching and learning acts are carried out.

learning strategies Techniques and processes used by students to receive and store information to help them become autonomous, self-regulated learners.

level of actual development A concept attributed to Lev Vygotsky that identifies a learner's level of current intellectual functioning.

level of potential development A concept attributed to Lev Vygotsky that identifies the level at which a learner could function intellectually with the assistance of a teacher or more advanced peer.

link-word method A mnemonic which creates a mental image that links a familiar word with a word that is unknown; used mainly in foreign language instruction.

long-term memory The place in the mind where information is stored, ready for retrieval when needed.

management demands Demands made on a teacher's management system by various instructional approaches and particular learning tasks.

management system The overall structure a teacher uses to organize and manage instruction so students remain engaged in learning tasks.

massed practice Practice assigned to students to be done during a single extended period of time.

mastery teaching Another term for *direct instruction*.

matrix note taking An elaboration learning strategy and way of taking notes that places information in a matrix; facilitates encoding and making comparisons of complex information.

meta-analysis A research methodology for reviewing a number of experimental studies and synthesizing the results.

metacognition The process of knowing about and monitoring one's own thinking or cognitive processes.

metacognitive strategy Strategies used for recognizing one's cognitive processes and ways of thinking about how information is being processed.

mnemonic A learning strategy to assist memory by forming associations between new materials and patterns that are familiar or already exist.

momentum The force and pace of a lesson.

numbered heads A technique of assigning numbers to involve all students in the review of learning materials.

observational learning Another term for *behavioral modeling.*

observational study A research procedure in which the researcher watches and records behaviors of teachers and students.

opportunity to learn Another term for *allocated learning time.*

organization strategy A learning strategy that help increase the meaningfulness of new materials by imposing new organizational structures on the materials.

overdwelling A situation in which a teacher goes on and on after a subject or a set of instructions is clear to students.

overlappingness The ability of teachers to spot disruptive behavior and deal with it without interrupting the flow of the lesson.

overlearning Working or practicing a task or skill until it is learned completely and can be performed automatically.

pacing The momentum and flow of a lesson or instructional activity.

performance assessment Assessment procedures that have students demonstrate their abilities to perform particular tasks in testing situations.

planned academic time The amount of time teachers set aside for different subjects and academic activities.

planning cycle The span of time considered for various aspects of planning: daily, weekly, unit, term, and yearly.

postinstructional planning Teacher planning in which decisions are made about how to provide feedback to students and how to assess and evaluate student learning.

PQ4R method A strategy used to help learners remember what they have read; the letters stand for *preview, question, read, reflect, recite,* and *review.*

preinstructional planning Teacher planning conducted before instruction during which goals, content, and approaches are decided.

preventive management Actions taken by teachers, such as planning, allocating time and space, and building positive learning environments to gain student cooperation and to prevent disruptive behavior.

prior knowledge Information and knowledge held by students before they receive instruction on a topic.

problem-based instruction An approach to instruction in which students work on authentic problems for the purpose of constructing their own knowledge, developing inquiry and higher-level thinking skills, and becoming autonomous, self-regulated learners.

problem solving Finding ways to apply new solutions to complex problem situations rather than relying on fixed rules or recipes.

procedural knowledge Knowledge about how to do something; can pertain to specific behavioral skills or to complex cognitive strategies.

procedures Systems established by teachers for dealing with routine tasks and for coordinating student talk and movement.

process-product research An approach to educational research characterized by studying relationships between teacher behaviors *(process)* and student achievement *(product).*

productions The way basic units of procedural knowledge are organized and linked in the memory system.

propositions The way basic units of declarative knowledge are organized and linked in the memory system.

reciprocal teaching An approach to teaching in which students and teachers take turns leading discussions about reading materials and practicing four cognitive strategies: summarization, question asking, clarification, and prediction.

recitation An approach to teaching characterized by a teacher's asking questions of the whole class, getting an individual student to respond, and providing feedback by praising or correcting.

reflection Careful and analytical thought by teachers about what they are doing and the effects of their behavior on their instruction and on student learning.

rehearsal strategy A learning strategy that assists the encoding process by connecting new information with prior knowledge.

reliability The degree to which a test produces consistent results over several administrations.

repertoire of teaching practices The number of teaching approaches and strategies teachers are able to employ for the purpose of helping students learn.

reward structures The ways rewards can be distributed within a classroom; the three types are individualistic, competitive, and cooperative.

rote rehearsal strategies Strategies that help learners remember simple information by repeating aloud or to oneself information to be remembered.

row-and-column formation A classroom arrangement in which desks are organized in straight rows and columns, used effectively when a teacher is presenting or demonstrating and when student exchange is not required.

rules for behavior Statements that specify expected classroom behaviors and define behaviors that are forbidden.

scaffolding The process in which a learner is helped by a teacher or more accomplished person to master a particular problem beyond his or her current developmental level.

schema An individual's knowledge structure or the way information has been organized and stored in memory;

schemata The plural form of *schema.*

scientific inquiry The process used by scientists and by many educational researchers to produce new knowledge.

seatwork Independent work done by students at their desks, such as reading, answering questions, and completing work sheets.

self-regulated learner A learner who can diagnose a learning situation, select an appropriate learning strategy, monitor the effectiveness of the strategy, and remain engaged in the learning task until it is accomplished.

set induction A technique used by teachers at the beginning of a lesson to prepare students to learn and to establish a communicative link between the learner's prior knowledge and the new information to be presented; same as *anticipatory set* and *establishing set.*

short-term memory The place in the mind where conscious mental work is done; also called *working memory.*

smoothness A teacher's ability to keep the flow of a lesson going smoothly and without interruptions.

social interaction The interaction and exchange among individuals; Lev Vygotsky believed that interaction and exchange spurred learning and intellectual development.

social learning theory The perspective that learning occurs observationally from modeling done by others.

Socratic method An approach to teaching in which teachers help students think and inquire by asking questions that require inductive reasoning.

strategic learner A learner who is proficient in the use of learning strategies; another term for *self-regulated learner.*

structural approach An approach to cooperative learning in which a teacher employs certain techniques designed to make student interaction patterns more cooperative and broadly shared.

structures of knowledge The way particular subject matters or disciplines are organized; the major concepts, ideas, and relationships that define a particular field.

student accountability Holding students responsible for their learning and for their behavior.

student cooperation A situation in which students are cooperating with the teacher and with other students on particular learning tasks.

student teams achievement divisions (STAD) An approach to cooperative learning in which students work in mixed-ability groups and rewards are administered and recognized for both individual and group effort.

study skills The skills possessed by students, such as note taking and underlining, that make them more proficient learners.

summative evaluation Evaluation done after instruction and used to make judgments about program effectiveness or the worth of students' work.

syntax The overall flow, sequence, or major steps of a particular lesson.

task structures The way lessons are arranged and the learning demands they place on students.

taxonomy   A classification system or device that helps identify and show relationships among objects and ideas.

taxonomy of educational objectives   A system developed by Benjamin Bloom for classifying objectives into three domains: cognitive, affective, and psychomotor; also can be used to classify the types of questions teachers ask.

teaching model   A term use by Bruce Joyce to describe an overall approach or plan for instruction; the attributes of teaching models are: a coherent theoretical framework, an orientation toward what students should learn, and specific teaching procedures and structures.

think-pair-share   A technique used by teachers to slow down the pattern of discourse and to increase student participation.

time-on-task   Another term for *engaged time.*

time tokens   An activity specifying permitted talking time that teaches students how to take turns and share participation.

U-shape seating pattern   An arrangement used for discussions in which students' chairs form a U and the teacher is seated in the front at the open end of the U.

validity   The degree to which a test measures what it claims to measure.

wait-time   The time a teacher waits for a student to respond to a question (wait-time 1) and the time a teacher waits before responding back (wait-time 2).

web   Another term for *conceptual web.*

wisdom of practice   Personal knowledge accrued by teachers as a result of their experiences and reflections on their work.

with-itness   The ability of teachers to spot disruptive student behavior quickly and accurately.

work involvement   The time and degree to which students are engaged in their academic work.

working memory   The place in the mind where conscious mental work is done; same as *short-term memory.*

zone of proximal development   A concept attributed to Lev Vygotsky that represents the area between a learner's level of actual development and his or her level of potential development.

REFERENCES

Adams, R. S., & Biddle, B. J. (1970). *Realities of teaching: Exploration with video-tape.* New York: Holt, Rinehart & Winston.

Airasian, P. W. (1996). *Assessment in the classroom.* New York: McGraw-Hill.

Albanese, M. A. & Mitchell, S. A. (1993). "Problem-based learning: A review of literature on its outcomes and implementation issues. *Academic Medicine.* 68, 52–81.

Allport, F. (1924). *Social psychology.* Boston: Houghton Mifflin.

Allport, G. (1954). *The nature of prejudice.* Cambridge, Mass.: Addison-Wesley.

Anderson, J. R. (1985). *Cognitive psychology and its implications.* New York: Freeman.

Anderson, L. M. (1985). What are students doing when they do all that seatwork? In C. Fisher & D. Berliner (eds.), *Perspectives on instructional time.* New York: Longman.

Anderson, L., Evertson, C., & Brophy, J. (1979). An experimental study of effective teaching in first-grade reading groups. *Elementary School Journal, 79,* 193–223.

Arends, R. I. (1994). *Learning to teach* (3d ed.). New York: McGraw-Hill.

Aronson, E., Blaney, S. C., Sikes, J., & Snapp, M. (1978). *The jigsaw classroom.* Beverly Hills, Calif.: Sage Publications.

Atkinson, R. C. (1975). Mnemotechnics in second-language learning. *American Psychologist, 30,* 821–828.

Ausubel, D. P. (1960). The use of advance organizers in the learning and retention of meaningful verbal material. *Journal of Educational Psychology, 51,* 267–272.

Bandura, A. (1977). *Social learning theory.* Englewood Cliffs, N.J.: Prentice-Hall.

Barzun, J. (1991). *Begin here: The forgotten conditions of teaching and learning.* Chicago: University of Chicago Press.

Bloom, B. S. (ed.). *Taxonomy of educational objectives. Handbook 1: Cognitive domain.* New York: David McKay.

Bloom, B. S., Hastings, T. J., & Madaus, G. F. (1971). *Handbook on formative and summative evaluation of student learning.* New York: McGraw-Hill.

Bredderman, T. (1983). Effects of activity-based elementary science on student outcomes: A quantitative synthesis. *Review of Educational Research, 53,* 499–518.

Brooks, J. G., & Brooks, M. G. (1993). *In search of understanding: The case for constructivist classrooms.* Alexandria, Va.: Association for Supervision and Curriculum Development.

Brophy, J. E., & Evertson, C. (1974). *Process-product correlations in the Texas Teacher Effectiveness Study: Final report.* Austin, Tex.: University of Texas R & D Center for Teacher Education.

Brophy, J. E., & Good, T. L. (1986). Teacher behavior and student achievement. In M. C. Wittrock (ed.), *Handbook of research on teaching* (3d ed.). New York: Macmillan.

Brown, A., & Palincsar, A. (1985). *Reciprocal teaching of comprehension strategies.* Technical Report no. 334. Champaign-Urbana, Ill.: University of Illinois.

Bruner, J. S. (1960). *The process of education.* Cambridge, Mass.: Harvard University Press.

Bruner, J. S. (1962). *On knowing: Essays for the left hand.* Cambridge, Mass.: Harvard University Press.

Bruner, J. S. (1966). *Toward a theory of instruction.* New York: Norton.

Cazden, C. B. (1986). Classroom discourse. In M. C. Wittrock (ed.), *Handbook of research on teaching* (3d ed.). New York: Macmillan.

Cazden, C. B., & Mehan, H. (1989). Principles from sociology and anthropology: Context, code, classroom, and culture. In M. C. Reynolds (ed.), *Knowledge base for the beginning teacher.* New York: Pergamon Press.

Cognition and Technology Group at Vanderbilt. (1990). *Anchored instruction.* Unpublished paper. Nashville, Tenn.: Vanderbilt University.

Coleman, J. (1961). *The adolescent society.* New York: Free Press.

Collins, A. (1977). Processes in acquiring knowledge. In R. C. Anderson, R. J. Spiro, & W. E. Montague (eds.), *Schooling and the acquisition of knowledge.* Hillsdale, N.J.: Erlbaum.

Cooper, H. (1989). *Homework.* New York: Longman.

Cooper, J. D. (1993). *Literacy: Helping children construct meaning* (2d ed.). Boston: Houghton Mifflin.

Costa, A. L. (1985). *Developing minds: A resource book for teaching thinking.* Alexandria, Va.: Association for Supervision and Curriculum Development.

Cruickshank, D. R., Bainer, D., & Metcalf, K. (1995). *The act of teaching.* New York: McGraw-Hill.

Cuban, L. (1982). Persistent instruction: The high school classroom, 1900–1980. *Phi Delta Kappan, 64,* 113–118.

Cuban, L. (1984). *How teachers taught.* New York: Longman.

Cypher, T., & Willower, D. J. (1984). The work behavior of secondary school teachers. *Journal of Research and Development, 18,* 17–24.

Dashiell, F. F. (1935). Experimental studies of the influence of social situations on the behavior of individual adults. In C. Murchison (ed.), *A handbook of social psychology.* Worcester, Mass.: Clark University Press.

Dewey, J. (1916). *Democracy and education.* New York: Macmillan.

Dewey, J. (1933). *How we think* (rev. ed.). Boston: D.C. Heath.

Doctorow, M., Wittrock, M. C., & Marks, C. (1978). Generative processes in reading comprehension. *Journal of Educational Psychology, 70,* 109–118.

Doyle, W. (1979). Classroom tasks and students' abilities. In P. L. Peterson & H. J. Walberg (eds.), *Research on teaching; Concepts, findings and implications.* Berkeley, Calif.: McCutchan.

Doyle, W. (1986). Classroom organization and management. In M. C. Wittrock (ed.), *Handbook of research on teaching* (3d ed.). New York: Macmillan.

Doyle, W., & Carter, K. (1984). Academic tasks in classrooms. *Curriculum Inquiry, 14,* 129–149.

Duckworth, E. (1964). Piaget rediscovered. In R. E. Ripple & V. N. Rockcastle (eds.), *Piaget rediscovered: A report of the Conference on Cognitive Skills and Curriculum Development.* Ithaca, N.Y.: Cornell University.

Duckworth, E. (1987). *The having of wonderful ideas and other essays on teaching and learning.* New York: Teachers College Press.

Duckworth, E. (1991). Twenty-four, forty-two, and I love you: Keeping it complex. In K. Jervis & C. Montag (eds.), *Progressive education for the 1990s: Transforming practice.* New York: Teachers College Press.

Duffy, G. G., & Roehler, L. R. (1987). Improving reading instruction through the use of responsive elaboration. *Reading Teacher, 40,* 514–520.

Dunkin, M. J., & Biddle B. J. (1974). *The study of teaching.* New York: Holt, Rinehart & Winston.

Edwards, D., & Mercer, N. (1987). *Common knowledge: The development of understanding in the classroom.* London: Methuen.

Emmer, E. T., Evertson, C., & Anderson, L. M. (1980). Effective classroom management at the beginning of the school year. *Elementary School Journal, 80,* 219–231.

Emmer, E., Evertson, C., Clements, B., & Worsham, W. E. (1989). *Classroom management for secondary teachers* (2d ed.). Englewood Cliffs, N.J.: Prentice-Hall.

Emmer, E., Evertson, C., Clements, B., & Worsham, W. E. (1994). *Classroom management for secondary teachers* (3d ed.). Englewood Cliffs, N.J.: Prentice-Hall.

Evertson, E. T., & Emmer, E. (1982). Preventive classroom management. In D. Duke (ed.), *Helping teachers manage classrooms.* Alexandria, Va.: Association for Supervision and Curriculum Development.

Evertson, E. T., Emmer, E., Clements, B. S., & Worsham, W. E. (1989). *Classroom management for elementary teachers* (2d ed.). Englewood Cliffs, N.J.: Prentice-Hall.

Evertson, E. T., Emmer, E., Clements, B. S., & Worsham, W. E. (1994). *Classroom management for elementary teachers* (3d ed.). Englewood Cliffs, N.J.: Prentice-Hall.

Evertson, E. T., Emmer, E., Sanford, J., & Clements, B. S. (1983). Improving classroom management: An experiment in elementary classrooms. *Elementary School Journal, 84,* 173–188.

Fenstermacher, G. D. (1986). Philosophy of research on teaching: Three aspects. In M. C. Wittrock (ed.), *Handbook of research on teaching* (3d ed.). New York: Macmillan.

Fenton, E. (1967). *The new social studies.* New York: Holt, Rinehart & Winston.

Fisher, C., Filby, N., Marliave, R., Cahen L., Dishaw, M., Moore, J., & Berliner, D. (1978). *Teaching behavior, academic learning time and student achievement: Final report of phase III–B, beginning teacher evaluation study.* San Francisco: Far West Laboratory.

Flanders, N. A. (1970). *Analyzing teaching behavior.* Reading, Mass.: Addison-Wesley.

Flavel, J. H. (1985). *Cognitive development* (2d ed.). Englewood Cliffs, N.J.: Prentice-Hall.

Fleener, A. (1989). Sample lesson plan format. Unpublished manuscript. Minneapolis, Minn.: Augsburg College.

Floyd, W. D. (1960). *An analysis of the oral questioning activity in selected Colorado primary classrooms.* Doctoral dissertation. Fort Collins: Colorado State College.

Fosnot, C. T. (1989). *Inquiring teachers, inquiring learners.* New York: Teachers College Press.

Gagné, E. D. (1985). *The cognitive psychology of school learning.* Boston: Little Brown.

Gagné, E. D. et al. (1993). *The cognitive psychology of school learning* (2d ed.) New York: HarperCollins.

Gagné, R. M. (1977). *The conditions of learning and theory of instruction* (3d ed.). New York: Holt, Rinehart & Winston.

Gagné, R. M. (1985). *The conditions of learning and theory of instruction* (4th ed.). New York: Holt, Rinehart & Winston.

Gagné, R. M., & Briggs, L. J. (1979). *Principles of instructional design.* New York: Holt, Rinehart & Winston.

Gagné, R. M., & Briggs, L. J. (1987). *Principles of instructional design* (2d ed.). New York: Holt, Rinehart & Winston.

Gall, M. (1970). The use of questions in teaching. *Review of Educational Research, 40,* 707–721.

Gall, M. (1984). Synthesis of research on teachers' questioning. *Educational Leadership, 42,* 40–47.

Glass, G. (1976). Primary, secondary, and meta analysis of research. *Educational Researcher, 5,* 3–8.

Good, T. L., Grouws, D. A., & Ebmeier, H. (1983). *Active mathematics teaching.* New York: Longman.

Goodlad, J. (1984). *A place called school.* New York: McGraw-Hill.

Gronlund, N. E. (1978). *Stating objectives for classroom instruction.* New York: Macmillan.

Gronlund, N. E. (1982). *Constructing achievement tests.* Englewood Cliffs, N.J.: Prentice-Hall.

Gronlund, N. E., & Linn, R. L. (1990). *Measurement and evaluation in teaching* (6th ed.). New York: Macmillan.

Hebert, E. A. (1992). Portfolios invite reflection from students and staff. *Educational Leadership, 49,* 59–62.

Hertz-Lazarowith, R., & Miller, N. (1992). *Interaction in cooperative groups.* Cambridge, Eng.: University of Cambridge Press.

Hunter, M. (1982). *Mastering teaching.* El Segundo, Calif.: TIP Publications.

Jervis, K., & Montag, C. (eds.). (1991). *Progressive education for the 1990s: Transforming practice.* New York: Teachers College Press.

Johnson, D. W., & Johnson, R. T. (1986). *Learning together and alone: Cooperation, competition, and individualization* (2d ed.). Englewood Cliffs, N.J.: Prentice-Hall.

Johnson, D. W., & Johnson, R. T. (1994). *Joining together: Group theory and group skills* (5th ed.). Boston: Allyn & Bacon.

Joyce B., & Weil, M. (1972). *Models of teaching.* Englewood Cliffs, N.J.: Prentice-Hall.

Joyce B., Weil, M., & Showers, B. (1992). *Models of teaching* (4th ed.). Englewood Cliffs, N.J.: Prentice-Hall.

Kagen, S. (1993). *Cooperative learning.* San Juan Capistrano, Calif.: Resources for Teachers.

Kaplan, M. (1992). *Thinking in education.* Cambridge, Mass.: Cambridge University Press.

Kounin, J. S. (1970). *Discipline and group management in classrooms.* New York: Holt, Rinehart & Winston.

Krajcik, J. (1994). *Project-based instruction.* Unpublished paper. Ann Arbor, Mich.: University of Michigan.

Krajcik, J. S., Blumenfeld, P. C., Marx, R. W., & Soloway, E. (1994). A collaborative model for helping middle grade science teachers learn project-based instruction. *Elementary School Journal, 94,* 483–497.

Lyman, F. (1985). *Think-pair-share.* Unpublished paper. College Park, Md.: University of Maryland.

Lyman, F. (1986). *Procedures for using the question/response cues.* Unpublished paper. College Park, Md.: University of Maryland & The Howard County Public Schools.

MAACIE. (1990). Swing into teams. *Cooperative News, 3,* 5.

Madden, N. A., Slavin, R. E., Karweit, N. L., Dolan, L. J., & Wasik, B. A. (1993). Success for all: Longitudinal effects of a restructuring program for innercity elementary schools. *American Educational Research Journal, 30,* 123–148.

Mager, R. F. (1962). *Preparing instructional objectives.* Palo Alto, Calif.: Fearon.

Mastropieri, M. A., & Scruggs. T. E. (1991). *Teaching students ways to remember.* Cambridge, Mass.: Brookline Books.

Mayer, R. E. (1984). Aids to prose comprehension. *Educational Psychologist, 19,* 30–42.

McTighe, J., & Lyman, F. T. (1988). Cueing thinking in the classroom: The promise of theory-embedded tools. *Educational Leadership, 45,* 18–24.

McWhorter, K. T. (1992). *Study and thinking skills in college* (2d ed.). New York: HarperCollins.

Meyer, B. J., Brandt, D. M., & Bluth, G. J. (1980). Use of top-level structure in text: Key for reading comprehension of ninth-graders. *Reading Research Quarterly, 15,* 72–103.

Meyer, C. A. (1992). What is the difference between authentic and performance assessment? *Educational Leadership, 49,* 39–40.

Mitchell, R. (1992). *Testing for learning: How new approaches to evaluation can improve American schools.* New York: Free Press.

Moely et al. (1986). How do teachers teach memory skills? In J. Levin & M. Pressley (eds.), *Educational Psychologist, 21* (special issue).

Morine-Dershimer, G. (1985). *Talking, listening, and learning in elementary classrooms.* New York: Longman.

Mosenthal, P. B., Conley, M. W., Colella, A., & Davidson, R. (1985). The influence of prior knowledge and teacher lesson structure on children's production of narratives. *Elementary School Journal, 85,* 621–633.

Moyer, J. R. (1966). *An exploratory study of questioning in the instructional processes in selected elementary schools.* Doctoral dissertation. New York: Columbia University.

Norman, D. A. (1980). Cognitive engineering and education. In D. T. Tuma & F. Reif (eds.), *Problem solving and education.* Hillsdale, N.J.: Erlbaum.

Palincsar, A. S., & Brown, A. L. (1984). Reciprocal teaching of comprehension-fostering and comprehension-monitoring activities. *Cognition and Instruction, 1,* 117–175.

Palincsar, A., & Brown, A. (1989). Instruction for self-regulated reading. In L. Resnick & L. Klopfer (eds.), *Toward the thinking curriculum: Current cognitive research.* Alexandria, Va.: Association for Supervision and Curriculum Development.

Paris, S. G., Lipson, M. Y., & Wixson, K. K. (1983). Becoming a strategic reader. *Contemporary Educational Psychology, 8,* 293–316.

Posner, G. J., & Rudnitsky, A. N. (1986). *Course design: A guide to curriculum development for teachers* (3d ed.). New York: Longman.

Pramling, I. (1988). Developing young children's thinking about their own learning. *British Journal of Educational Psychology, 58,* 266–278.

Pressley, M. et al. (1989). The challenges of classroom strategy instruction. *Elementary School Journal, 89,* 301–342.

Pressley, M. et al. (1990). *Cognitive strategy instruction.* Cambridge, Mass.: Brookline Books.

Pressley, M. et al. (1991). *Cognitive instruction that really improves children's academic performance.* Cambridge, Mass.: Brookline Books.

Redfield, D., & Rousseau, E. (1981). A meta-analysis of experimental research on teacher questioning behavior. *Review of Educational Research, 51,* 237–245.

Resnick, L. B. (1987a). *Education and learning to think.* Washington, D.C.: National Academy Press.

Resnick, L. B. (1987b). Learning in school and out. *Educational Researcher, 16,* 13–20.

Resnick L. B., & Klopfer, L. E. (eds.). (1989). *Toward the thinking curriculum: Current cognitive research.* Alexandria, Va.: Association for Supervision and Curriculum Development.

Robinson, F. P. (1961). *Effective study.* New York: Harper & Row.

Rosenshine, B. (1971). *Teaching behaviors and student achievement.* London: National Foundation for Educational Research.

Rosenshine, B. (1980). How time is spent in elementary classrooms. In C. Denham & A. Lieberman (eds.), *Time to learn.* Washington, D.C.: U.S. Department of Education.

Rosenshine, B., & Furst, N. (1973). The use of direct observation to study teaching. In R. M. W. Travers (ed.), *Second handbook of research on teaching.* Chicago: Rand McNally.

Rosenshine, B., & Stevens, R. (1986). Teaching functions. In M. C. Wittrock (ed.), *Handbook of research on teaching* (3d ed.). New York: Macmillan.

Rothman, R. (1995). *Measuring up: Standards, assessment and school reform.* San Francisco: Jossey-Bass.

Rowe, M. B. (1974a). Wait-time and rewards as instructional variables, their influence on language, logic, and fate control. Part One: Wait-time. *Journal of Research in Science Teaching, 11,* 81–94.

Rowe, M. B. (1974b). Relation of wait-time and rewards to the development of language, logic, and fate control. Part Two: Rewards. *Journal of Research in Science Teaching, 11,* 291–308.

Rowe, M. B. (1986). Wait time: Slowing down may be a way of speeding up. *Journal of Teacher Education, 37,* 43–50.

Rugen, L., & Hart, S. (1994). The lessons of learning expeditions. *Educational Leadership, 52,* 20–23.

Ryle, G. (1949). *The concept of mind.* London: Hutchinson University Library.

Sanford, J., & Evertson, C. (1980). Classroom management in a low SES junior high. *Journal of Teacher Education, 32,* 34–38.

Schmuck, R. A., & Schmuck, P. A. (1989). Adolescents' attitudes toward school and teachers: From 1963–1989. Unpublished paper. Eugene, Oreg.: University of Oregon.

Schon, D. A. (1983). *The reflective practitioner.* San Francisco: Jossey-Bass.

Schreiber, J. E. (1967). *Teacher's question-asking techniques in social studies.* Doctoral dissertation. Iowa City: University of Iowa.

Schwab, J. J. (1965). *Biological sciences curriculum study, Biology teachers' handbook.* New York: Wiley.

Shaefer, W., & Lissitz, R. (1987). Measurement training for school personnel: Recommendations and reality. *Journal of Teacher Education, 38,* 57–63.

Sharan, S., Kussell, P., Hertz-Lazarowitz, R., Bejarano, Y., Raviv, S., & Sharan, Y. (1984). *Cooperative learning in the classroom.* Hillsdale, N.J.: Erlbaum.

Shavelson, R., & Baxter, G. (1992). What we've learned about assessing hands-on science. *Educational Leadership, 49,* 20–25.

Sirotnik, K. A. (1983). What you see is what you get. *Harvard Educational Review, 54,* 16–32.

Slavin, R. (1983). *Cooperative learning.* New York: Longman.

Slavin, R. (1984). Students motivating students to excel: Incentives, cooperative tasks and student achievement. *Elementary School Journal, 85,* 53–62.

Slavin, R. (1986). *Student team learning* (3d ed.). Baltimore, Md.: Center for Research on Elementary and Middle Schools, Johns Hopkins University.

Slavin, R. E. Madden, N. A., Dolan, L. J., & Wasik, B. A. (1992). *Success for all: A relentless approach to prevention and early intervention in elementary schools.* Arlington, Va.: Educational Research Services.

Slavin, R. E. Madden, N. A., Dolan, L. J., & Wasik, B. A. (1994). Roots and wings: Inspiring academic excellence. *Educational Leadership, 52,* 10–14.

Smith, H. (1995). Rogue eco-system project. *Education Connection, 1,* January-February, 3–4.

Stallings, J., & Kaskowitz, D. (1974). *Follow-through classroom observation evaluation 1972–1974.* (SRI project URU–7370.) Stanford, Calif.: Stanford Research Institute.

Stevens, R. (1912). *The question as a measure of efficiency in instruction: A critical study of classroom practice.* Teachers College Contributions to Education, no. 48. New York: Teachers College Press.

Stiggins, R. J. (1987). *Profiling classroom assessment environments.* Paper presented at the annual meeting of the National Council on Measurement in Education, San Francisco.

Suchman, R. (1962). *The elementary school training program in scientific inquiry.* Report to the U.S. Office of Education. Urbana, Ill.: University of Illinois.

Thelan, H. A. (1954). *Dynamics of groups at work.* Chicago: University of Chicago Press.

Thelan, H. A. (1960). *Education and the human quest.* New York: Harper & Row.

Thomas, E. L., & Robinson, H. A. (1972). *Improving reading in every class: A sourcebook for teachers.* Boston: Allyn & Bacon.

Weinstein, C. F., & Meyer, R. F. (1986). The teaching of learning strategies. In Wittrock, M. C. (ed.), *Handbook of research on teaching* (3d ed.). New York: Macmillan.

Weinstein, C. S., & Mignano, A. J., Jr. (1992). *Elementary classroom management: Lessons from research and practice.* New York: McGraw-Hill.

Wittrock, M. C. (ed.). (1986). *Handbook of research on teaching* (3d ed.). New York: Macmillan.

Yinger, R. (1980). A study of teacher planning. *Elementary School Journal, 71,* 143–151.

NAME INDEX

SUBJECT INDEX